BACK ON TOUR

CONTENTS

ACKNOWLEDGMENTS

This book is a cooperative effort involving many people over three years. Philip Laird would especially thank research assistants Ms Moya Collett and Ms Gabriella de Battista and colleagues of the School of Mathematics and Applied Statistics of the University of Wollongong. He would also thank the Australian Research Council and the Rail Infrastructure Corporation of NSW, for support of related research, and his father John Laird, and family, Anna, Martin and Helena for encouragement. Thanks are also due to the Bureau of Transport Economics for the data for the graphs in Chapter 2, and other Federal and State agencies in Australia, and government agencies in New Zealand for other data.

Mark would like to thank his wife Kim Morland for all her support over the past few years, and Peter Newman and Dr John Peet for their unwavering support in pursuing his PhD.

Peter and Jeffrey thank their long-suffering families and the ISTP at Murdoch University for continuing to provide support. All the authors thank John Elliot of UNSW Press for valuable assistance from start to finish of the book.

PREFACE

Transport affects every area of the Australian and New Zealand economies and is a daily part of everyone's lives. That the transport sector is worth in the order of $100 billion each year should be enough motivation for rethinking the direction of Australian and New Zealand transport policy and practice. But there is also much more, as transport impacts on the quality of life in our communities and is increasingly the attention of global policy in a world constrained by such matters as climate change and vulnerability to oil imports.

Most people have strong views on what we should do about transport. Yet few people have any role to play in deciding how we shape our transport systems. We believe that there are far better solutions to our transport problems than we are currently pursuing. These solutions will ultimately be better for our economies, our environment and our communities. The new approach will also involve a lot more people working out the detail.

This book attempts to pursue these solutions by examining the past, present and future of transport in Australia and New Zealand. It provides a perspective on the history of transport and how it relates to the changing economy. Against this background, we argue that the new economy increasingly favours a more balanced transport system with flexible use of cars and trucks for some functions and fixed-track rail systems that provide mass movement for other functions. The book provides data on freight, inter-city and urban transport to show that Australian and New Zealand transport systems have become heavily out of balance. It shows, for example, that the Australian vehicle fleet has one of the lowest fuel-efficiency levels and one of the highest level of road-based freight in the world. The book suggests we need to get 'back on track'.

Cities, regions and nations don't develop transport systems through simple logic. The resulting systems are the product of a policy debate. The book therefore examines the transport process and shows how heavily it is influenced by narrow road-based interests, to the point that the system now suffers from 'policy paralysis'. Moreover, there are hidden subsides to road users in excess of $8 billion a year and this 'road deficit' is growing. We simply cannot afford to allow this to go on, and need a more democratic and transparent approach to transport decision making.

Transport policy in cities is shown to be dependent on integrating transport and land use, as well as providing alternatives to excessive car use. In the regions, the key need is to improve rail infrastructure. The whole transport system needs to be priced to more accurately reflect the total costs of road vehicle use.

Throughout this book, frequent reference is made to the Department of Transport in Australia. This is taken to mean the Federal Department of Transport in one of its many forms, which during the 1990s was the Department of Transport and Communications, and in 2000 was the Department of Transport and Regional Development. This book shows that this Department of Transport is in need of major reform.

Overall, a new approach to transport funding that is more community-based is needed. This can provide a more balanced system that helps us to get 'back on track'.

Philip Laird, Peter Newman, Mark Bachels and Jeffrey Kenworthy

AUTHORS

Dr Philip Laird is an Associate Professor in the School of Mathematics and Applied Statistics at the University of Wollongong and an Honorary Visiting Fellow of the Centre for Resource and Environmental Studies at the Australian National University, Canberra. He is a member of the Chartered Institute of Transport, and a Companion of the Institution of Engineers, Australia. Philip is involved in land transport research and consulting, has served on three NSW Government advisory committees and was recently National Chairman of the Railway Technical Society of Australasia.

Dr Peter Newman is the Professor of City Policy and Director of the Institute for Sustainability and Technology Policy at Murdoch University, Perth. He has served as a councillor with the City of Fremantle, worked with the WA Premier and the Minister for Transport in the 1980s, and is perhaps best known in that state for his advocacy for and success in rebuilding Perth's rail system. Peter is also a Visiting Professor at the University of Pennsylvania and works on an international level, studying global cities for organisations such as the World Bank and the United Nations.

Dr Mark Bachels originally hails from California and is a graduate of the University of California in Santa Barbara and the University of Canterbury, New Zealand. His PhD thesis focused on urban transport and land-use planning in New Zealand cities. Mark is now the Project Manager for Central City Revitalisation with the Christchurch City Council.

Dr Jeffrey Kenworthy is an Associate Professor in Sustainable Settlements in the Institute for Sustainability and Technology Policy at Murdoch University, Perth. He has 20 years' experience in urban transport and land-use policy with more than 150 publications in the field. He is internationally recognised for his comparisons of cities worldwide based around the theme of reducing automobile dependence.

LIST OF ABBREVIATIONS

AAA	Australian Automobile Association
AADT	Annual Average Daily Traffic
AATSE	Academy of Technological Sciences and Engineering
ABARE	Australian Bureau of Agricultural and Resource Economics
ABC	Australian Broadcasting Commission
ABS	Australian Bureau of Statistics
ACG	Apelbaum Consulting Group
ACT	Australian Capital Territory
AGM	Average gross (operating) mass
AGO	Australian Greenhouse Office
ALGA	Australian Local Government Association
ALP	Australian Labour Party
AMA	Australian Medical Association
AN	Australian National Railways Commission
ANTS	A New Tax System
ANZ	Australia and New Zealand
APRA	Australian Prudential Regulatory Authority
ARA	Australasian Railway Association Inc.
ARRB	Australian Road Research Board
ATA	Australian Trucking Association
ATC	Australian Transport Council
ARTC	Australian Rail Track Corporation
ATEC	Australian Transport and Energy Corridor Limited
BHP	Broken Hill Proprietary Ltd
BTCE	Bureau of Transport and Communications Economics (now BTE)
BTE	Bureau of Transport Economics

btkm	billion tonne kilometres
BTS	Bureau of Transportation Statistics
CBD	Central Business District
COAG	Coalition of Australian Governments
CPA	Competition Policy Agreements
CSIRO	Commonwealth Scientific and Industrial Research Organisation
CSO	Community Service Obligations
CTC	Consumers Transport Council
CTP	Compulsory Third Party (Insurance)
ECC	European Communities Council
EPA	Environmental Protection Authority
ESA (L)	Equivalent Standard Axle (Loading)
ESD	Economically Sustainable Development
FBT	Fringe Benefit Tax
FFT	Fast Freight Train
FIRS	Federal Interstate Registration Scheme
FORS	Federal Office of Road Safety
GDP	Gross Domestic Product
GPS	Global Positioning Satellites
GRP	Gross Regional Product
GST	Goods and Services Tax
GVM	Gross Vehicle Mass
HORSCCTA	House of Representatives Standing Committee on Communications, Transport, and the Arts
HSRE	High Speed Rail Engineers
IAC	Industries Assistance Commission
IC	Industry Commission
ICE	Inter-City Electric
IRTP	Integrated Regional Transport Plan
ISC	Inter-State Commission
ISTEA	Intermodal Surface Transportation Efficiency Act 1991 (US)
ISTP	Institute for Sustainability and Technology Policy, Murdoch University
IT	Information technology
ITS	Intelligent Transport Systems
LCV	Light Commercial Vehicles
LPG	Liquified Petroleum Gas
MANS	Major Airport Needs of Sydney
MJ	Megajoule
MLU	Main Line Upgrade
MT	Million tonnes
MTAA	Motor Trade Association of Australia
NAASRA	National Association of Australian State Road Authorities
NCC	National Competition Council

NCP	National Competition Policy
NGRS	National Greenhouse Reduction Strategy
NHS	National Highway System
NIMT	North Island Main Trunk (NZ)
NLTC	National Land Transport Commission
NRFI	National Rail Freight Initiative
NRMA	National Roads and Motorists Association NSW
NRN (FA)	National Railway Network (Financial Assistance) Act 1978 (Cth)
NRTC	National Road Transport Commission
NSW	New South Wales
NT	Northern Territory
NTPT	National Transport Planning Taskforce
NTS	National Transport Secretariat
NZ	New Zealand
OAG	Over-Arching Group
OECD	Organisation for Economic Cooperation and Development
PC	Productivity Commission
QANTAS	Queensland and Northern Territory Aerial Services Ltd
Qld	Queensland
QR	Queensland Rail
RACV	Royal Automobile Club of Victoria
RTA	Roads and Traffic Authority of NSW
RTF	Road Transport Forum
RTIF	Road Transport Industry Forum
RTSA	Railway Technical Society of Australasia
SA	South Australia
SACTRA	Standing Advisory Committee on Trunk Road Assessment,
SALAD	Save-A-Life-A-Day
SEQ	South East Queensland
SMH	*Sydney Morning Herald*
SMVU	Survey of Motor Vehicle Usage
TEA	Transportation Equity Act (US)
TGV	Train à Grand Vitesse
tkms	tonne kilometres
TMO	Transport Management Organisations
TNT	Thomas Nationwide Transport
TWU	Transport Workers Union
USA	United States of America
VFT	Very Fast Train
WA	Western Australia
WWII	World War II
XPT	Express Passenger Train

1

HOW WE GOT HERE: THE ROLE OF TRANSPORT IN THE DEVELOPMENT OF AUSTRALIA AND NEW ZEALAND

PHILIP LAIRD AND PETER NEWMAN

The twentieth century has seen incredible changes in transport in Australia and New Zealand

From text

TRANSPORT IN THE 21ST CENTURY

Australia in the year 2000 could hardly be thought of without reference to the Olympic Games. Held in Sydney, the Games were judged to be a triumph and transport arrangements pronounced a success. Olympic Park coped with the influx of over 1 million visitors a day. At times 70 000 people per hour were reaching Olympic Park without major hold-ups. Most of these people (50 000 per hour) arrived by train. This was in stark contrast to the problems of congestion that plagued Atlanta. The key difference between Sydney and Atlanta was that Atlanta tried to do it all with buses and cars. A few of the outlying Sydney venues without rail access did have problems.

The sheer mathematics of how rail can so efficiently move large numbers of people to key centres, where road systems cannot, is part of the message of this book. One rail line can move 50 000, a busway up to 7000 and a freeway lane 2500 people an hour. Far from being an old, obsolete form of transport, rail is critical to how a modern efficient city can work.

However, the reality is that in Australia and New Zealand, probably only Sydney (and Melbourne at a pinch) could have managed to pull off the modern Olympic transport achievement. The rest of our cities just do not have the option available to them to enable a major part of their city population to choose a train.

The other feature of Australia and New Zealand in 2000, along with the rest of the world, is that transport suddenly faced escalating petrol prices. It is not that we weren't warned, as experts pointed to the 'end of the golden era of oil' for decades before (see Chapter 4). But Australia had to blame oil producing countries or Federal Government taxes for a problem that we created ourselves. We are to blame. It is we in Australia and New Zealand who have chosen to go with cars and trucks at the expense of enhancing rail options. This is the other major theme of our book: how we have an endemic problem that is just not going to be easily solved. We were warned in a series of government inquiries and we should have done something about it.

Australian and New Zealand transport needs to change. In the last decades of the 20th century the patterns of car and truck use became disturbingly out of balance. The following trends highlight the problems:

- Between 1976 and 1996 population in Australia grew by 50 per cent but car use almost doubled with car use per capita growing by 27 per cent. Urban car use tripled between 1976 and 1996. In the same period public transport use was near static.

- Freight has grown substantially in all modes but trucks in particular have become the dominant way of shifting goods. As shown in Appendix A, between 1970–71 and 1994–95 truck traffic has grown by more than four times, rail traffic less than three times and sea traffic has been relatively static.

- In the 20 years to 1990 there had been a growth in Australian transport fuel use of nearly 60 per cent. In the following 20 years in response to global concerns over climate change, we are supposed to be stabilising our greenhouse gas emissions, or keeping to no more than 8 per cent growth. However, by the year 2000, transport trends showed no sign of changing to be more sustainable.

- In New Zealand the trends are similar with public transport remaining near static or declining and road traffic apparently out of control. Auckland has severe road congestion and arguably the worst public transport levels of any western world city with a population of more than one million.

How did we get into this predicament? Are we so different from other places that we must be so dominated by cars and trucks? What can we do to get back on track? These are some of the questions we will be examining in this book. To begin with, we need to see where we have come from. What did Australian and New Zealand transport look like as we entered the 20th century? How did Australians and New Zealanders move themselves, and their goods, one hundred years ago?

TRANSPORT IN 1900

Australia in the year 1900 had a population of about 3.8 million people living in the six British Colonies of New South Wales (NSW), Victoria (Vic), Queensland (Qld), South Australia (SA), Western Australia (WA) and Tasmania (Tas). Their capital cities of Sydney, Melbourne, Brisbane, Adelaide, Perth and Hobart had about 33 per cent of Australia's population and ranged in size from about 27 000 people in Perth to some 484 000 people in Melbourne, which was then slightly larger than Sydney.

All of these cities, plus Newcastle (NSW) and Zeehan (Tas), had tram services in 1900. The most common trams then were horse-drawn trams. Steam trams were in use in 1900, along with cable trams in Melbourne. Sydney had recently acquired the then most modern electric-powered trams, and the first two decades of the 20th century were to see the introduction and extension of electric tram networks in many cities. The electricity was provided by coal-fired power stations, with their pollution in major coastal cities adding to that from steam ships and steam locomotives.

Horses were a valued means of transport in cities and in the country. Australia had an estimated 1.6 million horses in 1900, along with roughly 7000 bullocks and over 5000 camels (BTE, 1995a). Horses were put to work in many different ways, including moving trams in cities and coaches in the country. At the start of the 20th century, Cobb and Co were still doing good business moving people in remote regions and to connect with railway stations.

Sea transport remained essential in 1900 for everyone who came and went from Australia, or moved from Tasmania and Western Australia to other parts of Australia. Shipping sustained all exports, imports and much intercity freight, including the movement of over 2 million tonnes of coal in 1900 from Newcastle to destinations around Australia, with Melbourne as the biggest customer. The remnants of a once flourishing Murray River boat trade were still in place, but were mainly reduced to serving railheads.

In the more populated regions of Australia, the preferred mode of travel was by rail. By 1900 railways, which were mostly public although some were privately owned, extended for more than 21 000 route kilometres. In that year, over 100 million passengers and over 15 million tonnes of freight were moved by rail in Australia.

The first inter-colonial rail link was between Sydney and Melbourne in 1883, albeit with a change of gauge in Albury. For more on Australia's costly burden of different rail gauges, see Box 1.1 and Appendix B. The next rail link was Melbourne–Adelaide in 1887 followed by Sydney–Brisbane through Wallangarra in 1888, with another change in gauge. These rail links acted as an important catalyst for Federation in 1901 and it is worth noting that rail is the only mode of transport that is expressly mentioned in the Australian Constitution.

BOX 1.1
AUSTRALIA'S GAUGE MUDDLE

The story of Australia's different railway gauges has already filled several books. In brief, the Colony of New South Wales in the early 1850s changed its preference from the standard gauge of 4' 8.5" (1435 mm) to the Irish broad gauge of 5' 3" (1600 mm) but later, in 1855, opened its first railway in standard gauge, leaving Victoria and South Australia with the broad gauge. Not content with either of these two gauges, Queensland settled on a third and narrower 3' 6" gauge (1067 mm) for its first railway in 1865. The net result was that each colony got the gauge that it wanted, but at significant long-term cost to the national interest.

During the 1880s, three inter-capital city railways met at the Colonial borders, two with a break of gauge. The linking of Adelaide, Melbourne, Sydney and Brisbane by rail assisted the process of Federation. However, the Colonies were unwilling to transfer their railways to the new Commonwealth, as had been agreed for defence, postal and telegraphic services.

Although most other countries had made good progress in gauge standardisation by the end of the 19th century, progress in gauge standardisation in Australia was still slow during the 20th century. In 1917, the Commonwealth completed a standard gauge railway between Port Augusta and Kalgoorlie. However, standard gauge did not reach Perth until 1968, and it did not reach Adelaide until 1982. With Commonwealth assistance and agreements with the relevant States, construction of a standard gauge link from Kyogle (NSW) to South Brisbane was completed in 1930, followed by Port Augusta to Port Pirie in 1937.

At the outbreak of World War II, there were 11 locations where tracks met with a break of gauge. These differences in gauge added immense cost to the Australian war effort. Even so, it then took until 1962 to extend standard gauge into Melbourne, and 1969 to extend it to Broken Hill. This allowed standard gauge trains to move from Sydney to Perth from 1970. Finally, Adelaide and Melbourne were directly connected by standard gauge in 1995.

There is still scope for gauge standardisation of the entire Victorian and South Australian broad gauge systems – at least those that are not used for urban rail services. The case for conversion of Queensland, South Australia (Eyre Peninsula), Western Australian and Tasmanian narrow gauge tracks is often raised. However, in most cases, gauge standardisation is not as compelling as improving the speed-weight restrictions of the interstate mainlines.

It is of interest to note that New Zealand in 1873 had the three different railway gauges, but by 1877 had converted them to a uniform narrow gauge. One can ask why gauge standardisation has taken so long in Australia. The answer has to rest with parochial Colonial governments in the 19th century, followed by narrow State viewpoints, and coupled with a weak approach by the Federal Government to rail transport in the 20th Century.

Air transport did not exist in 1900, and the first powered flight in Australia was not made until 1910. A basic road system had been developed in the 19th century for use by horses and coaches. Thus when the first cars were being imported into Australia in 1900, they found the going hard. As we have noted, sea transport, railways and tramways, and horses and coaches were then paramount.

Across the Tasman in New Zealand a similar transport situation prevailed in 1900. Horses were important for trams and coach services. Sea transport was very much alive and well, as were government and private railways which in 1900, although not having a link between Auckland and Wellington (finally completed in 1908), did have a rail link between Christchurch and Dunedin (completed 1878) which was extended (in 1879) to Invercargill (Yonge, 1985). Each of these five cities had horse-drawn tram services in 1900. Like Australia, the first decade of the 1900s would see a growth of tram networks in New Zealand cities of various types – horse, cable and steam, with Auckland gaining the first electric trams in 1902. Electric trams proved the most popular, and by 1916 were to be found in Gisborne, Napier, New Plymouth and Wanganui as well as in the major cities. In 1900, aviation and cars ranged from the unknown to a novelty in New Zealand as well as Australia.

The 20th century has seen incredible changes in transport systems in Australia and New Zealand. The motivation for people wishing to move themselves, or their goods, has changed to reflect the increasing ease of mobility at lower real costs. Thus, there has been an enormous growth in moving people. The growth in road vehicle usage has far outstripped population growth and has also been faster than real economic growth. The movement of freight has also grown astronomically, with a large increase in the tonnages moved, and an increase in the average length of haul. Most, but not all, of the growth in transport outputs has depended on plentiful supplies of cheap oil. As we shall see in later chapters, there is a real question as to how sustainable the present land transport systems in Australia and New Zealand are.

We can gain a brief appreciation of the extent of change during the 20th century, by the following 'snapshots' taken at mainly 20-year intervals in Australia. Our approach here will be to look separately at each of the following: urban passenger transport, intercity land passenger transport, aviation, and freight transport.

URBAN PASSENGER TRANSPORT

By 1920, Australia's six State capitals had shown significant growth in the twenty years from 1900. In fact, during this time, their combined population had doubled. Sydney was Australia's largest city by 1920 with a population approaching 900 000 and had developed what was regarded by many as one of the world's largest tram systems. In 1920, Australia's trams were then mostly electric services with some steam, horse and cable trams. State governments provided most tram services, but local government and also private companies ran trams in some cities and towns. The growth in electric trams was supplemented by a growth in urban rail services. The electrification of Melbourne suburban trains had already started in 1919 (Sydney had to wait until 1926, Brisbane 1979 and Perth until 1992). The extensive city railway and tramlines built in the early 20th century were to shape land use and the development of city suburbs for many decades to come.

By 1920, only 87 000 cars were registered for use on Australia's roads. By 1940, however, despite the constraints imposed by the Depression, the number of motor vehicles had grown to some 562 000 cars, 258 000 commercial vehicles and some 79 000 motor cycles. Roads had also improved, with some valuable additions both during and after the Depression. Trams continued to do well in the larger cities, although Rockhampton in 1939 lost its trams to buses.

World War II was to cause irrevocable changes to urban transport in Australia and New Zealand. Although the tram and urban rail systems performed well during and after this war when they achieved record passenger loadings, they were to face fierce and growing competition from cars. Indeed, the inevitable change from public transport to cars was retarded by World War II and related factors such as petrol rationing in Australia which was only lifted in 1949.

By 1960, when Australia's population had grown to over 10 million, car numbers had risen to nearly 2 million. In addition, tram services had been rapidly losing patrons in the 1950s and were being closed down in favour of buses and ever more cars. Notable exceptions to the loss of trams were the solitary Adelaide line to Glenelg, and the extensive Melbourne system. The last of the other major tram systems to go was that of Brisbane, in 1969. In some cities, electric trolley buses came and went. Other factors would come into play including the emergence of the motorway, dispersed outer city suburbs heavily dependent on road transport, and the widespread development of regional suburban shopping centres such as Roselands in Sydney. A major increase in women's participation in the workforce, and the growing numbers of women holding drivers licences and owning cars, would also drive the growth to more cars and more vehicle kilometres.

The post-World War II growth in car use and its attendant problems drew a decisive response from the Whitlam Government, whose

Prime Minister's December 1972 policy speech had noted a '... recognition of the need for national Government to accept a share of responsibility for the public transport systems of Australian cities. This was essential if the serious deterioration in our urban environment attributable to over-reliance on the motor car as a means of transport was to be overcome'.

Following negotiations with the States, a *States Grants (Urban Public Transport) Act 1974* was passed. Prior to this, there had been no Commonwealth funding of urban public transport in Australia's major cities. The Act ratified an agreement between the Commonwealth and States to upgrade urban public transport. However, Federal funding of urban public transport in the 25 years from 1974 to 1999 has been characterised by 'on-again, off-again' funding.

Partly as a result of an extended period of declining public transport patronage from the 1950s, Government rail systems have seen a rise in aggregate deficits. These deficits peaked at about $2.1 billion in 1984. The States have continued to invest in urban public transport, and in recent years, most urban rail systems have seen an increase in passenger numbers. The increase was most noticeable in the lead-up to Brisbane's 1988 Expo, and in Perth following completion of the Northern Suburbs' Railway. Urban buses have shown only modest overall growth in recent years.

However, despite the two major oil price 'shocks' of the 1970s when the security of supply of cheap oil was seriously threatened (in 1973–74 and 1978–79), car use has continued to grow. By 1980, Australia's 15 million people very much preferred cars for both urban and intercity travel. Both car ownership and car use had grown. The cost of servicing Australia's road vehicle use in the early 1990s had grown to an estimated $80 billion a year (Allen Consulting Group, 1993). This included outlays on roads by Australia's three levels of government and an allowance for the cost of road crashes. Despite more road building, road congestion in major cities has worsened during the 1990s.

INTER-CAPITAL CITY PASSENGER RAIL TRANSPORT

In 1900, the rail systems, supplemented by an extensive network of coach services, were the main means of intercity transport. However, shipping remained essential for overseas transport and continued to do well with interstate passenger movements.

Throughout Australia, and despite World War I, the rail network had extended from some 21 000 km to about 37 000 km by 1920. This included the completion of the Trans-Australian Railway from Port Augusta to Kalgoorlie in 1917 by the Commonwealth Government, thus fulfilling a promise made at Federation. Other notable works included the duplication of many NSW mainlines to meet growing traffic demands. In 1920, rail passenger journeys throughout Australia had grown to 320 million.

Trains moved 379 million passengers in 1940. Anticipating that competition would emerge from the use of cars and planes, the Victorian Railways developed the *Spirit of Progress* for the Albury–Melbourne run. When it was commissioned in 1937, it was the fastest and finest train in the Southern Hemisphere. The introduction of *The Comet*, which had air-conditioning, between Parkes and Broken Hill in 1937, was also worthy of note. Australia's rail tracks had continued to grow until 1940, with notable additions including a through-link to Cairns finally completed in 1924, a standard gauge link from Kyogle to South Brisbane in 1930, and another from Port Augusta to Port Pirie in 1937. This gave Port Pirie the unique distinction of being the only station in the world with three railway gauges.

For rail, the net result of World War II was to run down the rail system. In places where the rail system could not fully cope, new roads were constructed. The Americans, with an Allied Roads Council formed in February 1942 favoured this. Coastal shipping was risky in World War II. Although some overseas aviation services were cut, air transport was also important. Today, it may seem hard to believe that from 1942 to 1945 personal interstate travel by rail, bus or air actually required a Commonwealth Government permit issued under an Interstate Travel Permit Scheme.

By 1960, rail had lost much of its appeal for interstate travel, although it was still preferred by many of the travelling public to buses. Efforts would be made over the next decade to revive the Melbourne–Sydney trains in 1962 and Sydney–Perth trains in 1970 as a follow-on to major gauge standardisation projects. Although some modernisation was in progress with replacement of steam locomotives by diesel locomotives, and extension of electrification from Sydney, too often the new trains followed 'steam age' track alignment that had rarely been straightened for improved running. Instead, flying was gaining increasing appeal, and as cars and roads began to improve, more people were tempted to complete long journeys by car.

A further transport initiative of the Whitlam Government was the passage of the *Australian National Railways Act 1975*. This followed agreements with the States of South Australia and Tasmania under Section 51 (xxxiv) of the Constitution, and the Commonwealth formed the Australian National Railways Commission, or Australian National. However, although Australian National inherited passenger train services in both States, along with the Indian Pacific, Ghan and Overland trains, its main focus was the development of long-distance rail freight services.

This land transport initiative was supported by the Fraser Coalition Government, which in 1980 was prepared to electrify the Sydney–Melbourne railway line. However, the Hawke Labor Government put much more emphasis on highway development at the expense of rail development (Stevenson, 1987). It was left to the CSIRO in 1984 to propose an ambitious Sydney–Canberra–Melbourne Very Fast Train, or VFT.

Long-distance bus travel was also on the rise in 1980. This was boosted by better roads and unrestricted competition for interstate trips and resulted in severe price-cutting. Long distance buses were to face tougher times in the 1990s, and a slight decline from their peak passenger task. Long distance trains were hit even harder, with their market share reduced to a mere 4 per cent on a passenger-kilometre basis. However, as we examine in the next chapter, in recent years, some services, such as the Brisbane–Rockhampton new tilt train service operating over upgraded track, have done well.

INTERCITY ROADS

In 1900, the condition of intercity highways, after years of neglect in favour of railways, was poor. Roads were then the responsibility of local government, and to this day, are not mentioned in the Australian Constitution. In 1912, the Victorian Government had formed a Country Roads Board; this was followed by the NSW Department of Main Roads in 1922 and similar bodies in other states. A popular interest in motor vehicles led to the formation in 1920 of the NSW National Roads Association (later NRMA). Other State-based motoring organisations were also formed in the 1920s. The first Commonwealth Government grants for roads were made in 1922, and have continued ever since.

Some intercity roads received a boost during the 1930s as part of Depression relief schemes, and other intercity roads were improved during World War II. Although some improvements were made during the 1950s and 1960s, it was still possible to encounter dirt roads in 1970 on the main road between Adelaide and Perth, and between Melbourne and Brisbane on the Newell Highway via Parkes in NSW. Increased intercity car use, coupled with growing numbers of trucks, prompted the Whitlam Government to commence full Federal funding of a National Highway System linking Australia's mainland capital cities under the *National Roads Act 1974*. The formation of a National Highway System, with the outlay of some $18 billion over the 25 years to 1999, has seen a major transformation of inter-capital city roads. The large-scale road projects included the reconstruction of most of the Hume Highway linking Melbourne and Sydney, and the sealing of the remote parts of the National Highway System in Western Australia and the Northern Territory by 1989.

AIR TRANSPORT

The 1910s had seen a growing interest in the feats of aviation in war and peace. The first flight from Britain to Australia was made in 1919, and QANTAS (Queensland and Northern Territory Aerial Services Ltd) was formed in 1920. The Commonwealth was to take an active interest in regulating and supporting aviation. However, relatively few people had ever flown in a plane until World War II.

Developments in aviation meant that it was possible to fly between England and Australia by the late 1930s. Whilst World War II was to close down some international services, it was also to lay the groundwork for better planes after the war.

By 1960, aviation was available, if not easily affordable, for much of the population. Planes were also getting bigger and better, and QANTAS had in service 707 jet aircraft, the first being acquired in 1959. In 1980, the domestic air passenger task had easily outgrown the combined intercity bus and train passenger task, and would continue to grow at a very rapid rate. By 1990, and with the advent of cheaper airfares prompted by the brief and spectacular entry of Compass Airlines, domestic air transport was set for a decade of further and spectacular growth. This included air transport becoming the dominant mode for Sydney–Melbourne passenger trips in 1990, having displaced cars. However, cars remained dominant on the shorter Sydney–Canberra corridor.

The rise of domestic aviation has gone hand in hand with increasing numbers of international passengers.

FREIGHT TRANSPORT

In the early part of the 20th century, shipping remained essential for overseas transport and dominated interstate freight movements. The growth in the number of cars and trucks in the 1920s and the early impact of the depression led all State governments to introduce legislation in the early 1930s to restrict the movement of freight by road. This was in part to protect the effective monopoly enjoyed by the State railways. The efforts to try and coordinate land freight transport were to prove difficult over the years.

A further concern, as noted in a Queensland Royal Commission on Transport and Harbour Problems (Ffrost, 1997), along with ensuring a return on railway capital, was that of '… men working very long hours on truck driving, often to the detriment of their health and with grave danger to the public'. Such a theme was to be very apparent for the remainder of the 20th century and has continued into the 21st century.

In the 1930s, ships remained essential for imports and exports, and did well with interstate trade until World War II. During this war, rail and road began to take more freight, and after the war, a weakened rail system was struck down with coal shortages resulting from miners' strikes and/or railway strikes. Although the road system was very basic by today's standards, many truck drivers were on the road able and willing to assume a much larger freight task. The regulations to try and restrict road transport were used by each State, and the road transport industry showed much tenacity in the resulting challenges. These included 'Barney's Barrow' which was pushed from Sydney to Melbourne in 11 days in July 1952 carrying a copy of the Constitution, arriving two days earlier than a parcel consigned by rail between the two cities (Ffrost, 1997, p56). Ongoing litigation ensued, and a Special Court was established in Redfern NSW to deal exclusively with road tax cases. Years later, in 1967, the Federal Minister for Transport, the Hon. G. Freeth was noted as observing (Ffrost, 1997, p84) that '... no other section of industry had figured so often as the long distance road industry had done in the Commonwealth Law Reports'.

In 1954, the Privy Council in London struck down restrictions on interstate trucking, on appeal from Australia's High Court. This was on the basis that they contravened part of Section 92 of the Constitution that required trade between the States to be 'absolutely free'. Further legal cases established that the States could only levy a very modest charge on interstate trucking for road maintenance, which was set at one third of one penny for each 'tonne mile'. This new charge was much less than a previously levied road tax of three pence per tonne mile. It was never indexed for inflation, and subject to increasing evasion over time.

By 1960, a strong interstate trucking industry was developing at the expense of coastal shipping and the railways. The introduction of more powerful diesel engines, the development of articulated truck technology, and better roads facilitated the growth in road freight. In this regard, in 1962, less than 2 per cent of the trucks on the Hume Highway had more than four axles, whilst by 1980, every second truck had five or six axles, with a marked increase in the number of six-axle articulated trucks (Lonie, 1980).

During the 1960s, regulations that attempted to restrict some intrastate freight to rail were lifted in South Australia. Slowly but surely other States followed, thus putting to an end such practices as 'border hopping'. This practice, which was extensive over the NSW/Victorian border, and occurred on the NSW/Queensland border (Ffrost, 1997) sought to convert an intrastate haul, that was subject to regulation, to an interstate haul that was not subject to regulation. By the 1990s, with some prompting by the Commonwealth in the late 1980s for grain transport, the process of land freight transport deregulation was virtually complete, except for the reservation of some coal to rail in NSW for environmental reasons. The result, with arguably low road-user charges imposed on heavy trucks, was to lead to a rapid growth in Australia's road freight task. However, this came at a high cost including over-representation of articulated trucks in fatal road crashes, noise, air pollution, and additional road construction and maintenance costs. Overloading by some truck operators exacerbated the road maintenance costs. The Annual Report of the NSW Department of Main Roads for 1984–85 estimated truck overloading to cost some $24 million, which was at that time some 13 per cent of the NSW road maintenance budget.

Further problems in the road freight industry surfaced as intense competition within the industry gave some operators incentives for speeding, overloading, driving excessive hours, and avoiding the modest road maintenance charge. Following major truck blockades in 1979, this road maintenance charge was removed by all State governments. In place of this charge, and in time, all States except Queensland imposed a modest diesel fuel franchise fee.

The growth of the road freight task was assisted by a succession of Federal governments putting much more emphasis on highway development at the expense of rail development. We shall trace this in later chapters, along with other problems in the road freight industry.

One area where the railways were able to grow their freight was in the area of bulk haulage of coal, iron ore and wheat. Since 1970, there has been a strong growth in coal exports from NSW and Queensland, which had grown from less than 20 million tonnes (MT) in 1970 to a massive over 150 MT moved by rail for export in 1997–98. Over the same period of time, increasing tonnages of iron ore were being moved from mines to ports in the Pilbara region of Western Australia. The growth was again spectacular, from less than 20 MT in 1970 to 149 MT in 1998–99.

To service the growing exports of coal, Queensland Rail during the 1980s embarked on their giant Mainline Electrification project that was then the largest in the Western world. As a result of the spectacular growth in iron ore exports from the Pilbara, Australia developed the most efficient freight trains in the world.

The situation with regard to the haulage of general freight by rail in Australia over the last three decades of the 20th century was not so good. For interstate operations, impressive gains were also made in the 1980s by Australian National with their Adelaide–Perth freight trains and by the late 1990s, National Rail and other rail operators were winning over 70 per cent of the share of intercity land freight on this corridor. However, by the end of the 1990s, the interstate rail freight system linking Australia's three largest cities of Melbourne, Sydney and Brisbane was only attracting about 20 per cent of intercity land freight. The reasons for limited rail performance and the excessive reliance on road transport in Australia are examined in later chapters.

NEW ZEALAND DEVELOPMENTS

During the 20th century, New Zealand as well as Australia has seen the rise and fall of its urban tram systems and strong growth in road use. The railways' dominant position for intercity passengers has gone, aviation has grown, and trucks are now essential for many freight movements. Sea transport in New Zealand also has a special role, given that the country is divided into two main islands separated by Cook Straight. Some interesting differences between Australia and New Zealand land transport are worth noting.

The first difference is that New Zealand, favoured by not having State and Federal Governments, has been quicker than Australia to make government transport investments when the private sector would not invest. This includes the introduction of a new Cook Straight ferry in 1962, and investing in rail freight productivity measures such as the North Island Main Trunk upgrading in the 1980s. New Zealand was also quicker than Australia to introduce reforms such as integration of international and domestic air carriers, and to privatise air and rail transport operations.

A major difference between Australia and New Zealand has been in road pricing for heavy trucks. Before deregulating land freight by lifting rail protection, New Zealand chose, under the *Road Users Charge Act 1977*, to introduce an advanced system of mass-distance charges for all heavy vehicles. This required a truck operator to purchase a pre-paid distance licence before the haulage of goods. The net result is that demand for intercity road upgrading away from major cities has been lessened, and New Zealand Rail freight operations, on a narrow traffic base, have been profitable, whilst intercity rail passenger operations have held their own. As we shall see later, Australia retains low road pricing for heavy trucks.

FINDING PERSPECTIVE — TRANSPORT TECHNOLOGY AND ECONOMIC CYCLES

The rise in the use of motor vehicles and planes in the history of Australia and New Zealand may be seen as somewhat inevitable due to the global move towards these technologies. However, not all countries have made such a dramatic shift away from trams and trains and in many countries they are rapidly growing again. Is the shift away from fixed-track transport to road-based transport an inevitable process that will dominate our future as it has dominated our past?

It is possible to analyse the historical patterns of transport over the past century through the cycles of economic change which have occurred worldwide. These cycles can then be seen in the light of present world economic trends to help us answer the above question.

The world economy has been through four major cycles of change or different periods of industrialisation and we are now entering the fifth; these changes are sometimes called Kondratiev Cycles, Economic Cycles or Business Cycles and they are summarised below in Table 1.1.

TABLE 1.1

THE FIVE CYCLES OF ECONOMIC ACTIVITY. BASED ON: FREEMAN AND PEREZ (1988)

Wave Time	Description and main industries	Key factor	Business paradigm
1 1770s/80s–1830s/40s – 'Industrial Revolution' 'Hard Times'	Early mechanisation era Textiles, potteries, canals	Cotton and iron	Capital-based local industries
2 1830s/40s–1880s/90s 'Victorian prosperity' 'Great Depression'	Steam-power and railway era Trains, steamships, machine tools	Coal	Large firms
3 1880s/90s–1930s/40s 'Belle Epoque' – 'Great Depression'	Electrical and heavy engineering era Electricity, cable and wire, trams, radio…	Steel	Giant firms, monopoly, oligopoly
4 1930s/40s–1980s/90s Golden age of growth and Keynesian full employment – 'structural adjustment' crisis and worse (?)	Fordist mass production era Cars, trucks, tractors, aircraft, petrochemicals, fertilisers	Oil	Multinational firms, sub-contracting, hierarchical control
5 Late 20th century 'Global recession' – next wave of economic activity	Information technology (communication and control systems) Environmental technology (renewables, recycling, zero emissions) and sustainable transportation	IT and sustainability	Networking, systems, flexible specialisation, 'community' scale

The economic cycles outlined above are all based on technology. The analysts who examine technology in history show that it both changes the way we live and work and is also an expression of our fundamental values (Metcalfe, 1990; Freeman, 1996; Linstone and Mistroff 1994; Freeman and Soete, 1997). The phases outlined above can be seen to have certain key technologies in each phase: the first stages of industrialisation were based on cotton and iron, the next phase on coal, then steel and finally oil. However the technologies were also associated with different ways of doing the production process and different social values.

The phase we are now entering, the fifth cycle, is clearly related to the microchip, to information technology and how it can be used to control all production and the transfer of knowledge and services. Moreover, the fifth cycle is also about how our society is more based on networks and systems. The fourth cycle was based on simple mass production lines; this old form of production is called 'Fordism' after Henry Ford who installed the first industrial production line in his Detroit car plant. Part of the new paradigm of networks and multiple goals rather than simple lines of production, is sustainability. This is setting the new direction for how all forms of technology and social interaction progress. It is the ultimate approach to 'network' thinking rather than 'linear' thinking as it integrates not only natural capital and financial capital but also social capital (Selman, 1996, Putnam, 1993).

Transport is also a key technology. The economy is not formed by its mode of transport but transport develops in close connection to the new phases of technology and is also an expression of our fundamental social values. It is not hard to see how transport has developed in its broad patterns due to the large economic cycles outlined above; but it is also possible to see how different social values are expressed and prioritised in the combinations of various transport technologies.

The broad patterns in terms of transport technology are summarised in Table 1.2.

TABLE 1.2
TRANSPORT TECHNOLOGY ADVANCES AND THEIR LINKS TO ECONOMIC CYCLES

Economic cycle	Major intercity transport technology	Major intra-city transport technology
1st cycle: 1770s/80s–1830s/40s	Ships and horse/carriages	Walking
2nd cycle: 1830s/40s–1880s/90s	Steam trains	Trains
3rd cycle: 1880s/90s–1930s/40s	Electric trains	Trams
4th cycle: 1930s/40s–1980s/90s	Trucks and planes	Cars

The early stages of industrialisation were closely linked to the transport of raw materials by barges on ship canals and by global shipping. People also travelled by ship but on land the main transport was by horse, particularly horse-drawn carriages. In cities the horse-carriage was there but most people walked. Cities were similar in form throughout the past few thousand years, being constrained by how far people could walk in half an hour, ie. they grew no more than an average of about 5 km in diameter.

The settlement of Australia and New Zealand began in the first cycle of industrialisation. Indeed, the transportation of convicts and the opening up of new land for raw materials were a part of the social and economic consequences of this new industrial world. Sea transport determined where the first cities would be built and rivers were the first economic arteries for transporting goods and people. Horses provided the major inland transport (Cobb and Co coaches only ceased running in 1924) and the central cities of Sydney, Hobart, Wellington and Fremantle still retain their classic 'walking city' characteristics.

The second stage of industrialisation, based on coal, saw the introduction of steam trains. These were able to transform the quantity of materials transported, though they did not replace the ship and the barge where water transport was still viable. They did open up land in new ways and hence vast areas of the New World in the Americas and Australia could be developed for agriculture and mining. They were able to service large industries and to link the inland to ports. They were the symbol of power and speed for the new industrial age.

They were also able to provide a solution for cities that had become vastly overcrowded in the 5km 'walking city' diameter. The city was able to develop rail corridors where passenger trains could bring people 20 kms in half an hour. Thus the railway suburbs were born and visionaries planned new Garden Cities linked together by these trains. Trains in cities provided the first mass transit, a necessary solution to the transport of every big city, then and now. No technology before or since has been able to provide a better solution to mass movement in a city than the train.

Steam trains were a huge boost to development in the New World. Railways were built from the 1850s and soon became the main activity of governments in terms of infrastructure for development. They opened up vast areas as they linked towns and brought produce to the ports. It is even possible to understand something of the different demographics of the various regions in Australia and New Zealand, through an understanding of how rail was used for development.

In Europe there are some large cities but also many, many small towns and villages. In Australia and New Zealand there are far fewer small towns and villages because these developed in Europe in the pre-industrial era when villages were a few hours' walk apart and a market town was a day's walk from a series of villages. Then, when the railways came and most development was linked to them, the possibilities of concentrating development were even greater. Rail could bring produce and people from hundreds of kilometres away to a main port and service centre. Thus in Western Australia, there is now a population of 1.6 million of which 1.3 million live in Perth because once the rail was built it focused all development on this city. And as wheat and

wool were the main agricultural products they could be brought slowly by long rail lines from a vast interior stretching in an 800 km arc.
However in Queensland and in New Zealand the products of agriculture included dairy and sugar which needed quick processing and
shipping so that smaller processing/port towns had to be developed
in the regions.

The building of train lines across large areas of each of Australia's
States has left an important economic and social legacy. The valuing
of this resource takes up a large part of this book. However, there is
also another side of this legacy that reveals a side of Australia's transport problem: the states were unable to agree on a standard gauge and
hence there are now a variety of systems that are not able to work as
a national system. The story of how this occurred (as outlined in Box
1.1 and Appendix B) raises the serious question of how national decisions about transport continue to be made and whether a better system could not be created that is more able to achieve integrated
transport goals.

All the Australian and New Zealand cities were influenced by the
development of rail suburbs and tram corridors built in the second
and third periods of industrialisation. They are all still heavily influenced by their train connections, especially in Melbourne, but it is
obvious in all cities that they still retain the strong lines of mixed use
development so characteristic of tram streets even after they were
removed as transport systems. There are few of these in Australia or
New Zealand that are not thriving areas of urban activity.

The third stage of industrialisation built on the first two stages and
added the technologies related to steel, particularly electricity. Thus
electric trains could replace steam trains and give extra power and
speed. This was also evident in cities where electric trains were more
acceptable to the movement of people. But this era in cities was particularly marked by electric trams, which spread rapidly to every part
of the industrial world from the 1890s. These gave rise to the tram
suburbs that were the characteristic mixed use, dense corridors of
development that can be seen in most cities today. Such linear 'urban
villages' are often the most sought after area of cities and are a constant source of inspiration to the New Urbanism urban designers
(Katz, 1994; Calthorpe, 1993; Duany and Plater-Zyberk, 1991).

The story of Australian and New Zealand transport, which began
(above) in 1900, can be seen to illustrate these economic cycles. The
world, including Australia and New Zealand, in 1900 still had remnants of each of the first two economic cycles (walking city areas,
water transport, horse drawn transport, and steam railways) but was
about to be drawn into the third and fourth cycles. The era of trams
and trains grew rapidly for several decades and then as the Depression
and World War II struck the fourth cycle was unleashed.

The fourth stage of industrialisation added the truck and the car to our transport systems. Although they had been invented at the turn of the century they were not mass-produced until the past fifty years of economic development created their need in large numbers. The truck and the car (supplemented by the bus) were able to add a new dimension of flexibility to the movement of freight and to the movement of people.

In regions and in cities the chance to create flexibility in freight gave flexibility to the placement of industries. Yet the continuing value of fixed rail systems remained essential for mass movement as not all economic problems are solved by flexibility, indeed many are solved by economies of scale. Thus choices needed to be made about the extent to which mass transport by rail and flexible transport by truck could be balanced. The same choices were required in relation to intercity passenger movement between the train and bus.

In cities the movement of people by cars enabled cities to expand outwards in all directions for 30 to 40 kms; the density of suburbs could be further lowered and employment located virtually anywhere. The new flexibility over space created the sprawling car-based cities that today dominate North America, Australia and New Zealand. The fact that they are not so obvious in Europe and are not common in Asia (even where wealth levels are high) is an indication that the economic cycles are not so deterministic as this brief overview may have begun to suggest.

The economic cycles are indeed powerful in that they bring new technology. However they do not replace the former technologies, they generally add to them. And in some countries, regions or cities, the choice is often made to set the balance between new and old technologies in ways that reflect their social values differently to others. Some cities continue to emphasise their 'walkability', some their trams and trains. The dynamic combinations of transport technologies all provide different market niches and express different social values. This book will argue that the balance of emphasis in Australia and New Zealand has gone too far towards the truck and car. It will also argue that the fifth cycle of economic change, where sustainability must be a central value, demands that we do something serious about redressing the balance.

The most obvious impact of transport on urban and regional development in Australia and New Zealand has been the fourth phase of industrialisation: the car and truck phase, based on the era of cheap oil. The growth of North American cities and regions based on these technologies was well under way in the 1930s and 1940s but was not really unleashed 'down under' until the post-war removal of petrol rationing and the release of the Holden car in 1948. Until then Australians could only buy a car using overseas funds. Thus from the 1950s a technology was freely available to service the new suburbs, subsidised by governments through housing loans, and generally built without much concern for access by public transport. But to the average Australian and New Zealand family, the car and the suburbs appealed (as probably did the promise provided at the early stages of each cycle of economic activity).

The era of the fourth cycle is now ending. The 'oil, truck and car' cycle has clearly begun to be phased out in terms of how employment and economic growth is generated. It is also clear that a change of social values is occurring. Data on the patterns of transport and land use in the fifth cycle era will be given in Chapter 2 on Australian and New Zealand cities and regions; this will then be put into a global context in Chapter 3.

The broad patterns of how technology, and in particular transport technology, has influenced Australian and New Zealand history, can be discerned. Where the fifth economic cycle may be leading us, or more hopefully how we can make the most of the future potentialities of technology, is therefore an important question for us to ask.

THE FIFTH CYCLE AND THE FUTURE

There is much speculation about the direction of the fifth stage of industrialisation. There is little doubt that information technology is the key element which underlies much of the technological momentum driving economies at the turn of the new millennium (Castells, 1996). However, what it means for cities and transport systems is very much open to debate (Brotchie et al, 1999).

The debate seems to revolve around several key social characteristics of cities and transport systems, and echoes the changes that have already been occurring. These social characteristics concern the question of whether flexibility is the dominant driving force in the economy or whether economies of scale and hence mass transit/fixed rail systems, also continue to matter. Flexibility favours the use of motor vehicles both because they are more inherently flexible in their transport character, and because they create or facilitate more flexible (scattered) land uses. Economies of scale mean that mass transport systems (especially rail) are more inherently able to service either freight requirements or people movements, and the places that are facilitated (in regions and in cities) are more concentrated. Those who seem to favour flexibility are academics such as Ogden (1992), Troy (1996) and Hensher (2000) as well as the various arms of the road lobby (Hamer, 1987). Those who seem to favour rail solutions and economies of scale, include academics such as Klaasen et al (1981), Lowe et al (1998), Diesendorf et al (1999) and the authors of this book.

Central to the basis of the latter group, however, is a common belief in the growing importance of sustainability in the fifth cycle of industrialisation. The decisions on technology are no longer seen as purely a one-dimensional market approach based on what seemed to work before. Decisions now need to incorporate a more global perspective on technology which can simultaneously improve the economy, the environment and the community (Newman and Kenworthy, 1999b). This means in reality that transport decisions which unilaterally favour trucks and cars, which extend urban sprawl and increase the consumption of fossil fuels and the production of greenhouse gases and smog, can no longer be seriously contemplated. This will be further enunciated in Chapter 4, then the structural reasons that favour cars and trucks will be outlined in Chapters 5 and 6. The transport decision-making frameworks to reverse the patterns and get us 'back on track' will follow in Chapters 7 and 8.

An awareness that transport decision making is part of this changing social and political process is now quite common; there are few conferences or professional duty statements that do not draw attention to sustainability. However, there is a widespread belief that the fundamental economics of transport, if it could somehow separate itself from these 'external' factors, would always end up favouring the truck and the car. We would want to seriously challenge this assumption and our book provides evidence to support our case that more balanced transport systems are better for economies in the fifth economic cycle, and are distinctly better for the environment and for ordinary people in communities.

We will provide hard data to show why we believe this to be the case. Also, one of the keys to our approach is to show that the fifth cycle information technologies can favour transport systems that are improving flexibility in an economy *and* those that are favouring economies of scale in movement and place. There is no doubt that information technology (IT) will:

- Improve just-in-time production;
- Improve management through things like GPS (global positioning satellites) which can keep track of truck movements;
- Improve traffic flow through ITS (intelligent transport systems) which can help put more cars on freeways and help navigate trips, and
- Improve transport pricing through better electronic payment and monitoring of road use.

But it is also possible to see how IT will:

- Enable mass transit to be more efficient through better tracking of trains and buses (GPS and track signalling);

- Provide instantaneous customer feedback on transit times, and

- Enable 'smart card' payment and monitoring on all transit systems.

Clearly, the use of new technology engines in all vehicles can be of equal benefit to all transport modes. Thus, it is possible to see how IT can help all modes to function better at their particular role.

In terms of issues to do with place or land use, the fifth cycle IT systems were thought initially to provide the basis for an increase in the scatter of land use. People could locate in small country towns or settle on hobby farms, and not require the advantages of agglomerations in cities. We were thought to be entering a 'post city' age where we could make cities into 'non-place urban realms', where community was no longer place-based but net-based (Webber, 1963, 1964, 1968). But the reality has been different. Evidence will be presented later that cities are re-urbanising and the new economy is favouring those places where there is not only significant agglomerations of people, but also where there are real networks of community based on a local sense of place (Putnam, 1993). As Peter Hall (1997, p89) said: 'The new world (of information technology) will largely depend as the old world did, on human creativity; and creativity flourishes where people come together face-to-face.'

The need for a spatial expression of the new economy that is more urban and less suburban, should not really be a surprise. The problem was that for years the debate was dominated by American theorists whose perceptions of the future were seriously affected by deteriorating central and inner-urban areas. This is not the case in Australian and New Zealand cities where the new economy has always been expressed in a greater concentration of wealth in more central locations (Newman et al, 1996). How issues of social justice are incorporated into the new economy and the new city in Australia and New Zealand is a different problem to that faced by American cities. This will be pursued in later chapters.

Thus the question becomes one of not seeing the next era of technology as setting a determined path which we must inevitably follow. The challenge is to choose the path we want that will create better economies, better communities and better environments (globally and locally). This requires us to balance the issues of flexibility and concentration in land use and in flexible/fixed modes. It requires us to create decision-making systems that are open to public discourse and which can more fully reflect social values. We do not have this kind of system in Australia and New Zealand.

2

WHERE WE ARE NOW: NATIONAL PATTERNS AND TRENDS IN TRANSPORT

PHILIP LAIRD

The National Highway System has been improved beyond recognition since its formation in 1974, and road freight has grown in Australia to the point that it is the highest, per capita, in the world. Meantime, trains struggle to operate over substandard national track.

From text

Any resident of Australia or New Zealand cannot help but notice how traffic has increased in recent years. In fact, the total vehicle kilometres driven in Australia has doubled in the 27 years to 1999. There are various reasons for the substantial growth in traffic. These include population growth, increasing real disposable income for more people, a tendency for some people to commute to work by car over longer distances, the power of the car culture as portrayed in the media, and social factors such as the greater participation of women in the workforce. Other major causes for the increase in traffic also include: the relative increase in the ease of use of cars as compared with much public transport, land use planning that has assumed car dependence, and a tax system that favours car ownership and use. Before we can assess these factors in more detail we want to look more closely at how these trends have occurred over the last two decades.

Road traffic can be measured in several ways. For a given location on a road, and a given year, the most basic indicator is the Annual Average Daily Traffic (AADT) factor. This simply gives an estimate, derived from vehicle counters placed on the road of the daily traffic averaged out between weekdays and weekends, and throughout the year. The busiest section of road in Australia in 1996 was the Sydney

Harbour Crossing (bridge plus tunnel) with an AADT exceeding 220 000. By way of contrast, on some rural roads, the AADT may be as low as 100 or less. Indeed, remote sections of national highways such as Port Hedland to Mt Newman in WA have an AADT of only about 250.

Another basic indicator of vehicle movements for a region, an entire State, or even a nation, are estimates in a given year (or twelve-month period) of the total vehicle kilometres which are simply estimates of the sum of the distances driven by each vehicle. In Australia, this information is collected from time to time by the Australian Bureau of Statistics in a Survey of Motor Vehicle Usage (SMVU). In 1999, there were 11.7 million vehicles registered for use on Australian roads, and these vehicles were driven a total of about 178 billion kilometres in 1998–99. This is an average of nearly 9400 km for every man, woman and child in Australia, whose average vehicle ownership was then 616 per 1000 persons.

FIGURE 2.1
AUSTRALIAN CITIES BILLION PASSENGER KILOMETRES

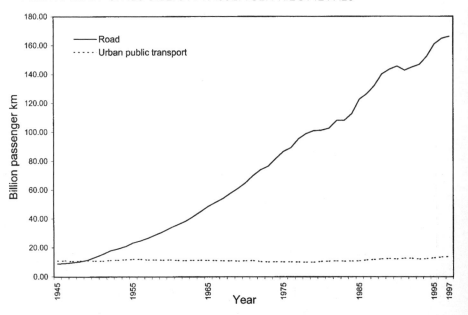

SOURCE Bureau of Transport Economics trend estimates. Road includes cars and other road; urban public transport includes rail, buses and ferries

In New Zealand, there was a total of nearly 2.7 million vehicles in 1999 (NZ Year Book), giving an average of 710 vehicles per 1000 people. According to the NZ Land Transport Safety Authority, these vehicles were driven a total of about 36.4 billion kilometres in 1998. This is an average of some 9600 km for each person in New Zealand.

When vehicles are driven to move people and one needs to take distance factors into account as well the number of people in a vehicle; measures such as passenger kilometres are used. The rule is that one passenger kilometre is generated when one person (driver or passenger) moves a distance of one kilometre. Figure 2.1 shows the strong growth of passenger kilometres in recent years that far outstrip population or economic growth. As noted by the Bureau of Transport Economics (BTE, 1999b), since the end of the Second World War, Australian cities have been transformed and '... total travel in the urban areas of Australia has grown remarkably — almost nine-fold over 50 years. Almost all of that growth came from cars and "other" road vehicles (mostly light commercial vehicles used for private purposes and motorcycles). As of 1995, private road vehicles represent about 93 per cent of city passenger transport'.

In the next chapter we will see how the trends in urban transport in Australia and New Zealand compare with other cities in other parts of the world. The remainder of this chapter is concerned with intercity passenger transport and freight transport.

FIGURE 2.2
AUSTRALIAN NON-URBAN BILLION PASSENGER KILOMETRES

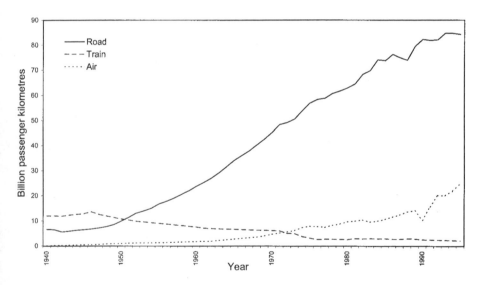

SOURCE Bureau of Transport Economics, see also Rail Projects Taskforce (1999). Road includes buses

NON-URBAN PASSENGERS

As shown by Figure 2.2, cars now dominate non-urban passenger movement including Sydney–Canberra trips, although air transport is now used by most people for moving between state capital cities. During and after World War II, rail was the dominant mode for non-urban passenger journeys in Australia. This situation continued until 1952, when rail's passenger kilometres (pkms) were overtaken by cars. Since then, cars have been the dominant travel mode. By 1973, rail passenger kilometres were overtaken by air passenger kilometres, and two years later in 1975, by bus passenger kilometres. The situation where car passenger kilometres have more than 50 per cent of market share (and so more than all the other modes put together) followed by air, bus, and then train, has persisted in Australia throughout the fourth quarter of the 20th century. To some extent, these trends have been influenced by the fact that Australia has a relatively small population, reaching 19 million in 1999, for a large land area of about 7.7 million square kilometres.

The development of non-urban transport in New Zealand has followed a similar pattern.

During the 1990s, the real growth in non-urban transport in Australia has occurred in domestic aviation. Non-urban bus travel, that showed a strong growth in the 1980s, has been pegged back in the 1990s. Overall, non-urban rail travel has gone backwards in Australia. We look at each mode in turn.

INTERSTATE ROAD PASSENGER TRANSPORT

One reason for the domination of non-urban transport by cars and other passenger vehicles in Australia is that the proportion of passenger vehicles has grown from roughly 120 cars per 1000 persons in 1950 to over 500 cars per 1000 persons in 1999. In addition, there has been an increase in the percentage of the population holding a driver's licence, a marked increase in the reliability of cars, and in their ease of use. Finally, the road system in Australia has seen extensive improvements. This applies not only to the condition of the pavement, with the sealing of more roads, but also to major increases in highway capacity near cities with the construction of more lanes. Major improvements in the quality of road alignments, allowing for faster and safer car journeys, have also progressed.

One striking example of road upgrading in Australia is the ongoing development of the National Highway System (NHS). Such a system was initially proposed in the mid-1950s by the NSW Department of Main Roads and subsequently received the support of a Commonwealth Bureau of Roads during the 1960s. The NHS was formed by the Whitlam Government under the *National Roads Act 1974* which provided for full Federal funding of approved NHS projects. At its time of formation, the NHS included the major roads linking all mainland capital cities, plus certain main Tasmanian roads, with a combined length of about 16 000 kilometres. Between Melbourne and Sydney, the Hume Highway was chosen, and from Sydney to near Newcastle, the Pacific Highway was used along with the New England Highway to Brisbane. However, the Pacific Highway north of Newcastle did not form part of the NHS. At the time of the formation of the NHS in 1974, almost 25 per cent of its length was unsealed, and of those sections that were sealed, 66 per cent were of a width less than 6.7 metres. This often required one of two passing vehicles to move off the sealed surface (Waslin and Widdup, 1988).

The major achievements resulting from sustained Commonwealth funding of the NHS since 1974 have included the sealing of the entire length of highway by 1989, and the reconstruction of most of the Hume Highway between Sydney and Melbourne. The upgrading of the NHS has led to a vast improvement in intercity highway driving for motorists. However, in the absence of comparable upgrading of intercity rail track, the NHS upgrading has gone hand in hand with an increase in interstate freight being moved by heavy trucks.

In November 1992, the NHS was extended to 18 500 kilometres to include the Sturt Highway (Adelaide–Wagga Wagga) and the Newell Highway between Tocumwal and Boggabilla followed by the Gore Highway between Goondiwindi and Toowoomba. As of January 1994, the NHS was extended to include certain urban arterial roads in the mainland State capital cities.

The reconstruction of the Hume Highway is of particular interest. In the early 1970s, the Hume Highway was a basic two-lane sealed road. The Commonwealth Bureau of Roads (1975) noted that

> ... the majority of the Hume Highway between Goulburn and Albury is deficient when compared with not only the proposed standard for a four-lane National Highway, but also the standard for a two-lane rural highway with a design speed of 110 kph ... Deficiencies include those related to both vertical and horizontal alignments, pavement and formation width, pavement performance, and periods of closure (due to flood).

The NRMA (1975) also gave details of the poor condition of the Hume Highway in the 1970s — including grades, alignment (tight curves), narrow shoulders and basic bridges, along with high road crash fatalities and injury numbers. In 1971, no less than 101 km of the then total length of the Hume Highway of 878 km was then in urban areas.

The reconstruction of the Hume Highway started from each of the major cities of Sydney and Melbourne. By 1980, there was 318 km of divided carriageway on the Hume Highway and by 1991, better highways with four or more lanes extended to 523 kilometres. By 1994, with the bypassing of Wangaratta, the entire Hume Highway in Victoria north of Melbourne was dual carriageway. The net result of the massive reconstruction to date has been a reduction in overall length by some 32 kilometres, along with a marked improvement in grades, alignment and capacity. By the end of 2000, dual carriageways accounted for 713 km or 86 per cent of the entire length of the Hume Highway in NSW and Victoria. However, a major problem has now occurred at Albury. Here, plans for a new internal bypass costed in the mid-1990s at about $200 million resulted in much ongoing community opposition. An external bypass was announced in February 2001, resulting in a major cost blowout.

Today, one can drive throughout all of Victoria, and over 300 km from Sydney to south of Yass, on dual carriageways without passing through a town. By 2006, about 90 per cent of the Hume Highway is expected to be dual carriageway.

The transformation of the Hume Highway required many years of planning as well as construction. Numerous reports, planning documents, internal reports, and Environmental Impact Statements and Assessments accompanied the work. It is clear that Federal funding and support since 1974 have been crucial in rebuilding most of the Hume Highway. In the 25 years from 1974 to 1999, nearly $4 billion in 1999 constant dollars was outlaid by the Federal Government on the Hume Highway (Laird, 1999). This outlay was mostly for new construction, although maintenance is now an emerging demand. This enormous commitment to the Hume Highway now needs to be extended to an upgrade of the rail line between Sydney and Melbourne.

The Hume Highway is not the only major National Highway System project in recent years. North of Sydney, the F3 highway has been substantially upgraded over the last 25 years to a high standard of at least four lanes at a cost exceeding $1 billion. However, the section between Berowra and Gosford is now under pressure to be augmented to three lanes each way. As an interim measure, the Federal Government will contribute towards the installation of variable message signs to try and ease occasional highway congestion. This freeway congestion occurs with increasing regularity at peak holiday times and on Friday evenings when commuting traffic mixes with people leaving Sydney for weekends away. Such traffic problems lead one to question the wisdom of the NSW Government agreeing to the request of the Federal Government to remove the tollgates at Berowra. This occurred in December 1988 and left the entire NHS free of any tolls. There is no rush on the part of either the Federal or NSW Government to reinstate a toll at Berowra, despite the need for vehicle demand management, and additional funds for highway expansion.

The New England Highway is also part of the NHS. Improvements over recent years have included work on general upgrading, widening pavement and providing passing lanes along with bypasses of Maitland and Armidale, duplication through Tamworth in NSW, and the improvement of the western approach to Cunningham's Gap in Queensland.

Funding for the Pacific Highway is primarily the responsibility of the NSW and Queensland Governments, and has been much more limited than funding for the NHS. Whilst some improvements in the Pacific Highway were made during the 1980s, these were offset by increasing car, bus and truck traffic. The worsening conditions, in part, are shown by road crash fatalities throughout the 1980s, where 1011 people were killed on the Pacific Highway and 276 people were killed on the New England Highway between Sydney and the Queensland Border (NRMA, 1991). These fatalities on the Pacific Highway in NSW included the tragic crashes involving a truck and bus in October 1989 and two buses in December 1989. Subsequently, the NSW State Coroner (1990) recommended that the entire Pacific Highway be reconstructed to provide dual carriageways. In place of this, a modest $300 million Pacific Highway upgrade program was undertaken in NSW in the early 1990s.

In January 1996, the NSW, Queensland and Federal Governments agreed to commit to a $3 billion upgrade over 10 years. The result was that many Pacific Highway major projects have been expedited, with a view to gaining a four-lane highway for most of the way between Sydney and Brisbane by 2005. The work includes the massive Brisbane–Gold Coast $850 million upgrade that was opened in October 2000, and includes some 35 km of eight-lane highway.

Other NHS roads have been transformed. A significant gain was the sealing of the entire length of the NHS including the Eyre Highway from Port Augusta to near Kalgoorlie, the Sturt Highway from Port Augusta to Darwin, and the Great Northern Highway from Perth to Kununurra. The final seal was made in December 1989 between Newman and Port Hedland. The Bruce Highway from Brisbane to Cairns was also one of many roads that were substantially upgraded from a very basic flood prone road to a good quality road.

The Federal Government's support of roads is not confined to the NHS. The outlay by the Federal Government from 1974 to 1999 on the NHS has been nearly $18 billion in 1999 terms. As shown in Appendix C, the total outlay of the Federal Government on all roads from 1974 to 1999 has been nearly $43 billion, in 1999 terms. This comprises $37.5 billion of 'tied' grants and $5.3 billion of 'untied' grants to the States and Local Government between 1991 and 1999. In November 2000, the Howard Government announced a further $1.6 billion for roads followed in January 2001 with $350 million towards a major Western Orbital toll road in Sydney.

In addition to generous Federal Government outlays on roads, State and local governments also fund roads. By way of example, in 1997–98, the respective road expenditures were $1.6 billion, $3.4 billion and $2.0 billion (BTE, 1999a). This now results in at least $7 billion being outlaid each year on Australian roads.

Intercity bus operations have been a major beneficiary of upgraded highways and enjoyed growth during the 1980s. This, in part, was fuelled by aggressive competition from new bus operators in the early 1980s, with low fares on the Sydney–Melbourne and other major corridors. However, by the 1990s, much of this business had been lost to air transport.

In New Zealand, intercity highway development has been very restrained by Australian standards. In the North Island, the road linking the two major cities of Auckland and Wellington is a basic two-lane highway, except for four-lane motorways that extend south from Auckland for about 50 km, through the Hamilton and Taupo urban areas (no bypasses) and to less than 30 km north of Wellington. Indeed, in 1995, the North Island had a total of just 142 km of motorway out of a network of 5611 km of State Highways in the entire North Island road network of 46 785 km (New Zealand Ministry of Transport, 1996). The main road system in the South Island remains in a basic two-lane condition for most of its length (40 001 km).

AIR TRANSPORT

Domestic air transport by scheduled air services has been the big growth industry of the late 20th century in Australia. From 1987, domestic flights more than doubled to nearly 27 million in 1999–2000. This strong growth was only interrupted by the so-called 'pilots' dispute' in 1989 which set back domestic aviation, and impacted heavily on many regional tourist operators. However, this setback was more than offset by the entry, albeit temporary, of Compass Airlines following government deregulation of domestic aviation in 1990. In two brief corporate lives, Compass Airlines gave many people in Australia their first air flight and led to lower average domestic airfares. Further aviation developments included Ansett offering limited overseas service in the 1990s, the merger of QANTAS and Australian Airlines (formerly TAA) by the Federal Government in 1993, the privatisation of QANTAS in 1995, and competition on major routes offered by Impulse and Virgin airlines in 2000.

Coupled with an increase in international passenger movements (from about 8 million in 1990 to 15 million in 1999), Australia's major airports have had unprecedented demands placed on them. The Federal Government funded much of the growth in airport capacity. Airport expansion, although partly funded by users, required a capital injection of some $1.4 billion by the Federal Airports Corporation between 1988 and 1996. During the 1990s, the Commonwealth had privatised all of the larger airports except Sydney, and transferred the smaller ones to local government or other interests under an Aerodrome Local Ownership Plan.

Nowhere in Australia has the growth of aviation been more keenly felt than in Sydney. Almost half of all scheduled domestic flights in

Australia involve a take-off or landing at Sydney's Kingsford Smith Airport and in 1998 some 45 per cent of all international passengers to and from Australia used this airport. The resulting pressure on Sydney, and the ongoing search for a second Sydney airport site, could fill a book. However, air transport is outside of the scope of this book except to mention some brief facts. In the 1970s, a Major Airport Needs of Sydney (MANS) inter-governmental group worked long and hard at site selection. In 1983, a newly elected Labor Federal Government hoped for a quick decision. By 1986, the choices for a major second Sydney airport site had been narrowed down to two: Wilton or Badgerys Creek. The Hawke Government chose Badgerys Creek. The decision by the Hawke Government in 1989 to construct a third runway at Kingsford Smith had appreciable political fallout and the Keating Government made limited moves to develop a site at Badgerys Creek. After the 1996 election, the Howard Government explored the option of Holsworthy, but rejected this in 1998, and reaffirmed Badgerys Creek in 1999. During this time, many commentators doubted if a major second Sydney airport would actually be built at Badgerys Creek. An interesting report quoted in the *Financial Review* of 10 August 1999 considered that the Government should, among other things:

- Shift regional air traffic from Kingsford Smith to Sydney's Bankstown airport by 2004 (by which time the proposed M5 East motorway will have been completed).
- Build a new general aviation airport at Badgerys Creek.
- Develop the proposed fast train between Sydney and Canberra, and fast track its extensions to Melbourne and Brisbane.

A long-delayed Federal Government decision on a second major Sydney airport was given in December 2000. In effect, the decision was not to proceed with a new airport at Badgerys Creek, maintain regional airline access at Kingsford Smith and seek to expand airports at both Bankstown and Canberra. It was also decided to privatise Sydney's airports, and to subject rail options to further studies.

NON-URBAN RAIL

For non-urban passenger transport, we have noted that trains have changed from being the most important transport mode up to 1952, to being the least important mode by 1975. This fall is mainly due to significant improvements in roads, cars, and air transport in recent decades, and relatively declining levels of rail service and transit times. This is well illustrated by the fact that in the mid-1950s, Sydney–Melbourne rail transit time at 13.5 hours compared very favourably with a bus transit time of about 18 hours using a somewhat basic Hume Highway. This superior service allowed rail to charge higher fares than buses between Sydney and Melbourne.

For many decades, the Sydney–Melbourne rail transit time tended to remain at about 13.5 hours, whilst the bus time was lowered to 12 hours or less by the 1980s and a car trip of 10 hours was quite possible. Whilst XPT trains put into the Sydney–Melbourne service in 1993 allowed for a 10-hour journey, the XPT train performance is severely limited in many sections by poor 'steam age' track alignment. The XPT train is also found by many passengers to be uncomfortable for journeys over six hours, and arguably poor on-board food services do not help. The Sydney–Brisbane XPT rail service has also been taken to task by both local and international travellers, with comment on the XPT sleeper cabins as 'cement mixers' (eg Ellis, 1998).

On a brighter note, the former Commonwealth rail system, Australian National, was able to do well with its passenger services *The Ghan* and the *Indian Pacific* between Sydney, Adelaide, Perth and Alice Springs. Improvements made in the 1990s included refurbishing the trains, offering good service, and marketing the train journeys as ones of world class. In 1997, these services were privatised and taken over by Great Southern Railway, who have made further improvements, and extended the operation of the *Ghan* to Melbourne and Sydney. Queensland Rail (or QR) have also made advances in developing intercity rail services, to include the premium *Queenslander* service between Brisbane and Cairns, an Inter-City Electric (ICE) service between Brisbane and Rockhampton in 1989, along with 'outback' services such as that between Brisbane and Longreach. By such initiatives, Queensland Rail has been able to buck the downward trend for non-urban rail and has actually increased rail passenger journeys since 1995.

A major initiative of Queensland Rail was the commissioning on 6 November 1998 of the first regular tilt-train service in Australia. These services operate between Brisbane and Rockhampton. To cover the 630 km distance, with 11 intermediate stops, a time of 7 hours is allowed. This service is very popular, and had carried 600 000 passengers within the first two years of operation. The maximum speed of the tilt train on the better quality track is set at 170 km per hour. This tilt train set the current Australian rail speed record of 210 km per hour on a trial run north of Bundaberg in May 1999.

Along with high levels of on-board service, the two basic requirements of any good passenger train service are the train and the track. Two QR tilt trains were constructed by Walkers of Maryborough at a cost of about $72 million. The QR tilt trains are electric trains drawing 25 000 volts AC from overhead catenary (as opposed to the much older 1500 volts DC system used in NSW and Melbourne), and have regenerative braking. As such, they are energy efficient.

Each QR tilt train has a first class car and five economy cars seating a total of 310 passengers. The interior of the cars looks more like that of a small jet aircraft cabin. As well as providing normal aircraft audio-visual services, there are telephones and power points. On-board television monitors, when not showing video movies, may show the view from the front of the train.

The Brisbane–Rockhampton track was progressively upgraded. The upgrading has included the following: Brisbane suburban and intercity electrification during the 1980s; Mainline Upgrade (MLU) during the 1990s; 95 per cent of track laid on concrete sleepers; and improved level-crossing protection for the tilt trains. The MLU project saw a total of 120 km of high-quality rail deviations and the replacement of hundreds of old timber bridges to achieve higher axle loadings between Brisbane and Cairns. The main reason for the MLU project was to improve rail freight efficiency with faster and heavier trains. The introduction of the highly successful tilt train was an MLU bonus.

Queensland Rail also entered into a partnership with Venice–Simplon–Orient to operate the Great South Pacific Express. This luxury new train service started regular services between Kuranda, Cairns, Brisbane and Sydney in April 1999, and has attracted much media interest.

Australia has also shown a keen interest in the concept of a Very Fast Train, or VFT. The concept as initially proposed in 1984 by CSIRO was simple and appealing — by use of existing French TGV (Train à Grand Vitesse) technology, build a completely new railway that would go through Canberra, and convey people between Sydney and Melbourne in just three hours. Although the concept generated much media interest, and some private sector capital to undertake feasibility studies in the 1980s, the proposal was suspended in 1990. The project also attracted some opposition on cost and environmental grounds, despite the billions outlaid in that decade on intercity highways with their environmental impact. At the conclusion of investigations, a number of valuable reports had been published.

From the rise and fall of the Sydney–Canberra–Melbourne VFT in the 1980s came the impetus for the development of a VFT proposal between Sydney and Canberra in 1995 called Speedrail. This new VFT proposal led to expressions of interest being formally invited in March 1997 by the Commonwealth, New South Wales and ACT Governments from six proponents. Four detailed proposals, each with a $100 000 deposit, were made to Government by December 1997: one Maglev (by Transrapid), one by Speedrail, and two tilt trains (Capital Rail, and Inter Capital Express) using an upgrade of the existing track. In August 1998, the Prime Minister announced that the preferred option was Speedrail, which then went into a 'proving-up' stage on the understanding that if the project were to proceed, it would be '... at no net cost to the taxpayer'. The feasibility reports were presented to Government in October 1999 with media speculation that Speedrail would require $1 billion of Government assistance or tax concessions.

In December 2000, after protracted review by the Federal Government, the Speedrail project was rejected. There was understandable disappointment shown by both the Speedrail consortium, and the city of Canberra.

The Australian market to support the VFT dedicated track and trains is very much weaker than the European or Japanese market. Moreover, during the 1990s, the United States settled on better trains on existing tracks as a means to win back intercity passengers to rail on numerous corridors. Here, tilt trains are in use between Seattle and Portland on the West Coast, and between Washington, New York and Boston on the East Coast. The new Acela tilt-train services on the East Coast were introduced in November 2000 with trains moving at up to 240 km per hour, and the New York–Washington train taking 2 hours and 28 minutes.

Clearly, a better Sydney–Canberra passenger train service to complement a good highway is highly desirable. However, this new four-lane highway between Sydney and Canberra, which was completed in August 2000, has no tolls south of Liverpool. Perceptions of cheap car travel, upgraded highways with no tolls, and new competition in domestic aviation, were all factors that negatively impacted on the economics of a French-style TGV between Sydney and Canberra.

In the meantime, the people of NSW have had little other than the prospect of a VFT on new tracks ever since 1984 with the occasional promise of a fast tilt train. A Swedish X2000 tilt train was brought to NSW by State Rail in 1995 following the success of a trial of this train in the United States. Some wondered if the 1995 NSW State elections were a factor — after all, the XPT had performed brilliantly in regional NSW for the 1981 State election. In early 1995, the X2000 was put on an eight-week trial between Sydney and Canberra. As well as demonstrating the potential of fast tilt train operations in Australia, the Swedish tilt train also highlighted the excessive track curvature of NSW mainline track.

In summary, it was a fast train on slow track with an even slower political process.

At the start of the 21st century, non-urban rail in Australia after some decades of decline has had some recent success including the Queensland tilt train. There is exciting potential for improvement in all mainline states.

NEW ZEALAND RAIL SERVICES

Long-distance rail passenger services were prospering in New Zealand and able to operate without Government subsidy during the 1990s.

These services were expanded in the early 1990s and appeal to both domestic travellers and overseas tourists. For example, the 1995 Annual Report of Tranz Rail Ltd notes that:

> Long-distance rail is establishing itself in the tourism and domestic marketplaces by promoting travel packages rather than purely rail journeys ... The Tranz-Alpine between Christchurch and Greymouth continued its phenomenal success with an increase in patronage ...

New Zealand railways were privatised in 1993 and shares were offered to the public in 1996. In the late 1990s, Tranz Rail Ltd could broadly be described as a United States and New Zealand-owned public company that paid taxes to the Government and dividends to its shareholders. These results were due to high service levels and largely supported by vertical integration, relatively good intercity track compared with basic intercity highways, and reasonable road cost recovery from heavy vehicles with mass-distance charging. However, in October 2000, Tranz Rail Ltd announced its intention to restructure the company and to sell its passenger operations. This led to some critical comment such as 'Track record costly to public' (*New Zealand Herald*, 21 October 2000) suggesting in part that:

> Fay, Richwhite, one of Tranz Rail's controlling shareholders, has never been on the wrong end of a transaction with the public sector and the sale of the corridors (in Auckland and possibly Wellington) to the local authorities is not expected to break this trend.

Thus, the future of Tranz Rail Ltd is uncertain. However, the fact that New Zealand still has a viable rail system to perform a small freight and passenger task by world standards is of interest. The actual annual rail freight task in New Zealand amounts to less than a day's work by the combined Class I railroads of the United States. As such, heavy trucks could easily perform New Zealand's land freight task, albeit at the expense of more road wear and tear, road crashes, noise and air pollution. In a similar way, buses could undertake New Zealand's intercity passenger task. New Zealand's largest urban rail passenger task is in Wellington where people could also be diverted to buses and cars, whilst Auckland's rail passenger task is very small, and Christchurch and Dunedin have not had urban trains for some decades now.

Coupled with rail deficits during the 1970s, this led some Treasury bureaucrats in the early 1980s to consider closure of all rail services. By then, many branch lines had been closed and services withdrawn. Within 15 years, it was thought, the entire rail system could be closed. This was despite the then recent investment in a new 8 km Kaimai tunnel to service the Port of Mt Manganui near Tauranga.

What turned the rail system around from the threat of closure prior to general elections in 1983 to privatisation in 1993, was a series of events we will describe below. This was coupled with a steady application of mass-distance charges for heavy trucks, so that rail could compete fairly with road for freight traffic.

The first main event was in 1983 when the Government sought to lift rail protection which reserved to rail the carriage of most goods moving a distance of more than 150 kilometres. The response of the rail unions was to embark on a public Save Rail campaign. This was strongly taken up by the Labor Party in opposition. When Labor won the 1983 election, under Prime Minister David Lange and Treasurer Roger Douglas, it was made clear that rail could stay only if New Zealand Railways became much more efficient. New Zealand Rail, which had been corporatised in 1982, was then massively downsized and restructured to lift its performance. This message was reiterated by Transport Minister Richard Prebble who in 1986 threatened to close down the entire system unless it was prepared to embrace technological change and become more efficient. However, in keeping faith, the New Zealand Government increased road-user charges for heavy trucks and heavily invested in the North Island Main Track modern high voltage electrification (25 000 volts AC) and civil works between Palmerston North and Hamilton. The extent of work over the 408-km section between Palmerston North and Hamilton is well described in an unpublished article by a NZR journalist Philip Hoskin in 1985.

> The decision to proceed with electrification has led to many major civil engineering projects, including massive earthworks, to improve the NIMT central section.

> Some have been necessary to install the traction overhead and cope with electric locomotive axle loads, and others to obtain maximum benefit from the power potential of the locomotives which can haul longer, heavier trains faster than the current diesel powered fleet.

> These track improvements include making it straighter and flatter through easing curves and gradients; alterations to 10 tunnels either by lowering floor or 'daylighting' — removing the earth about a tunnel; bridge and viaduct strengthening; and providing longer, and some new, crossing loops.

> An example of the scale of earthworks involved is the daylighting of the Makohine tunnel between Hunterville and Taihape. Another project, which alone cost $14 million, is the nine-kilometre deviation replacing a tunnel and two ageing viaducts between Ohakune and Horopito.

> It is improvements to the track such as these, together with the new signalling and communications systems, which will enable trains to travel faster.

> Electrification and modern electronics allow energy conservation through regenerative braking — locomotives when going downhill can convert energy to electricity for use by other trains in the area. In the hilly country in the centre of the North Island as much as a fifth of the energy required could be recovered in this way.

These and other track improvements help to provide good levels of intercity rail services in New Zealand. It is to be hoped that they will continue.

SEA PASSENGER TRANSPORT

Domestic sea transport is now reduced to serving niche markets in Australia. These include ferries (overnight and day) that run between Melbourne and Tasmania, medium distances such as Queenscliff to Portsea in Victoria, along with longstanding urban passenger ferries in Sydney, Hobart, and now Brisbane. The cruise market is also worthy of note.

Inter-island ferries play a larger role in non-urban transport in New Zealand. The main services run between Wellington and Picton and were operated from 1963 to 1993 by New Zealand Railways. The services now operated by Tranz Rail Ltd carried over one million passengers in 1997–98 and were later complemented by services offered by a competing operator.

FREIGHT

As we have seen in Chapter 1, the movement of goods by truck was once confined mainly to the nearest port or rail station. Over the years, road freight has grown to the extent that trucks move over 1400 million tonnes of goods each year in Australia (ABS, 2000b). This amount

FIGURE 2.3
THE INTERSTATE NON-BULK LAND FREIGHT TASK

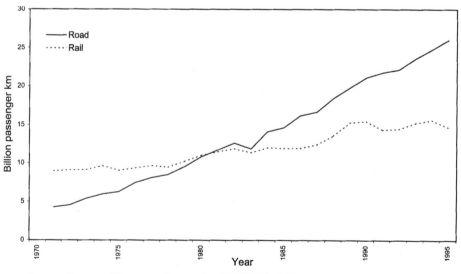

SOURCE Bureau of Transport Economics (1999, Table 1.1)

is far in excess of the tonnages moved by sea or rail. Although most road freight tonnages move over shorter distances, there has been an increasing amount of road freight moved using articulated trucks.

In discussing freight movements, it is better to take distance factors into account as well as the tonnages moved. This gives rise to the concept of one net tonne kilometre (or tkm), that occurs when one tonne of freight is moved one kilometre. Data about freight tasks is given in Appendix A that shows road, rail and sea now having roughly equal shares of Australian domestic freight transport if pipelines are excluded. Figure 2.3 shows the large growth of interstate road freight.

Australia's road freight industry is large and diverse, and uses a wide variety of trucks to perform different transport tasks. By far the largest tonnages are moved within urban areas over short distances and may be moved either by Light Commercial Vehicles (LCVs) including panel vans, rigid trucks with an in-built trailer having at most four axles, or by larger articulated trucks with five or more axles. Articulated trucks have one or more trailers coupled to a prime mover. During 1998–99, throughout Australia, LCVs moved 107 million tonnes (mt) of goods; rigid trucks moved 660 mt; and articulated trucks moved 653 mt, a total of 1421 mt. Taking into account the distance of haul as well as tonnages, the respective freight tasks, measured in tkms, for all freight in Australia in 1998–99 were: 4.9 billion tkm (btkm) for LCVs; 23.3 btkm for rigid trucks; and 99.1 btkm for articulated trucks.

For non-urban road freight, the use of articulated trucks has increased in importance. The Australian 'workhorse' is now a six-axle articulated truck, with a three-axle prime mover, and a tri-axle trailer. This design, which distributes a heavy load of as much as 30 tonnes over a truck with unladen or tare mass of up to 16 tonnes, has current standard Gross Vehicle Mass (GVM) limits of 42.5 tonnes. The development of these six-axle trucks, initially with a GVM of 36 tonnes, owes much to Australian initiative. So also do lifting their GVM to 38 tonnes in 1979 (assisted by truck blockades), and then 41 to 42.5 tonnes by the 1990s. By 2000, all States except NSW allowed modern six-axle articulated trucks with 'Road Friendly Suspension' (RFS) such as air bags, to lift their GVM to 45.5 tonnes. Following some persuasion by the Federal Government, NSW conditionally allowed RFS trucks to lift their mass in mid-2001.

Australia has also been a world leader in the development and use of large road trains in remote areas. These included Type 1 road trains with two large trailers and Type 2 road trains with three large trailers. As an example, by the mid-1980s, Type 2 road trains carrying liquid fuel in the Northern Territory had a GVM of 115 tonnes and a payload of 78 tonnes. Today, a modern Type 2 road train with RFS could have a GVM of 123 tonnes.

Relaxation of mass and dimension limits has allowed for the intro-duction in the 1990s of two different types of vehicle. These are even bigger road trains for remote areas, and, the widespread use of B-Doubles for use on most, but not all highways. An example of a very large road train, in use in 1999 on main highways in the North of Western Australia to haul bulk liquids, had no fewer than five trailers and twenty-two axles.

B-Doubles were initially developed in Canada, as B-Trains. The Australian road freight industry was able to persuade Governments to call them B-Doubles. This was to reduce potential confusion with road trains, and also help overcome some public opposition that persisted, in some urban areas, to the mid-1990s. One such area was Melbourne, another area was Wollongong where the local council was taken to task by a National Transport Planning Taskforce (1994, page 57) for hav-ing the temerity to oppose the extended use of B-Doubles. As we shall see, Wollongong has had more than its fair share of road haulage of coal with adverse environmental impact and loss of life.

B-Doubles began appearing on some major highways in the 1980s. To ease public acceptance in NSW, the State Government required modern equipment and specially trained drivers. B-Doubles were ini-tially restricted to eight axles with a maximum length of 23 metres. During the 1990s, the use of B-Doubles became more widespread, and permission was sought, and gained, to move to the heavier nine axles with a maximum GVM of 62.5 tonnes, and a maximum length of 25 metres.

The advances in Australian road freight productivity are heavily dependent on massive road upgrading and maintenance. As we have seen, road works are now costing Australia over $7 billion a year. A sig-nificant part of this cost, which we examine later, is due to heavy truck operations. Quite simply, lightly built roads — sealed or unsealed — quickly deteriorate under sustained heavy loads. To accommodate rel-atively large tonnages on intercity highways, the tendency is to con-struct new highways with easier grades, dual carriageways and concrete pavements. Where possible, towns on intercity highways may also be bypassed to overcome problems caused by large-scale trucking.

URBAN FREIGHT

Large urban areas generate the movement of large tonnages of freight, although often only over short distances. Appendix A gives data on the urban road freight task with data showing that the urban freight task, in tkms has almost tripled within 19 years to 1995 (with an average growth rate of 5.6 per cent per annum).

Urban road freight includes all manner of goods deliveries to shops, offices and homes, which are often performed by the LCVs, or the smaller rigid trucks. There is also the movement of materials needed for factories, which may use rigid trucks, and in some cases, the larger articulated trucks. Large seaports now have a capacity to generate much road freight, including the movement of imported shipping containers between a wharf and a warehouse, or, movement of commodities to a wharf for export. All types of road freight have to compete with cars for the same road space. However, the heavier articulated trucks cause the greatest environmental and social impact on cities.

All cities with a major container port have a story to tell about the movement of containers, often using old articulated trucks, and sometimes on narrow streets that were never designed for large trucks. One case in particular has been the movement of containers within Sydney, firstly from Mort Bay near Balmain, and then from Port Botany.

CONTAINERS

Most imports into New South Wales come through Sydney. The movement of containers to and from Sydney's ports by heavy trucks has presented severe problems since 1969. The operation of Mort Bay as a container terminal serviced only by trucks in the suburb of Balmain from 1969 to 1980 was one of the worst urban blights in Australia and even recognised by the NSW Maritime Services Board as '... a situation that is clearly unacceptable' (Kirby, 1981). The Mort Bay facility with container trucks persisted until Port Botany was handling containers.

The NSW State Cabinet resolved to have containers compulsorily moved by rail between Port Botany and the Western Suburbs, as recommended by a Commission of Inquiry (Kirby, 1981) with the unanimous support of seven affected local government councils. However, this plan was quickly overturned following industrial action involving the Transport Workers' Union. Road has since then continued to carry the majority of containers to and from Port Botany (except for those being moved interstate). This road haulage was accompanied by truck queues near the Port for many years, and ongoing severe environmental impact, despite the ability of rail to clear containers to decentralised depots away from the port. Although it was not in rail's comparative advantage to service short-distance movements, the use of such a system (with concentrated volumes, regular cycles and appropriate pricing structures) would offset the remoteness of Port Botany from the main industrial areas of Sydney and the tortuous road links that existed for many years (Inter-State Commission, 1989).

More use of rail for container movements between Port Botany and Sydney's Western Suburbs evolved in the late 1990s. However, the failure to reserve such container movements to rail has punished Sydney suburbs such as Bexley with large-scale trucking operations to move shipping containers through residential and commercial areas with severe adverse social and environmental impacts. The solution favoured by the NSW Government for two decades has been to construct a new urban freeway that was rejected by the Kirby Government inquiry of 1981. The proposed freeway met with strong local opposition in the 1980s and the 1990s, and was finally approved as the M5 East in 1998. It is due for completion in 2002 at a cost of some $400 million.

A second urban freight horror story was the movement of millions of tonnes of coal, for export, through the streets of Wollongong during the late 20th century. A major export from New South Wales is black coal, the volume of which had grown from about 12 million tonnes in 1970 to over 60 million tonnes in 1999. Most of this export coal is delivered to port by rail. However, for most of the 1970s, 1980s and 1990s, over 4 million tonnes per annum (mtpa) were delivered by road to Port Kembla with a smaller amount delivered by road to coal export terminals at Newcastle. In addition, significant quantities of coal were hauled by heavy trucks on public roads to rail loading points in the Hunter Valley until the commissioning in 1997 of a new coal loading facility near Muswellbrook.

Undoubtedly, Wollongong felt the most severe coal trucking impacts during the 1970s and 1980s. Laird (1986) gives the background, and the major points are outlined in the next section.

PORT KEMBLA COAL EXPORTS

In May 1979, no fewer than six lives were lost in two road accidents involving coal trucks. The public reaction was a massive petition signed by 40 000 people and presented to the NSW Parliament:

> We, the residents of Illawarra and Southern Tablelands living on the road haulage routes used by heavy transport hereby request your consideration of our petition. I, the undersigned, am appalled by the continuing carnage on our roads and in particular Mt Ousley, and join in demanding the local, State and Federal authorities take immediate action to ensure motorists' safety.

> I further demand the relevant authorities make provisions for the complete abandonment of coal haulage by road.

The immediate NSW Government response was a 40-km per hour speed restriction on heavy trucks descending Mt Ousley, and a thorough mechanical check of the entire coal truck fleet. The results as reported in 1980 (McDonell) by a Commission of Inquiry showed that some 30 per cent of the coal trucks had major safety defects, mostly in the braking and steering systems. This led to the ongoing efforts of the NSW authorities in annual and random safety checks of the mechanical condition of heavy trucks operating in NSW.

However, in 1983, Illawarra coal trucks were reportedly involved in fatal crashes at rates, per 100 million vehicle kilometres, that were up to three times higher than NSW averages for all articulated trucks. During the eight years from 1978 to 1985, trucks hauling coal to Port Kembla were reportedly involved in some 27 road fatalities. Further efforts by the NSW Government and the coal and trucking industry in the late 1980s, along with much road upgrading, led to an appreciable improvement in safety in coal trucking. However, the upgrading of main roads used by coal trucks and other vehicles came at a large cost, estimated to exceed $250 million.

In 1983, the NSW Government commenced work on a Maldon–Port Kembla railway. However, after an outlay of some $50 million on new track, half a bridge, and a start on a tunnel, the Greiner Government stopped the work in 1988.

Other external costs of coal trucking to Port Kembla include road congestion in urban areas, air pollution, vibration, and noise. The noise from coal trucks was found to exceed NSW Government roadside noise guidelines and was appreciably more than the noise from coal trains (Healthy Cities Illawarra/EPA, 1993). Subsequently, noise walls were installed extending for several kilometres along Mt Ousley and other roads used by coal trucks near residential areas in Wollongong City.

Along with Newcastle and Wollongong, many other cities and towns have had to deal with problems posed by haulage of bulk commodities by heavy trucks using public roads. The impacts were well summarised by a NSW Coal Development Strategies Industry Task Force (1990, page 59):

> Road haulage has significant community costs including noise and dust pollution, increased energy usage, increased road maintenance, safety hazards, negative effects on tourism and complaints from local residents.

NON-URBAN ROAD FREIGHT

There are many reasons for the growth of non-urban road freight in Australia. Firstly, there is the flexibility of door-to-door movement of goods using a single truck. This factor has become increasingly important with higher valued goods and smaller inventories or holdings of components held at factories. Next, there has been impressive and ongoing development in truck technology since World War II. Together with ongoing large-scale road improvements, these factors have allowed for heavier loads and faster intercity deliveries. As well, in a relatively deregulated environment, the Australian road freight industry has grown to be competitive by any world standards. Problems in the competing surface freight modes of rail and sea transport, including no fewer than five Government rail systems with inadequate investment in intercity track and problems on the waterfront over many decades, have increased road transport's appeal. All these factors, along with under-recovery of road system costs from the heavier long-distance trucks, have caused the

Australian road freight task to grow by leaps and bounds. By 1984, the road freight task in Australia — measured in tonne kilometres (tkms) — had outgrown, for the first time ever, the combined rail freight task. Further growth in road freight has now given Australia the dubious distinction of having the highest road freight, in tkm per capita, in the world (Austroads, 1997).

The non-urban articulated truck freight task almost quadrupled within the 19 years to 1995 (with a high average growth rate of 7.2 per cent per annum). The high growth in the road freight task, which is in excess of both gross domestic product, and the overall use of cars on Australian roads, has not been without its problems. These problems include: accelerated road pavement wear and tear; the need for more road construction; certain truck drivers have been induced to drive unduly long hours with a temptation to speed and/or overload; over-representation by articulated trucks in fatal road crashes, and the adverse impact of noise and air pollution on urban areas near truck routes.

Because of the importance of road freight to exports, industry and our way of life, these various problems tend to be lived with rather than properly addressed in a consistent manner. Occasionally, some problems become so severe that they demand attention. One problem was truck blockades, including the national ones in April 1979 starting at Razorback near Picton in NSW, and the blockades in mid-1988 at locations including Yass in NSW. Another problem has been the ongoing multiple fatal road crashes involving articulated trucks. Some government action in the early 1980s included NSW introducing both random and annual safety checks of the mechanical condition of heavy trucks. There have also been numerous government inquiries into the industry. These have included: a Commission of Inquiry into the NSW Road Freight Industry (McDonell, 1980); the National Road Freight Industry Inquiry, reporting in 1984; the inquiries of the Inter-State Commission from 1984 to 1990; the ongoing work of the National Road Transport Commission (or NRTC) formed in 1991; and a NSW Motor Accidents Authority inquiry in 2000.

The issues relating to heavy trucks, including road safety and road pricing, are important. We shall return to them in later chapters.

RAIL FREIGHT

Rail freight is an essential economic activity that is often given little thought. However, most people would probably agree that more freight should be moved by rail when it would take 'loads off roads'. Although most freight movements are small tonnages moved over short distances where road haulage is most appropriate, there is scope in Australia for rail to assume more of the nation's freight task.

Rail freight may be regarded as having two major components — bulk and non-bulk. In 1999, the Australian bulk rail freight task consisted mainly of two elements: the movement each year of nearly 150

million tonnes of iron ore from mines in the Pilbara to various ports,;
and the movement of over 150 million tonnes of coal from mines to
ports in Central Queensland and the Hunter Valley of NSW. Coal is
also moved from Ipswich to Brisbane's port and some NSW coal is
moved to Port Kembla. Apart from coal and iron ore, the other major
bulk rail freight task is the movement of grain in all mainland States.
This is seasonal traffic, peaking in summer, and can vary considerably
from year to year, reaching 20 million tonnes or more in a good year.
The efficiency of these bulk rail freight tasks range from world's best
practice for the haulage of iron ore in the Pilbara to 'text book' examples of difficult operations with poor performance.

The iron ore railways in the Pilbara region were built in the late
1960s to meet an emerging world demand for iron ore. This development followed the lifting of export bans on iron ore imposed by the
Federal Government in 1938. In the late 1960s, four railways were
completed: Goldsworthy's line between Yarrie and near Port Hedland;
Robe River's Pannawonica to Cape Lambert line; BHP's Mt Newman
to Port Hedland line; and Hamersley Iron's Mt Tom Price to Dampier
line. In 1970, the combined iron ore tonnage moved on these four
railways was less than 20 million tonnes.

In the next five years to 1975, there was a five-fold escalation of
iron ore exports. The new iron railways were pushed to their limits,
and track had to be strengthened to accommodate this burst of tonnage (see, for example, Vanselow, 1989). The demands placed on these
railways, with the much increased tonnages, resulted in Australia
undertaking research and development in heavier axle loadings for
wagons, along with increased efficiency and reliability of operations. In
this process, which drew on resources such as at BHP's Melbourne
Research Laboratory, Australia became a world leader in heavy rail
haulage. By 1990, the iron ore trains in the Pilbara were demonstrably
the most efficient freight trains in the world.

During the 1990s, these iron ore railways were further extended.
The use of new locomotives and the introduction of higher standards
of track maintenance have allowed these railways to become even more
efficient. In fact, they are so efficient that it takes less than one litre of
diesel fuel to move one tonne of iron ore over the 426 km of high quality railway track from Mt Newman to Port Hedland. This includes a
sustained climb with loaded trains over the Chichester Ranges, and
bringing back the empty wagons.

The non-bulk rail freight task includes the movement of containers, cars, steel products and general freight. The performance of this
task varies from near world's best practice down to inefficient operations over substandard track that are unable to compete with heavier
trucks operating over upgraded roads with low road pricing.

Non-bulk rail freight consists of two parts in Australia — interstate (between States) and intrastate (a freight movement within one state only). At the end of the 1990s, the interstate rail freight task was performed by no fewer than six rail systems and companies. The largest share was held by National Rail at about 15 billion tonne kilometres (btkm) in 1998–99, with some 5 btkm held by SCT, Toll, Patrick, Freight Corp and Freight Victoria. Interstate rail freight moves mostly over two corridors: either the East–West corridor linking Melbourne to Perth through Adelaide, or, the North–South corridor between Melbourne, Sydney and Brisbane. Some interstate rail freight also moves between Sydney and Perth through Parkes and Broken Hill.

Rail's share of interstate land freight varies from as low as 20 per cent or less on the shorter corridors such as Sydney–Melbourne (where trucks on the Hume Highway win 80 per cent or more) to as high as 80 per cent on the longer Melbourne–Perth corridors. Over the years, there have been many government- funded reports suggesting that rail could be wining higher modal shares. As seen by the National Transport Planning Taskforce (1995), an investment in the national rail highway of $3 billion was warranted, and, rail on a corridor such as Melbourne–Brisbane should be attracting a much higher share of land freight than a low 20 per cent.

As recognised by many Government inquiries, which we examine in Chapter 5, in order for rail to win more freight, it is necessary to upgrade the rail tracks. In short, it is no good having one of the world's best locomotive fleets (as does National Rail with its 120 new General Electric Dash 8 locomotives built in Australia) and a good wagon fleet if the track has too many sharp curves.

In many Australian railway situations in the 1980s and 1990s, Queensland showed the way. As Gough Whitlam observed (1997), although the Fraser Government had in 1980 offered to help electrify the 960 km Sydney–Melbourne railway, the NSW and Victorian Governments had let the opportunity pass by them. However, in contrast, by the end of the 1980s Queensland had electrified over 2000 km of track, including Brisbane–Rockhampton–Emerald — a longer distance than from Sydney to Melbourne. Moreover, as well as modern high voltage mainline electrification, as noted above much of Queensland's mainline track has been rebuilt to modern engineering standards. The benefits include lower maintenance costs, faster and heavier freight trains, and faster passenger trains.

In New Zealand, through a combination of a good balance in rail track and road investment, mass-distance charges for heavy trucks, and good rail management (both in public hands until 1993 and then privately owned), rail is successful in moving a near optimum share of freight. However, in the late 1990s, the New Zealand annual rail freight task at about 4 btkm is small in comparison with the Australian aggregate annual rail freight task of about 130 btkm.

3

HOW WE COMPARE: PATTERNS AND TRENDS IN AUSTRALIAN AND NEW ZEALAND CITIES

PETER NEWMAN, JEFFREY KENWORTHY AND MARK BACHELS

> ... total travel in the urban areas of Australia has grown remarkably — almost nine-fold over 50 years. Almost all of that growth came from cars and 'other' road vehicles ...
>
> Bureau of Transport Economics (1999b)

As shown in Chapter 1 there has been a 50-year history of building Australian and New Zealand cities around the car. This chapter examines the more recent trends, how the resulting transport patterns compare with other cities around the world and some of the implications of these patterns.

The data used in the chapter are from a longstanding *Global Cities* study by the Institute for Sustainability and Technology Policy (ISTP), first published for 1960–80 on 32 cities (Newman and Kenworthy, 1989), and more recently updated and extended in several separate exercises. The first update for 1990 on 46 cities is found in Kenworthy et al (1999). More recently, these data have been extended to include the three main New Zealand cities of Wellington, Auckland and Christchurch (Bachels, Newman and Kenworthy, 1999). Finally, these data are being brought up to 1995 and extended even further in a new study of 100 cities entitled the 'Millennium Cities Database', being conducted for the International Union (Association) of Public Transport (UITP — Union Internationale des Transports Publics) in Brussels. The detailed methodology used in the construction of these data and the cross-checking and validation procedures can be found in Chapter 2 of Kenworthy et al (1999) and further detail for the New Zealand cities can be found in Bachels, Newman and Kenworthy (1999).

For the 1980 data, the Australian cities included Sydney, Melbourne, Brisbane, Adelaide and Perth; Canberra was added for 1990, but for 1995 in the larger global data base only Sydney, Melbourne, Brisbane and Perth are included. Data are often for 1991 and 1996 in Australia and New Zealand due to census dates.

TRANSPORT PATTERNS

The detailed data on some of the key private and public transport parameters are summarised in Table 3.1. They are discussed below in comparison to other global cities for 1990. Trends are discussed later.

CAR USE

Australian cities have amongst the highest per capita car use (car passenger km per capita) in the world (See Figure 3.1). Only US cities exceed Australian cities in these factors. New Zealand cities are lower than Australian cities in car use and transport energy use, by considerable margins (24 per cent to 26 per cent).

These generalised data hide a plethora of detailed differences between each of the cities. Sydney's car use, for example, is significantly less than the other Australian cities, especially Perth and Canberra (9417 pass. km cf 12 029 pass. km and 11 194 pass km respectively). In New Zealand, Wellington and Christchurch are somewhat less than Auckland (7941 pass. km and 8115 pass. km, cf 8444 pass. km respectively). It is not surprising to see that Sydney is the highest public transport-using city in the Australian context and Wellington is the highest within New Zealand.

FIGURE 3.1
AVERAGE PUBLIC TRANSPORT TRIPS PER CAPITA (1991)

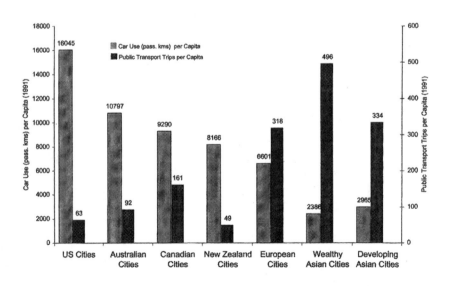

PUBLIC TRANSPORT

The Australian and New Zealand cities along with the US cities are the poorest achievers in terms of public transport use in the world. Figure 3.1 demonstrates this very clearly, showing that New Zealand cities are even lower than US cities in their average annual public transport trips per person. The outstanding Australian city is Sydney (160 trips per person per year) and Wellington for the New Zealand sample (77 trips per person per year). However, it should be noted that three of the Australian cities virtually equal or exceed Wellington's performance in public transport use, making New Zealand cities generally very poor in this factor.

The general association between cities with good rail systems and high levels of public transport is very strong. This is seen globally and in the sample here. Although there is debate about how effectively the rail systems are provided (Mees, 2000), there is no doubt that where a city has only bus services, that the level of car use is considerably higher.

The 40 developed cities in the international study are divided into strong rail cities and weak rail cities on the basis of the percentage of public transport travel that is achieved on rail (under 50 per cent are considered weak rail cities and over 50 per cent are strong rail cities). Table 3.2 shows that overall public transport use is more than twice as high in the rail-oriented cities in the world.

TABLE 3.2
DIFFERENCES IN PUBLIC TRANSPORT USE IN STRONG RAIL AND
WEAK RAIL CITIES (1990/1)

Public transport performance indicators	Strong rail cities	Weak rail cities
Percentage of pubic transport passenger kms on rail	73%	15%
Annual public transport passenger trips per capita	248	113
Annual public transport passenger kms per capita	1701	773

This pattern is certainly clear in the Australian and New Zealand (ANZ) cities where the stronger rail cities in both nations (Sydney, Melbourne, Brisbane and Wellington) tend to have higher per capita passenger kilometres on public transport.

Christchurch and Auckland are the poorest public transport cities in the sample with astonishingly low figures of 28 and 41 annual transit trips per capita. Auckland has a very small rail system based on quite old diesel rail cars that run on an hourly service (total 1.2 trips per person per year in 1991) and only succeed in capturing 7 per cent of Auckland's public transport passenger travel. The upgrading of this system has been discussed for many years and the funding has

TABLE 3.1
SOME KEY TRANSPORT PATTERNS IN AUSTRALIAN AND NEW ZEALAND C▮

City	Private pass energy use (MJ/capita)	Private pass vehicle pass (kms per capita)	% of workers using foot or bicycle	Transit pass (trips per person)
Australian cities				
Adelaide	31 784	11 173	5.4	76
Brisbane	31 290	11 188	5.1	69
Canberra	40 700	11 194	6.0	89
Melbourne	33 527	9 782	4.7	101
Perth	34 579	12 029	4.1	54
Sydney	29 491	9 417	5.5	160
Average	33 562	10 797	5.1	92
New Zealand cities				
Auckland	27 060	8 444	7.5	41
Christchurch	24 792	8 115	15.2	28
Wellington	22 359	7 941	10.6	77
Average	24 737	8 166	11.1	48

SOURCES Kenworthy et al (1999) and Bachels, Newman and Kenworthy (1999)
NOTE 'Transit' is used interchangeably with 'public transport' in this book

FIGURE 3.2
RAIL PROVISION IN THE GLOBAL CITY SAMPLE FOR CITIES WITH POPULATION BETWEEN 600 000 AND 1.7 MILLION (1991)

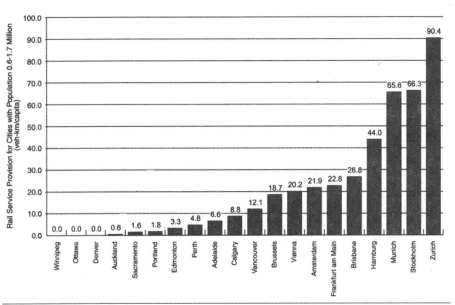

Transit pass ms per capita)	% of transit pass (kms on rail)	Average speed of traffic (km/h)	Average bus speed (km/h)	Average rail speed (km/h)	Average transit speed (km/h)
572	21.1	46.4	22.1	27.0	23.0
900	65.7	50.1	28.7	44.0	38.8
660	0.0	49.5	34.5	–	34.5
844	79.7	45.1	21.0	33.0	27.1
544	17.9	45.0	24.6	34.0	26.3
1 769	62.6	37.0	19.0	42.0	33.5
882	41.2	45.5	25.0	36.0	30.5
294	6.6	47.8	27.0	39.0	28.0
173	0.0	46.8	18.0	–	18.0
843	69.3	46.5	21.0	42.0	36.0
437	25.3	47.0	22.0	40.5	27.3

been cleared for a detailed plan to be prepared in 2000; history would suggest it will take a brave political move to overcome entrenched anti-rail forces in this city. In Christchurch there is no rail service, apart from a tourist-oriented short historic tram line in the central area.

For many years, cities like Auckland, Christchurch, Perth and Adelaide were denied good rail systems because they were considered not big enough. Figure 3.2 shows that for the smaller cities in the global sample (between 0.6 and 1.7 million) there is a huge variation in rail service provision. There is little obvious relationship between city size and rail service — it just appears that some cities choose to implement rail systems and others do not. Auckland, Christchurch and Adelaide continue not to opt for rail, whereas Perth has, since the late 1980s, chosen to revitalise its rail service. This trend continues with a government decision in 2000 to extend the suburban rail service south to Rockingham/Mandurah, along with some strategic smaller extensions of other lines. In the US it is interesting to see how the non-rail cities of Dallas, Denver, Houston, and Phoenix, have all chosen recently to build multi-billion dollar rail systems as their traffic has grown beyond control.

FIGURE 3.3
AVERAGE PRIVATE AND PUBLIC TRANSPORT SPEEDS (1991)

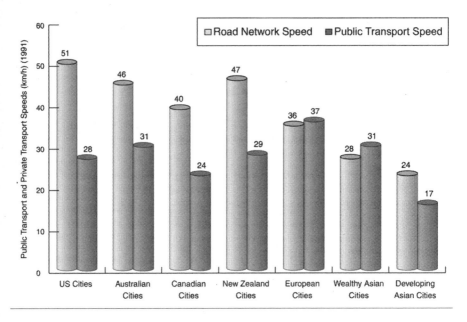

The reasons why rail is now preferred in more and more cities include rail's higher profile (patrons know where the service is located and where it is going), its extra comfort, the way land use tends to cluster around stations, and the extra speed it provides. Data on the relative speed of transit to traffic in the global sample of cities are provided above. This is a critical factor in people's mode choice decisions — where transit speed is inferior to car speed, only captive public transport riders tend to dominate and hence the systems achieve poorer usage. Where transit offers a speed competitive with the car, choice riders can be attracted to the system with good patronage results.

Rail-based cities tend to provide more realistic competition with the car because of the higher speed generally achieved by segregated rail systems. The same can be seen when the best and worst are compared in the Australian cities. Table 3.1 shows this for the ANZ cities where rail speeds generally match or even exceed road speeds, whereas average bus speeds are universally non-competitive with car speeds, often less than half as fast. The same patterns repeat themselves in the larger global sample as shown in Table 3.3. The data in this table show the best and worst city within the different regions in terms of the relationship between public transport speed (rail and bus), and car speed. We conclude that the only way to ensure speed competitiveness of public transport in any city is to develop a quality rail system. Bus systems as a whole cannot deliver this competitiveness, though they can play a critical role in supporting rail systems and providing local flexible movement similar to a car.

TABLE 3.3
AVERAGE SPEED BY MODE AND RELATIVE SPEED OF TRANSIT TO TRAFFIC IN GLOBAL CITIES (REGIONAL AVERAGES AND SELECTED CITIES, 1990)

Cities	Average speed (km/h)			Relative speed of transit to traffic
	Car	Train	Bus	
US cities (av.)	51	37	22	0.55
Houston	61	–	24	0.39
New York	38	39	19	0.89
Australian cities (av.)	45	36	25	0.67
Perth	45	34*	25	0.58
Sydney	37	42	19	0.91
Canadian cities (av.)	40	33	21	0.60
Ottawa	40	–	24	0.60
Vancouver	38	42	20	0.67
European cities (av.)	33	41	21	1.11
Copenhagen	50	59	24	0.94
Zurich	36	45	21	1.24
Wealthy Asian cities (av.)	28	40	17	1.12
Tokyo	24	40	12	1.58
Poorer Asian cities (av.)	24	37**	15	0.71
Bangkok	13	34**	9	0.70
Seoul	24	40	19	1.07

NOTES *Before the full electrified rail system in Perth. Rail system speed is now 51 km/h with the northern suburbs line considerably above this
** Poorer or developing Asian cities very small and mostly older, slower rail systems

BICYCLING/WALKING

All the ANZ cities are low in bicycling and walking compared to European and Asian cities (Table 3.4). Christchurch and Wellington are the best cities in the sample (15 per cent and 11 per cent). However, compared to US, Australian and Canadian cities, New Zealand cities perform comparatively well in the number of people getting to work using non-motorised transport. This may partly explain the rather low use of public transport in New Zealand cities, since the journey-to-work is a key market niche for public transport.

TABLE 3.4
WALKING AND CYCLING TO WORK IN THE GLOBAL SAMPLE OF
CITIES, 1990–91

City	% workers using foot or bicycle
US cities average	4.6
Australian cities average	5.1
New Zealand cities average	11.1
Canadian cities average	6.2
European cities average	18.4
Wealthy Asian cities average	20.3
Developing Asian cities average	18.4

TRANSPORT INFRASTRUCTURE

The dominance of the car in ANZ cities should not be unexpected when infrastructure is examined. In terms of CBD parking and length of road provided the cities are among the highest in the world. Table 3.5 details the transport infrastructure patterns in the nine ANZ cities.

TABLE 3.5
KEY TRANSPORT INFRASTRUCTURE PATTERNS IN ANZ CITIES, 1991

City	Road supply (m/person)	Parking spaces per 1000 CBD jobs
Australian cities		
Adelaide	8.0	580
Brisbane	8.2	322
Canberra	8.8	842
Melbourne	7.7	337
Perth	10.7	631
Sydney	6.2	222
Average	8.3	489
New Zealand cities		
Auckland	4.9	600
Christchurch	5.2	942
Wellington	5.7	966
Average	5.3	836

The availability of roads and parking are clearly key determinants of how much cars will be used. We have shown the strong links between these infrastructure factors and transport patterns over many years (Newman and Kenworthy, 1989, 1999b; Kenworthy et al, 1999).

LAND USE

The length of road in a city is closely related to density, both because a more dispersed city must necessarily have longer roads and also because of the close link between building roads and promoting urban sprawl (Newman and Kenworthy, 1999b). Thus the ANZ cities are generally low in density, though NZ cities are closer to Canadian cities than Australian cities. Figure 3.4 reveals the global patterns in urban density.

FIGURE 3.4

AVERAGE URBAN DENSITY BY COUNTRY/REGION (1991)

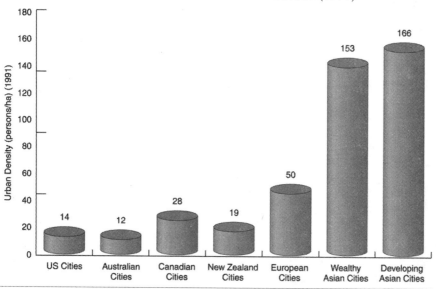

The variations again are considerable, with Sydney (17/ha) and Wellington (23/ha) having the highest density (and having the lowest car use and best public transport in their respective regions), whilst Perth is at the other extreme on all these variables. The implications are obvious, although many academics continue to wonder if there are any links between transport and land use (eg Brindle, 1994).

We can examine the patterns of land use in a little more detail in Table 3.6 below by looking at population and job density in different parts of each city, as well as the degree of centralisation of population and jobs. Our other studies show that car dependence is lowest in higher density areas and in more centralised areas which favour the provision of public transport over dispersed land uses.

Of all the cities in the study, New Zealand cities have the least intense CBDs or central city areas. The population component is very lean, averaging only 5.0 persons per ha, which makes even Australia's performance on this indicator (14 persons per ha) look healthy. Australian and New Zealand cities have similarly low proportions of

TABLE 3.6
URBAN FORM PARAMETERS IN ANZ CITIES AND OTHER GLOBAL CITIES, 19

City density	Whole city density		Central city density	
	Pop./ha	Jobs/ha	Pop./ha	Jobs/ha
Australian cities				
Adelaide	11.8	5.1	10.2	408.1
Brisbane	9.8	4.0	11.8	528.6
Canberra	9.6	5.0	4.3	160.9
Melbourne	14.9	5.9	27.1	530.6
Perth	10.6	4.4	9.5	131.5
Sydney	16.8	7.2	20.8	422.2
Average	12.3	5.3	14.0	363.7
New Zealand cities				
Auckland	18.1	7.1	3.7	129.9
Christchurch	16.1	5.8	4.1	137.7
Wellington	23.0	9.1	7.3	142.6
Average	19.1	7.3	5.0	136.7
US cities average	14.2	8.1	50.0	429.9
Canadian cities average	28.5	14.4	37.9	354.6
European cities average	49.9	31.5	77.5	345.1
Wealthy Asian cities average	152.8	87.5	86.6	881.9
Developing Asian cities average	166.4	65.1	281.9	279.3

total population in their CBDs (only 0.2 per cent to 0.3 per cent). Likewise, job densities are very low 137 jobs per ha, by far the lowest in the international sample (Australian cities average 364 jobs per ha). However, in terms of the proportion of metropolitan jobs found in the CBD, Australian and New Zealand cities are healthier than US cities (14 per cent and 19 per cent respectively, compared to only 10 per cent in US cities). Indeed, New Zealand cities rate quite favourably in this factor compared to Canadian, European and Wealthy Asian cities.

In terms of inner areas, Australian and New Zealand cities are quite similar and very low in their population densities (22 to 24 persons per ha on average). Job densities are similarly low with Australia doing a little better at 26 jobs per ha compared to 20 in New Zealand cities. However, by all accounts, Australian and New Zealand cities are low in their population and job densities, with only US cities coming close in average inner job density (27 per ha). When considering the relative importance of inner areas as sites for residential development and jobs,

Inner area density		Outer area density		Proportion of pop. in CBD (%)	Proportion of jobs in CBD (%)	Proportion of pop. in CBD (%)	Proportion of jobs in CBD (%)
Pop./ha	Jobs/ha	Pop/ha	Jobs/ha				
18.7	26.0	11.3	3.6	0.2	16.7	10.6	34.2
20.3	20.7	8.9	2.5	0.1	11.4	16.9	42.1
8.6	13.4	9.8	3.4	0.1	15.6	14.1	42.1
27.2	43.0	14.4	4.3	0.2	10.6	7.5	30.3
16.3	15.9	9.8	2.7	0.6	21.3	19.1	45.1
39.2	38.1	15.3	5.1	0.2	11.5	15.2	34.3
21.7	26.2	11.6	3.6	0.2	14.5	13.9	38.0
22.4	16.9	17.0	4.6	0.2	14.9	24.7	47.6
21.1	13.3	14.1	2.7	0.2	19.0	37.7	66.7
26.9	29.0	22.1	4.4	0.4	22.1	22.7	61.5
23.5	19.7	17.7	3.9	0.3	18.7	28.4	58.6
35.6	27.2	11.8	6.2	0.8	10.5	24.1	32.8
43.6	44.6	25.9	9.6	1.4	19.7	27.0	44.2
87.0	84.5	39.2	16.6	3.4	19.7	39.6	58.1
53.4	338.8	133.2	50.9	1.1	17.8	22.4	54.2
60.1	128.3	126.3	39.7	12.0	26.4	43.8	54.2

it is clear that New Zealand cities rate more highly than Australian cities in both these factors (28 per cent of population and 59 per cent of jobs in inner areas, compared to 14 per cent of population and 38 per cent of jobs). Likewise, New Zealand cities rate quite well in these factors compared to other international cities, whereas Australian cities generally do not (apart from the proportion of jobs in the inner area compared to US cities).

In the outer areas, however, New Zealand cities distinguish themselves a little more from their Australian neighbours in having an average population density of 18 per ha compared to only 12 in Australia (and the same in the US cities). While this is still low by international standards, it does give New Zealand cities an overall edge in urban density that is seen in the whole city figures and brings them closer to Canadian city densities. However, in job densities in outer areas, New Zealand cities are again low, like those in Australia and are significantly lower than US cities in this factor.

CONCLUSION TO PATTERNS

The data in the previous sections show a cluster of parameters in each city that are obviously closely linked. In Kenworthy et al (1999) a cluster analysis was conducted on the 46 cities in the study using 23 variables in order to determine their overall level of automobile dependence. The New Zealand cities have been added and the cluster analysis recalculated to show where the New Zealand cities fit in the range of automobile dependence found in this city sample.

From Table 3.6 it is clear that none of the New Zealand cities fall into the 'Extreme' class of automobile dependence, unlike Perth, Adelaide and Canberra in Australia. It should be pointed out that the order of the cities in this table is important. That is, Phoenix is classed as the most auto-dependent city in the sample, with cities becoming relatively less auto-dependent moving down the columns. Christchurch appears as the most auto-dependent city in the 'High' auto-dependence category, followed by another Australian city, Brisbane, and then Auckland. Melbourne is also in this category. As might be expected from the preceding discussion, Wellington, along with Sydney, make it into the 'Moderate' auto-dependence category, though they are nearer the top of this class, rather than the bottom. The cities in the Moderate auto-dependence category are in fact an interesting mixture of cities from just about every region. They include the majority of the Canadian cities (4 out of 7), the least auto-dependent US city, New York, as well as the most auto-dependent European cities and the most auto-dependent Asian city in the sample, Kuala Lumpur. The remaining 16 cities in the low and very low auto-dependence categories are all European and Asian cities.

TABLE 3.7
GROUPING OF CITIES INTO CLASSES OF AUTOMOBILE DEPENDENCE ACCORDING TO THE CLUSTER ANALYSIS

Extreme automobile dependence	High automobile dependence	Moderate automobile dependence	Low automobile dependence	Very low automobile dependence
Phoenix	Christchurch	Winnipeg	Amsterdam	Paris
Houston	Brisbane	Ottawa	Brussels	Stockholm
Detroit	Auckland	Wellington	Bangkok	London
Sacramento	Washington	Sydney	Vienna	Jakarta
Denver	Melbourne	Montreal	Munich	Seoul
San Diego	Boston	New York	Zürich	Tokyo
Portland	Vancouver	Toronto	Singapore	Hong Kong
Perth	San Francisco	Hamburg	Surabaya	Manila
Adelaide	Chicago	Copenhagen		
Los Angeles	Calgary	Kuala Lumpur		
Canberra	Edmonton	Frankfurt		

TRENDS

TRANSPORT TRENDS

It is important to understand how some of the major transport factors have changed in the Australian and New Zealand cities over recent times. Key data on car use, public transport and bicycling/walking are therefore examined to show how the seven cities in the sample have changed between 1991 and 1996.

TABLE 3.8
TRENDS IN SOME MAJOR TRANSPORT FACTORS IN ANZ CITIES FROM 1991 TO 1996

City	Car use (km per capita per annum)		Public transport use (boardings per capita per annum)		Bicycling and walking to work (% of workers using foot and bike to work)	
	1991	1996	1991	1996	1991	1996
Perth	8305	8260	54	60	4.1	3.3
Brisbane	7713	7756	69	60	5.1	4.2
Melbourne	7448	7649	101	101	4.7	3.9
Sydney	6614	6945	160	141	5.5	5.0
Auckland	6672	7398	41	35	7.5	6.0
Christchurch	5880	6326	28	24	15.2	13.2
Wellington	6062	6470	77	57	10.6	11.4

NOTE The car vehicle kilometres per capita include light commercial vehicles in all cities. The New Zealand city data were prepared in this way and the Australian city data have been adjusted to include light commercials so as to compare properly with these New Zealand cities. Kenworthy et al (1999) show only passenger car vehicle kilometres and total vehicle kms (all vehicles). In practice, a lot of light commercial vehicles are used for passenger travel.

The data show that all cities have continued to grow in car use per capita except Perth, which has a small decline, with most having a consequent decrease in public transport and bicycling/walking. Again, exceptions are Perth, which has experienced a small increase in public transport use per capita, and Wellington, which also showed a moderate increase in bike/walk. Brisbane hardly grew in car use from 1991 to 1996 (0.6 per cent), but still declined in public transport use by 13 per cent. Other Australian cities grew in car use by only small amounts over the five-year period (Melbourne 3 per cent, Sydney 5 per cent), whereas the New Zealand cities rose more (Auckland 11 per cent, Christchurch 8 per cent, Wellington 7 per cent). We have predicted elsewhere that the slowing of growth in car use in Australian cities, which has been occurring over a 35-year period, may be mainly due to continued strong urban consolidation processes (Kenworthy and Newman, 1993). Urban consolidation has also been occurring in NZ cities (see below) but the 1990's has seen the introduction of cheap secondhand Japanese cars into the New Zealand economy and these appear to have had a major impact on the rapid growth in traffic. Sydney's growth may be because of the building of the Harbour Tunnel and several large freeways which induced traffic growth, as would be expected from such road-building programs — see Chapter 7.

In terms of public transport, Melbourne remained stable, while Sydney lost ground by 12 per cent (consistent with its growth in car use), though in the late 1990's public transport again grew rapidly. For example, since 1993, a low point, Sydney's rail use has been steadily gaining ground each year. It has risen from 229 800 000 boardings in 1993 to 270 500 000 boardings in 1999. A similar situation exists in Melbourne, where a low point in rail use occurred in 1994 of 101 000 000 boardings but this has grown each year since to 115 000 000 boardings in 1999. The New Zealand cities all lost public transport patronage (Auckland 15 per cent, Christchurch 14 per cent, and Wellington with a big drop of 26 per cent).

One of the best performances in public transport has been the turnaround in the Perth rail system, which was the main contributor to Perth's overall improvement in public transport patronage since buses declined over this period. Figure 3.6 shows how the system grew dramatically after electrification of the three original lines to Fremantle, Midland and Armadale and extension to the northern suburbs to Currumbine. This

FIGURE 3.6
PERTH AND ADELAIDE RAIL PATRONAGE, 1991–97

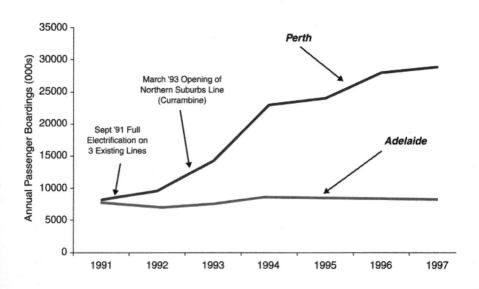

can be compared to Adelaide, which did little to upgrade its old diesel stock and hence its rail system has remained uncompetitive and declining in use. Also, Perth's success in rail is evident when compared to Auckland, a very similar city. Auckland, with its very small rail service has only 6 per cent of total public transport boardings in 1996 on rail, compared to 38 per cent of total boardings in Perth being on rail.

In terms of walking and cycling to work, the data show how each ANZ city except Wellington decreased quite substantially in this factor from what were already low levels in 1991. It is becoming increasingly difficult in all cities to maintain or improve mode share for non-motorised modes. The generally increasing distances of travel, the hostility of the public realm for pedestrians and cyclists and the diminishing amount of mixed land use, mean that walking and cycling struggles, especially for the journey-to-work. However, this is reversible with the right kind of transport and land use policies (Chapter 7).

LAND USE TRENDS

Available data on land use trends are set out in the tables below. The first and most important trend to examine is urban density. These data are available for the Australian cities between 1961 and 1996 and are shown in Table 3.9. The three New Zealand cities were added to the sample in 1998 and were only examined in detail for 1991 and 1996 so only these two years are shown for these cities.

TABLE 3.9
URBAN DENSITY CHANGES IN ANZ CITIES, 1961 TO 1996

| City | Urban density (persons per ha) | | | | |
	1961	1971	1981	1991	1996
Perth	15.6	12.2	10.8	10.6	10.9
Brisbane	21.0	11.3	10.2	9.8	9.6
Melbourne	20.3	18.1	16.4	14.9	13.7
Sydney	21.3	19.2	17.6	16.8	18.9
Auckland	na	na	na	18.1	18.9
Christchurch	na	na	na	16.1	17.0
Wellington	na	na	na	23.0	22.0

Metropolitan urban density in the Australian cities shows a continual decline in density from 1961 through to 1981, a stabilising of the rate of decline to 1991, and then either a reversal to 1996 (Perth and Sydney) or continued strengthening in the stabilisation trend (Melbourne and Brisbane). Sydney, the city that consolidated more strongly and effectively than most other Australian cities, rose in density by 12 per cent between 1991 and 1996. This is significant as it represents the first evidence of a reversal of a long established trend of declining urban densities. It is very difficult to reverse metropolitan-wide density declines and reflects a gradual build up over many years of the results of policies aimed at reducing urban sprawl, ie density is rising again due to re-urbanisation. The same pattern is clear for two of the three New Zealand cities: Auckland and Christchurch increased their densities from 1991 to 1996 by 4 per cent and 6 per cent respectively, whereas Wellington registered a decline of 4 per cent.

It should be noted that in the international sample, for which data are available up to 1990–91, that the ten-year period up to that time saw US cities' average urban density rise from 13.8 to 14.2 persons per hectare. Canadian cities rose fractionally from 28.2 to 28.5 persons per ha and wealthy Asian cities increased from 149.3 to 152.8 per ha. Thus, the metropolitan density reversal trend evident a little later in the ANZ cities, was beginning to happen in other cities in the previous decade. European and developing Asian cities did however continue to decline from 1980 to 1990, though with less rapidity than before.

This trend towards increasing densities is even more obvious in the re-urbanisation of the inner city, including the CBD, where significant reversal has occurred across all the ANZ cities. Table 3.10 summarises the beginning of this trend in the four Australian cities from 1981 to 1991. For the New Zealand cities, the trend in density in all areas for 1991 to 1996 is summarised as well in Table 3.10. In Australian cities, the trend in density in the CBD and wider inner area between 1981 and 1991 is mostly upwards and the declines in outer areas are generally quite small. All the New Zealand cities have quite marked increases in density in their CBDs and inner areas from 1991 to 1996 and even small increases in the outer areas of Auckland and Christchurch. The data indicate a significant re-urbanisation is underway, particularly in the central and inner areas.

TABLE 3.10

TRENDS IN DENSITY IN SECTIONS OF AUSTRALIAN CITIES, 1981 TO 1991, AND NEW ZEALAND CITIES, 1991 AND 1996

Australian cities	CBD density (persons/ha)		Inner area density (persons/ha)		Outer area density (persons/ha)	
	1981	1991	1981	1991	1981	1991
Perth	8.4	9.5	15.5	16.3	9.9	9.8
Brisbane	15.3	11.8	19.9	20.3	9.0	8.9
Melbourne	24.5	27.1	29.3	27.2	15.7	14.4
Sydney	10.7	20.8	39.1	39.2	15.8	15.3
New Zealand cities	1991	1996	1991	1996	1991	1996
Auckland	3.7	9.6	22.4	25.2	17.0	17.5
Wellington	7.3	14.2	26.0	28.9	22.1	20.5
Christchurch	4.1	6.0	21.1	22.4	14.1	14.9

Similar patterns are found across the world's cities (Newman and Kenworthy, 1999b). There does appear to be a process occurring where city populations are coming back in and concentrating around centres, particularly traditional centres. The reason for this reversal seems to be related to the newly emerging information/service-oriented economies of these cities (Newman et al, 1999). As discussed in Chapter 1, the transport system and the economy are closely related in broad cycles of change based on dominant technologies and business paradigms. The new cycle we are entering appears to be dominated by information and communication technologies and the business paradigm is related to networking/systems approaches and sustainability. How this relates to changes in urban forms has always been a matter of speculation with many Americans suggesting it would lead to further dispersal (Webber, 1964) and others less certain (Castells, 1996). The new data suggests that the city may need to be more agglomerated and centred to meet the needs of employees in the information and communications industries for interaction, personal networking and cross-fertilisation of ideas, as well as their desire to live in areas of rich urban diversity and opportunity.

As discussed in Chapter 1 there is evidence that face-to-face centres are more important, not less important in the fifth-cycle economy based on knowledge services, IT and sustainability. A century ago it was predicted that the telephone would end the need for cities but instead increased the need for face-to-face contact. The IT revolution may be doing this too, though now there is even more need to meet centrally together, with less industrial land uses preventing denser land development in inner areas.

The land-use planning implication from these trends is that a city is likely to facilitate its economic performance by enabling its density to increase, and particularly to enable centres of development to occur. As rail systems tend to facilitate centres and re-urbanisation, and roads tend to facilitate dispersal, the implications of these trends for transport planning are becoming obvious. They suggest that a policy of building up rail systems rather than road systems will be of economic benefit to a city as they facilitate the development of centres that encourage face-to-face contact.

ECONOMIC AND ENVIRONMENTAL COMPARISONS

The parameters below show a pattern of how automobile dependence is expressed in economic and environmental consequences. Table 3.11 provides a list of economic and environmental variables relevant to the discussions below.

First, the comparative wealth levels in the ANZ cities in terms of Gross Regional Product per capita are presented. This represents actual wealth

TABLE 3.11

ECONOMIC AND ENVIRONMENTAL VARIABLES IN THE ANZ CITIES, 1991

City	GRP per capita ($US, 1990)	Road Exp. (US $1990 per capita)	Road Exp. (US$1990 per $1000 of GRP	Public transport operating cost recovery from the farebox	% of GRP spent on operating passenger transport
Perth	$17 697	$133	$7.51	28%	16.8%
Adelaide	$19 761	$133	$6.73	40%	14.7%
Brisbane	$18 737	$167	$8.89	54%	11.1%
Melbourne	$21 088	$89	$4.22	24%	12.9%
Sydney	$21 520	$188	$8.74	55%	10.4%
Auckland	$12 236	$75	$6.13	51%	15.5%
Christchurch	$10 320	$76	$7.36	38%	15.4%
Wellington	$12 937	$91	$7.03	52%	14.0%
ANZ Average	$16 787	$119	$7.08	43%	13.8%
US cities	$26 822	$264	$9.84	35%	12.5%
Toronto	$22 572	$150	$6.65	61%	7.4%
European cities	$31 721	$135	$4.26	54%	8.1%
Wealthy Asian cities	$21 331	$88	$4.13	119%	4.8%
Developing Asian cities	$2 642	$39	$14.70	99%	13.9%

generated in the urban regions. These data form a basis for normalising some of the economic parameters examined in the following sections.

The New Zealand cities data come from airshed studies that use bigger metropolitan areas than for the other data. Correct populations have been used to standardise the data. However, the data are not totally representative of the urban regions used for the other data on New Zealand cities. Wellington and Christchurch data represent the 1996 situation, not 1991, as no data were available for that year. Auckland is 1993 data.

For CO_2, the average is for seven Canadian cities, not just Toronto.

ROAD EXPENDITURE

We can examine the total amount of money spent on constructing and maintaining roads in cities by all levels of government. Australian and New Zealand cities have generally quite high road expenditure per capita by international standards, especially when this is normalised for city wealth and compared as a proportion of each city's GRP per capita (gross regional product or city wealth). Australian cities (including Adelaide) average $7.18 per $1000 of GRP, while the three New

Transport deaths per 100 000 people	VHC Volatile hydro-carbons	NOx Nitrogen oxides	CO Carbon monoxide	SO_2 Sulphur dioxide	VP Volatile particulates	CO_2 emissions from transport kg per capitas
11.9	23.6	20.3	187.2	0.4	1.0	2980
12.9	21.2	18.2	168.1	0.4	0.9	2561
12.5	24.7	29.4	187.3	1.1	2.2	2899
11.6	22.7	18.0	179.2	0.5	1.3	2916
11.1	22.6	23.6	207.0	0.6	1.8	2588
11.4	43.9	32.9	329.1	0.4	0.9	2245
11.1	37.5	31.0	164.6	1.5	1.8	2241
7.3	24.7	21.1	101.8	0.8	na	1884
11.2	27.6	24.3	190.5	0.7	1.4	2539
14.6	22.3	22.3	204.5	1.6	1.0	4683
6.5	21.7	27.0	160.6	2.3	3.9	2764
8.8	11.6	13.0	72.6	2.0	0.8	1887
6.6	2.2	6.2	19.8	1.3	1.1	1158
13.7	13.6	8.7	61.8	1.3	3.4	837

Zealand cities average $6.84. Table 3.11 shows total annual road expenditure per capita in US$1990 in each of the ANZ cities and the average for other cities in the world, as well as per capita expenditure per US$1000 of GRP.

By way of contrast, US cities averaged per capita road expenditure of $9.84 per $1000 of GRP, the highest of all in the developed cities. Toronto, the only Canadian city for which data were gathered, spent $6.65, European cities $4.26, wealthy Asian cities $4.13 and developing Asian cities, because of their very low wealth level, $14.70 (Kenworthy, Laube et al, 1999).

PUBLIC TRANSPORT COST RECOVERY

One of the most emotional issues in transport debates, especially public versus private transport, is the degree to which public transport is 'subsidised'. The international data below support the view that those cities that have expansive public transport systems (rather than public transport systems that are forever being cut back to reduce costs) are the most financially successful. Unfortunately, ANZ cities, which average 43 per cent cost recovery, are at the lower end of cost recovery from their public transport systems, though there is a considerable range (24 per cent to 55 per cent). By comparison, US cities were worse with only 35 per cent, Toronto achieved 61 per cent, European cities 54 per cent, and wealthy Asian cities made a profit at 119 per cent. Developing Asian cities, with their captive bus riders, achieved a high 99 per cent cost recovery (Kenworthy, Laube et al, 1999).

PERCENTAGE OF GRP SPENT ON OPERATING PASSENGER TRANSPORT

When ANZ cities have all their direct transport costs added for both public and private transport, these costs are amongst the highest in the world as a proportion of their city wealth. Table 3.11 reveals that, on average, ANZ cities spend 13.8 per cent of their annual city wealth on passenger transport. US cities are also high in this factor with 12.5 per cent. However, Toronto spends only 7.4 per cent of its wealth on passenger transport, European cities 8.1 per cent, wealthy Asian cities 4.8 per cent and developing Asian cities, due to their extreme low wealth, 13.9 per cent, or about the same as the ANZ cities.

It would seem that car-dependent cities have high economic costs associated with running their cities, due to the direct costs of buying and running so many cars and due to the high costs of infrastructure for urban sprawl. Sprawl is, of course, one of the key reasons why cars are needed so much. On the other hand, as the above international data show, cities with good public transport systems, especially rail systems, have much lower total costs of transport as a proportion of city wealth. When the international city data are broken down according to strong rail cities and weak rail cities (strong rail cities having more than 50 per cent of public transport passenger kms on rail),they show that strong rail cities spend only 8.9 per cent of wealth on passenger transport, while weak rail cities spend 12.7 per cent (Kenworthy and Laube, 1999).

Why would car dependence be so costly for a city? The data above show the costs of travel are higher because car-dependent cities tend to be so sprawling. But there are other possible indirect economic feedbacks from sprawl-based car dependence.

There is a high opportunity cost when so much capital has gone into suburb building which means that the capital is not available for providing new wealth as it is directed into providing infrastructure in the highly dispersed city (Frost, 1991; Jacobs, 1984). Another way to look at the problem is in terms of disposable income. If families are dependent on cars they will have less disposable income for spending in the local economy than if they did not need a car, or at least did not need multiple cars.

There is clear evidence of very different travel patterns and local wealth associated with different land uses within cities. For example, in

Sydney people who live in inner and middle areas use cars less than people in outer areas. The 1996 Census revealed that only 16.5 per cent of outer-ring residents travelled to work by public transport, compared with 24.5 per cent for people in middle-ring areas, and 33.3 per cent for inner-ring dwellers. The patterns are similar in all Australian cities. Yet the low car-dependent areas of these cities are the most wealthy as indicated by Table 3.12 below.

TABLE 3.12
PERCENTAGE OF HOUSEHOLDS EARNING $70 000 OR MORE PER ANNUM BY URBAN SECTOR IN AUSTRALIA'S MAJOR CITIES, 1991
SOURCE ABS 1991 Census

	Sydney	Melbourne	Brisbane	Adelaide	Perth
Core	17.1	11.4	9.4	14.7	7.5
Inner	15.1	10.9	7.5	10.3	7.3
Middle	10.7	10.1	8.2	7.3	9.1
Outer	12.6	8.2	5.8	5.3	6.1

The gathering evidence that car dependence is not good for urban economies is even more striking when external costs of car use are considered. The external costs, such as road accidents, noise and pollution due to high car use still feed back into the city economy. Such parameters are rarely considered quantitatively in the development of urban policy and benefit-cost analyses of alternative urban futures.

These external costs are summarised below and are considered on a national basis in Chapter 4.

ROAD ACCIDENTS

The costs of transport crashes are estimated in Chapter 4. Here we show that ANZ cities have relatively high transport death rates due primarily to high exposure because of high car usage. Table 3.11 summarises the transport death rate in ANZ cities in 1991. This averages 11.2 deaths per 100 000 people compared to 14.6 in US cities, 6.5 in Toronto, 8.8 in European cities, 6.6 in wealthy Asian cities and a very high 13.7 in developing Asian cities considering their low level of car use. This figure in developing Asian cities is attributable to a host of other factors such as high motorcycle and pedestrian death rates, poor road conditions, poor driver training and weak road regulation enforcement.

SMOG EMISSIONS

Emissions from motor vehicles generally follow car usage, but Table 3.11 shows that the ANZ cities are even higher than expected compared to their level of car use; they are amongst the highest in the world in many emissions. This is probably due to a combination of the age of the vehicle fleet and the relatively poorly regulated emissions standards of the vehicle fleet compared to other countries.

Australia's fleet is now one of the oldest of any developed nation and this is one of the reasons why there has been a continued flattening or decline in vehicle fuel efficiency despite new cars having lower fuel consumption rates. The other reason is the growth in Sports Utility Vehicles (sometimes known as 'urban assault vehicles') which have been a rapidly growing portion of the new vehicle market and which have very poor fuel efficiency.

The data confirm that over a 35-year period where engineers have suggested that the fuel crisis could be solved quickly and easily by technological means, this policy has been a dismal failure. It is obvious that policies which mean people need to, or want to, use cars less are going to be a more important part of the policy mix for the future.

CO$_2$ EMISSIONS

The international community is finding new ways to limit climate change. Although not yet in place, there is likely to be a global process that pushes nations and cities towards carbon taxes. If this is so, then ANZ cities will be among the highest as their CO$_2$ emissions from transport are among the highest in the global sample. Table 3.11 shows the total CO$_2$ emissions per capita from urban transport in each of the ANZ cities. The data are derived from the energy used by each mode, taking into account relevant conversion factors according to the type and source of fuel.

The US cities do eclipse the ANZ cities in this factor by a considerable margin due to their higher energy use in transport (4683 kg per capita). The seven Canadian cities for which this item was available average 2764 kg per capita, or some 9 per cent higher than the ANZ cities. By contrast, European cities have 1887 kg of CO$_2$ per capita, wealthy Asian cities 1158 kg and developing Asian cities 837 kg per capita.

CONCLUSIONS TO COMPARISONS

The direct and indirect costs of ANZ cities from their in-built car dependence can be assessed from the above data. They indicate that car dependence is an economic drain on cities compared to cities that have a more balanced transport system. This is due to the extra direct costs of running the transport system (both public and private) and the indirect costs through the dispersed land-use patterns which are both hard to service and are not conducive to the new knowledge-based economy. External costs from accidents, noise and pollution add to this perspective on the economic handicaps associated with car dependence.

The cities that will be more competitive in the new global economy will be those which favour centres and have genuine options for non-car-based travel. These cities are more like Sydney and Wellington rather than Adelaide and Auckland.

The data outlined in this chapter do not reflect other parameters of importance such as the loss of community associated with neighbour-hoods where car-dependent, dispersed-land uses are not properly ser-viced and where few opportunities exist for people, especially youth, to participate in urban life in a meaningful way. Rebuilding community is now a major priority for cities and yet it is very difficult when car dependence continues to be the driving assumption in how suburbs are built. This is especially important now it is clear that the level of civic community life in a city is closely linked to its economic performance (Putnam, 1992).

Hope does exist, however, because of the economic forces that appear to be favouring community-based city planning where the city re-urbanises around sub-centres. This is increasingly being driven by New Urbanism designs such as Perth's 'community code'. However, it is easy for this process to leave whole urban areas behind in a car dependence which is increasingly associated with poverty (Newman, 2000).

The restructuring of cities to provide a more sustainable and more equitable future is the main urban agenda occupying planning author-ities in many cities today, especially those in the developed world. However, the funding of infrastructure to achieve this is not yet con-sistent with such a goal, nor are the financial incentives provided by governments for people and communities to make this transition.

4
WHY IT CAN'T GO ON: THE ROAD DEFICIT

PHILIP LAIRD AND PETER NEWMAN

> Perpetuation of existing arrangements will condemn the nation to ineffective results.
>
> National Transport Planning Taskforce (1994, p iv) commenting on the need for planning for transport in Australia into the 21st century.

In this chapter, we grapple with what could be done to moderate road traffic growth and reduce the social and environmental impact of car and truck use. This includes a brief look at the important issue of road safety, including heavy vehicle safety. We comment on taxation measures that favour road vehicle use. The aggregate costs of motor vehicle usage are discussed in this chapter, and compared with revenue to Government from vehicle-specific taxes and charges. These aggregate costs are found to exceed revenue to Government and their difference is a 'road deficit'. For Australia, perhaps for the first time, we give a 'road deficit' which is broadly estimated at $8 billion per annum. We also give updated estimates of a 'road freight deficit'. Finally, we look at potential international pressures that may force Australia to radically change the way it moves people and goods. These pressures include international obligations to reduce greenhouse gases, and high prices for petroleum products.

At this stage, the reader may well ask, if things are so bad, why has nothing been done to fix the problems? This question is explored in detail in the next chapter.

ROAD CRASHES

A very real cost to the community of motor vehicle usage on public roads is the pain and injury, some serious and some even fatal, resulting from road crashes. A detailed discussion of road crashes is outside the scope of this book. However, brief mention is given of some facts, with estimates of the total cost of road crashes in Australia.

Statistics relating to aggregate numbers of fatalities, serious injuries, and other injuries have been kept for many years by State Government agencies, as well as the Australian Bureau of Statistics until 1989, and then a Federal Office of Road Safety (FORS) which was absorbed during 1999 into a new Australian Transport Safety Bureau. These statistics show a general increase in the number of persons killed each year throughout the 1950s and 1960s until 1970 when 3798 people were killed in road crashes on Australian roads. This number of road fatalities was the worst ever in Australia, and led to the introduction of major counter measures with the compulsory fitting and use of seat belts in cars, and protective helmets for motor cycles riders (Year Book No. 61, 1977, p 395). Other factors identified by Searles (1986 see also Inter-State Commission 1990 Vol.2 p.182), included:

> ... the effects of the economic recession in bringing about an overall decline in vehicle usage, ageing of the population and increased unemployment resulting in less driving by young people, improvements to vehicles and tyres, increased availability of improved medical services, and road engineering improvements, including the widespread provision of multi-lane motorways.

These road safety measures assisted in reducing the number of persons killed each year during the 1970s, and in 1979, 3508 persons were killed in road crashes. The ongoing high level of road fatalities required further action and social change.

The second major advance was the introduction of random breath testing. Victoria was one of the first states to introduce this measure whereas NSW resisted for some years. A valuable contribution was made by the late Mr Ken Thomas, founder of Thomas Nationwide Transport (TNT) who formed the Save-A-Life-A-Day (or SALAD) movement in the 1970s. Mr Thomas also stood for election for the NRMA Council in 1979 to advance SALAD objectives and also promoted the advantages of rail for safer inter-capital city freight movements. In Spring 1982 the NSW 'Staysafe' Parliamentary Committee on Road Safety in its first report 'Alcohol, Drugs and Road Safety' recommended random breath testing, and the Wran Government was moved to introduce it in December 1982 for a three-year trial. Within the three-year period, random breath testing was seen to be saving almost a life a day in NSW, and it became an ongoing measure. This action was a major contributor to reducing the number of people killed on NSW roads from 1303 in 1980 to 960 in 1990.

On a national scale, the numbers killed on Australian roads fell during the 1980s from 3272 in 1980 to 2331 in 1990. The 1990s have seen an ongoing drive to reduce the number and severity of road crashes including a Ten Point Plan as outlined in Box 4.1. In return for the States and Territories giving a commitment to implement the package by 1 July 1990, the Commonwealth allocated an additional $100 million to road funding. The extra funding was for the purpose of eliminating known 'black spots' at intersections, bridgeworks or other traffic points noted for involvement in accidents. This conditional payment was an example of how the Federal Government could use a 'carrot' approach to the States on issues they consider to be of national significance. The approach could be extended to a number of the issues in this book. Even after a decade, the ten points are still relevant.

BOX 4.1
AUSTRALIA'S TEN-POINT ROAD SAFETY PLAN

- National 0.05 level of alcohol limit
- National licensing of heavy truck and bus drivers
- National uniform speed limits
- Adopt zero alcohol limits for young drivers
- Increase enforcement to ensure that 1 in 4 drivers are Random Breath-Tested for alcohol in a year
- Implement a graduated licensing system for young drivers
- Introduce compulsory wearing of helmets by cyclists
- Introduce daylight running of lights by motorcyclists
- Increase enforcement of wearing of seat belts and use of child restraints

Although there has been a general reduction in the number of fatalities in Australian road crashes to the year 1999, the rate is still unacceptably high as shown by the comparative data in Chapter 3. There are also large numbers of injuries. Road accident injuries are classified as either serious injuries or other injuries. In Australia during 1999, along with the loss of 1759 lives there were over 20 000 serious injuries from road accidents requiring hospitalisation. Of increasing concern is the growth in the numbers of long-term disabled persons who were injured in road crashes.

Further road safety initiatives in the late 1990s include a reduction in urban residential road speed limits to 50 km per hour. The fact that the limit was 60 km per hour for so long in Australia when most of the rest of the world, including New Zealand, used a 50 km per hour limit, raises some interesting questions. Australia was also slow by the standards of the Western world to introduce 40 km per hour or lower speed limits outside schools.

The numbers of people killed on Australian roads, coupled with serious injuries and other injuries, plus loss of earnings, pain and suffering, and vehicle damage was estimated by the Bureau of Transport Economics (BTE, 1995b) to be costing Australia some $6135 million in 1993. This estimate for road accidents far outweighed BTE (1995b) estimates for aviation accidents at $75 million, rail accidents at $69 million and maritime accidents at $316 million. However, this very conservative estimate for the cost of road crashes was later revised by the BTE (2000a) to be $14 980 million in 1996. The marked increase from $6 billion reflects inclusion of an estimated cost of $2 billion for long-term care, and, a more realistic estimate of nearly $1.5 billion of the costs of traffic delays resulting from road crashes. This is an almost daily phenomenon on freeways in any major city.

Even so, the new BTE estimate of the cost of road crashes of some $15 billion is considered to be conservative by the Australian Transport Council (2000). At the end of the day, there is no way that money can compensate for the loss of a dearly loved person in a road crash. Other road crash costs, not included in the BTE estimate, include veterinary costs for the injury of domestic pets, the work done by voluntary organisations to assist animals injured, or the death of domestic pets or native fauna.

Australian vehicle operators paid motor vehicle insurance premiums of some $8 billion in 1999. This amount is calculated by the Australian Prudential Regulation Authority (APRA) and includes Compulsory Third Party insurance (CTP) which is covered by the private and public sectors, plus domestic vehicle insurance (comprehensive) and commercial vehicle insurance. The difference between the cost of motor vehicle insurance, and the cost of road crashes to Australia is about $7 billion. This difference is ultimately born by society as a whole.

In November 2000, Australia's Transport Ministers (State and Federal) adopted a National Road Safety Strategy 2001–10 and a National Road Safety Action Plan for 2001 and 2002. As well as seeking to improve road-user behaviour through education, enforcement and information, and improving the safety of roads and vehicles, there is a suggestion to encourage alternatives to motor vehicle usage, including public transport. However, neither the strategy nor the short-term plan suggested more use of rail to move freight.

In January 2001, public attention in Australia was focused on the increase in NSW road fatalities during the summer holidays. In addition, the number of road fatalities on Australian roads had risen to 1823, as opposed to the loss of 1763 lives in 1999 (eight more than in 1998). This ended a thirty-year trend of declining numbers of road fatalities, and suggests that stronger road safety measures will be needed.

The cost of road injury crashes in New Zealand in 1998 was estimated by the New Zealand Land Transport Safety Authority to be $2.8 billion.

HEAVY VEHICLE SAFETY

Heavy vehicle safety has been of concern for most of the 20th century. One long-standing reason is drivers working very long hours on truck driving and related activities such as loading, or waiting for loads. During the 1970s, such concern gave rise to a House of Representatives Standing Committee on Road Safety (1977) holding an inquiry into Heavy Vehicle Safety. A concurrent 1977 study (Linklater, as reported by Staysafe, 1989) found '… evidence of fatigue amongst the drivers in the form of 40.7 per cent of the 615 drivers using stimulant drugs, 28.8 per cent reporting hallucinations whilst driving within the preceding year, and an average 71.6-hour working week'.

The Commission of Inquiry into the NSW Road Freight Industry (1980) and a National Road Freight Industry Inquiry (1984) addressed safety issues. Both inquiries found a case for operator licensing of heavy trucks. The National Inquiry found the number of fatal crashes involving articulated trucks was about 7.4 per 100 million kilometres in 1983, as compared with 2.1 per 100 million kilometres for cars.

Compulsory tachographs were also recommended for most articulated trucks by the National Inquiry in 1984. This was part of a package of 98 recommendations that included a proposal that interstate truck owners would cease to receive effectively free registration for their trucks. Partly on the grounds that many heavy trucks were already defying the 80-km per hour speed limit, the Inquiry found that there was a case for the lifting of legal speed limits for heavy vehicles. On 1 January 1987, as part of a package including a modest $675 registration fee for interstate semitrailers, the open road legal speed limit for trucks was lifted to 90 km per hour. This was followed by a report of the Federal Office of Road Safety giving strong support to the open road speed limit for trucks being lifted to 100 km per hour. On 1 July 1988, as part of another package, this speed limit was granted. However, the higher speed limit was without compensatory measures such as operator licensing and tachographs. The reasons for Australia not requiring tachographs for heavy trucks, whose installation has been compulsory in Europe since 1986, are explored in Chapter 6.

By 1989, as shown in Table 4.1, there had been an alarming increase in the number of fatalities from road crashes involving articulated trucks. There were also reports of problems on the Hume Highway linking Melbourne and Sydney where, in 1988–89, no fewer than 37 lives were claimed in such crashes. One report was that of the

Anglican Bishop of Canberra and Goulburn, Bishop Dowling (*Church Scene* September 29, 1989) who, as a frequent traveller on the Hume Highway found:

> ... Late night travelling on that road is an extraordinarily intimidating experience. The cumulative effect of a large number of enormous vehicles, travelling in many cases beyond the speed limit in the middle of the night, is terrifying ... The drivers are clearly pushed hard and the number of accidents, even on good sections of the road, show that errors of judgement are easily made in that dangerous environment. The more the road is improved, the more commercial traffic seems to increase, and the more tragedies that happen.

TABLE 4.1
FATALITIES FROM ROAD CRASHES IN AUSTRALIA 1986–2000

Year	Involving articulated trucks	Involving buses	Involving all vehicles
1986	232	46	2888
1987	243	51	2772
1988	320	57	2887
1989	335	104	2801
1990	263	46	2331
1991	183	32	2113
1992	181	39	1974
1993	204	49	1953
1994	179	40	1928
1995	199	23	2017
1996	194	38	1970
1997	171	27	1768
1998	179	29	1755
1999	191	32	1763
2000	208	24	1823

SOURCE Road Fatalities in Australia, Time Series Statistics supplied by the Australian Transport Safety Bureau. The time series for fatalities involving rigid trucks is only available between 1990 and 1995, with numbers of loss of life varying from 215 in 1995 to 320 in 1991

On Friday 20 October 1989 at Cowper, near Grafton, a tragic accident that claimed the lives of 20 people resulted from a collision between a semitrailer and a long-distance coach. This fatal crash highlighted excessive working hours — both loading and driving — for the truck driver. As well as recommending better roads, the NSW State Coroner (1990) recommended that consideration be given to quality licensing. This was to give entry controls as a means of removing from the industry that minority of truck operators who put safety at undue risk and persistently overloaded their trucks.

A study by the Australian Road Research Board (ARRB, 1991) found that throughout the 1980s about 400 lives a year were claimed in fatal crashes involving trucks, with a further 1700 serious injuries a year. The total cost of all accidents involving trucks was conservatively estimated at about $500 million a year. The ARRB report also noted that whilst comparisons are difficult, fatal truck accident rates in Australia were approaching double that of the United States, Britain and Finland. The National Transport Planning Taskforce (1994, p 27) noted that the number of fatal road crashes involving articulated vehicles had been almost halved from 1988 to 1992 and appeared to then remain at the lower level.

The reduction in fatal crashes involving articulated trucks was due to improved roads, better trucks, and more attention to truck-driver training. Despite the gains made during the 1990s, heavy vehicle safety remains an important issue in Australia. This is shown by the ongoing occurrence of tragic fatal crashes involving articulated trucks whose drivers were found to have been under the influence of drugs. The following are examples.

One driver, of WRB Transport, a company placed in voluntary liquidation in April 2000, was found to have been providing 'stay-awake' drugs to other drivers, including one who was involved in a fatal crash at Blanchetown, on the Sturt Highway, in South Australia. 'He was on his fourth trip between Sydney and Adelaide in five days when he fell asleep at the wheel, crossed to the wrong side of the Sturt Highway and hit two oncoming cars.' (The *Advertiser*, 27 May 2000).

A truck driver of Hoppers Crossing, Victoria, who had pleaded guilty in the NSW Supreme Court to the manslaughter of two persons at Strathfield in September 1998, was convicted and sentenced to jail.

> In the days before the accident, Ryan drove from Victoria to Brisbane to Sydney, back to Victoria and then again to Sydney during which time he had taken methamphetamine and had little sleep.
>
> He falsified his log book entries to pretend he had complied with his break requirements.
>
> While driving his 36-tonne semitrailer at about 80 km/h along the six-lane highway at Strathfield, Ryan crossed the median strip and drove along the wrong side of the road for 500 m before colliding with the two cars.
>
> *The Illawarra Mercury*, 15 July 2000

A further fatal crash involving an articulated truck occurred on the Hume Highway in Victoria on the night of 9 April 1999. The driver of the truck, bound for Brisbane, reportedly (*Owner/Driver*, April 1, 2000) '... drove his truck into the back of a caravan being towed by a 4WD, causing it to leave the road and roll over, killing one of the passengers'. The truck driver then diverted from the Hume Highway to the Newell Highway, and failed to stop at the accident or notify the police. It took the police many months of careful investigation to apprehend the truck driver, who was subsequently jailed for three years.

Faced with increasing problems of fatigue in road transport, and larger insurance payouts, the Motor Accidents Authority of NSW established in 2000 an inquiry into the long-haul trucking industry. The terms of reference included:

• lack of client responsibility for driving hours,

• driver performance and remuneration for drivers,

• extent of proper enforcement in the industry of driving hours,

• speeding and drug use, and, current forms of regulation in the industry, whether a self-regulation or external regulation model is most appropriate for the road transport industry and what forms this should take.

The NSW inquiry supplemented an inquiry by a House of Representatives Committee (2000) into fatigue in all modes of transport. Most of the 41 recommendations related to road transport, and included one to the effect that if there had '... not been an appreciable improvement in the way in which the road transport sector is addressing the problem of fatigue management' by mid-2002, a national operator accreditation scheme should be developed for the road transport sector.

The involvement of heavy trucks in fatal crashes may also result in the loss of life of the truck driver. According to the Australian Transport Safety Bureau, 34 truck drivers lost their lives in road crashes involving articulated trucks during 1996. This makes truck driving one of the most dangerous occupations in Australia.

The New South Wales Parliamentary Committee on Road Safety (Staysafe, 1989) noted a total annual heavy vehicle crash cost to NSW of $218 million. Based on the NSW road freight task, this resulted in an average unit accident cost of about 0.5 cents per net tonne km for road freight using heavy trucks.

As noted above, the incidence of trucks involved in road crashes has fallen. The Bureau of Transport Economics (1996) assumed the cost of accidents involving articulated trucks at 0.2 cents per net tonne km. However, with the revaluation of the cost of road crashes outlined above, this figure must now be regarded as conservative. In view of the recent BTE revision of the cost of all road crashes, and based on recent NSW road crash data, the earlier estimate of 0.5 cents per net tonne km road crash risk for road freight is now considered more appropriate.

New Zealand has also had to deal with excessive numbers of fatal truck crashes. An inquiry by the New Zealand House of Representatives Transport Committee (1996) noted that although fatal road crashes had been declining significantly, the number of deaths from truck crashes had been steadily growing to 1995. In that year, there were no fewer than 118 fatalities from crashes involving trucks. The inquiry report (page 9) further found that 30 per cent of the trucks on the road were taking 'unacceptable safety-related risks' including: drivers who have a high risk of being fatigued; steering faults; worn tyres; insecure loads; and overweight or over-dimension loads. The Committee concluded that 'Until truck drivers and management start respecting and obeying the law, no attempts to reduce truck crashes will succeed. At present, law-breakers are being given an economic advantage, which will not disappear until a commitment to safety has a greater economic benefit. This severely handicaps the majority of responsible operators who operate within the law'.

Four years later, in 2000, there was still cause for concern in New Zealand. An editorial headed 'Scary Statistics' in the magazine *Rails* for July 2000 noted that in May 2000, evidence was tendered by expert witnesses to a court hearing a charge resulting from a logging truck crash in which four people were killed. This evidence included the observation '... that nearly 30 per cent of trucks had been found to exceed 100 km/h during speed surveys', and that no fewer than 60 logging trucks had overturned in 1997 out of a national fleet of 650, with excessive speed being the primary cause of the fatal crash being examined by the Court.

As summarised by this editorial: 'It's clear that there is an element in road transport which persists in flouting the law — and rising fuel prices will put more pressure on marginal operations leading to more dodgy practices.'

TRANSPORT AND THE URBAN ENVIRONMENT

In a special NSW Government Sydney Summit on Air Quality held in 1991, Professor John Niland, then Chairman of the NSW Environment Protection Authority (EPA — previously the State Pollution Control Commission), noted that public concern about air pollution from factories and industry had prompted the NSW Government to introduce the Clean Air Act in 1961.

However, by the early 1970s, as pollutants from older industries in Sydney were brought under control and reduced, there was an increasing amount of pollution from a growing vehicle population, giving rise to other forms of pollution including carbon monoxide, nitrogen oxides and photochemical smog. Road vehicle use is now the major source of air pollution in Sydney. It is also a major source of noise.

A similar pattern has occurred in other major cities over the last three decades. Most large cities also have extensive use of heavy trucks that results in further noise and pollution problems. Of growing concern are the small particulates emitted by the combustion of diesel in urban areas. This is a growing concern that has not yet fully entered into policy discussions. Dr David Brand, former Federal President of the Australian Medical Association stated in 1999: '... diesel truck drivers are ten times more likely to contract cancers, plus exposure to diesel fumes is associated with increases in prostrate cancer, lung cancer and bladder cancer.' The World Health Organisation '... has found that traffic pollution kills more Europeans than road accidents with 21 000 pollution-related deaths compared with 10 000 traffic deaths' (Press release, AMA, October, 1999).

How can this be? Burning diesel produces a lot of carbon particles; the large particles are visible — as soot — and lead to urban haze, but it is the fine particles (PM10 and PM2.5) which are not visible and cause the health problems. Fine carbon particles penetrate the lung wall and carry with them other toxic material — microscopic (asthma inducing) allergens, metal fragments and carcinogens (at least 15 are known in diesel smoke including Nitrobenzanthron which is one of the most carcinogenic chemicals known). These are transferred to the lymph nodes and from there to other parts of the body.

A fundamental question is whether technology can be used to clean up diesel. This is particularly important for Australia as the GST deal concluded in 1999 between the Democrats and the Coalition included a policy to introduce 'clean diesel'. The deal gave rural truck drivers a reduction in diesel excise of some 23 cents per litre (which was quickly forgotten when world oil prices rose in 2000) and tax changes were made so that 'clean diesel' could be introduced.

Clean diesel is low in sulfur and has fewer large particles but some early assessments based on dynamometer tests suggest that this refined diesel has more fine particles, not less, as referred to in the AMA press release noted above.

Thus there is real and growing concern that the increased use of diesel in trucks, even if it is 'clean', will be creating a 'time bomb' in cities where most of the health impacts will be. For example, it is estimated that 87 per cent of London's fine particles come from diesel exhausts. In response, the World Health Organisation has said there is 'no minimum level below which there are no health effects from exposure to fine particles'. As well, the California Air Resources Board has said there is 'no safe exposure level for diesel exhaust' and that diesel fumes are a 'toxic substance'. It would be unwise for Australian transport policy not to minimise the growth in truck use when dealing with this potentially explosive health problem.

As well as the question of whether technology is solving or exacerbating the fine particle issue, there is the question as to whether reducing emissions per vehicle is likely to succeed when total vehicle use continues to grow. This is most obvious when it comes to large cities where smog issues continue after decades of technological improvements. Whilst the adverse environmental impacts, with growing health impacts (in addition to road crash trauma), have been most apparent in larger cities such as Sydney, they are also apparent in nearby regions. This is directly from regional road vehicle use; also, when car-generated air pollution from a major city may affect the region (eg some ozone generated by Sydney's cars is trapped in a valley at Albion Park near Wollongong, over 100 kilometres away).

It is hard to make an estimate of the cost of transport-generated noise, pollution, and the resulting health related impacts in Australia. The former Inter-State Commission (1990) found that the total 1989–90 cost in Australia for noise and air pollution was in the order of $534 million and $730 million respectively. It also noted that though such estimates should be treated with caution, '… it is increasingly important that an attempt be made to include these costs in road cost allocation'. Brindle et al (1999) quote a number of more recent estimates for the health costs of motor vehicle emissions, ranging from a low $20 — $100 million a year, to one by Manins (1997) estimating as much as $3.0 to $5.3 billion a year. However, none of these include the kind of data used to estimate the high costs due to fine particles that are now being seen in Europe. Here, as noted by the AMA, deaths due to fine particles from transport are greater than deaths from road accidents.

When an estimate (Simpson and London, 1995) of $255 — 462 million for the city of Brisbane is taken into account, we suggest that an amount in the order of $1 billion per year for Sydney is reasonable. Thus, an estimate in the order of $3 billion a year is reasonable for all of Australia. However, it is likely that in the future this will be seen as highly conservative.

THE GREAT TAX CONCESSION

In Australia, generous tax concessions are available for the operation, and in some cases, the lease and/or purchase of motor vehicles. Table 4.2 shows the extent of tax deductions recently allowed. These deductions are greater than the loss of revenue to Government. In turn, the loss of revenue is greater than Fringe Benefit Tax (FBT) payments for vehicles made by taxpayers. The aggregate gross deductions have been running in excess of $10 billion per annum for five years now.

TABLE 4.2
AUSTRALIAN MOTOR VEHICLE EXPENSES CLAIMED FOR TAX
DEDUCTIONS ($MILLIONS)

	Individuals	Companies	Partnerships	Trusts	TOTAL	FBT offset
1992–93	1535	4655	2135	1050	9375	606
1993–94	1613	5082	2272	1148	10 115	1 211
1994–95	1855	4986	2360	1232	10 433	1405
1995–96	2064	5802	2318	1325	11 509	1574
1996–97	2131	5876	2240	1384	11 641	1622
1997–98	2274	6223	2237	1488	12 222	1650

SOURCE Taxation Statistics 1997–98 and earlier years. Report and CD-ROM

For 1997–98, individuals, companies, partnerships and trusts were able to claim $12.2 billion in deductions. If we assume an average tax rate of 36 per cent for all classes of taxpayers, the cost to Government was $4.4 billion. When taking into account Fringe Benefit Taxes (FBT) for motor vehicles, the net loss of revenue to Government was $2.8 billion in 1997–98.

ROAD DEFICITS

As we have seen, the total cost of transport when all costs are measured is excessive. These costs, when added up, will be shown below to far exceed the revenue to Government from fuel excise, vehicle registration charges and sales taxes. As such, governments and the public alike are effectively paying, each year, for escalating 'road deficits' and 'road freight deficits'. Although these deficits are hidden, and impossible to put an exact monetary value on, they are very real.

Motoring organisations and road transport interest groups often claim that aggregate vehicle-related payments to Government exceed road outlays by Government. For example, in Australia, motor vehicle payments were $12.4 billion in 1997–98 (Bureau of Transport Economics, 1999a) comprising $8.6 billion fuel excise, $2.3 billion registration, and $1.5 billion in other payments (but excluding stamp duty which is not specific to motor vehicles). In 1997–98, the outlay on road maintenance and construction was $7.0 billion.

The net surplus to Government is then $5.4 billion. However, this should be offset by the net tax loss of about $2.8 billion in 1997–98 (see above), to leave $2.6 billion. In turn, this amount would be far exceeded by social or environmental costs of vehicles use. We have seen above that the road crash deficit is some $7 billion, and an environmental health cost of $3 billion is reasonable. However, there are other subsidies to consider as well.

For some years now, Queensland has had cheaper fuel than other States. Up to 1997, this was because Queensland was the only State that was not imposing a State Fuel Franchise fee. When such fees were declared invalid for tobacco by the High Court in 1997, the Federal Government then added 8.1 cents per litre to fuel excise, and made compensatory payments to the States. However, Queensland effectively chose to rebate this revenue to vehicle users in Queensland, at an estimated cost of $500 million a year. The Queensland Cabinet in June 2000 resolved to withdraw the 8 cents per litre fuel subsidy, and to lower car registration annual charges by at least $150 per car. This proposal received much condemnation within Queensland, by groups including the Royal Automobile Club of Queensland and the trucking industry. Although such a move to remove fuel subsidies of dubious constitutional standing was in the national interest, it was publicly attacked by two senior Ministers in the Howard Government. However, in the true spirit of Sir Humphrey Appleby, it was a 'courageous decision', and within four days, it had been reversed by the Queensland Government. Its retention means an ongoing fuel subsidy to road users of $0.5 billion per year in that State.

Estimates of road vehicle-related government revenue and community costs for Australia are given in Table 4.3. **In summary, the 'road deficit' is seen to be in the order of $19 billion a year if congestion is included and $8 billion a year if congestion is excluded.** This compares with an estimated road deficit including congestion for the United Kingdom in 1993 exceeding 30 billion pounds (Maddison et al, 1996). The case for including congestion is that road projects are usually justified on high benefit-cost ratios that have been inflated with travel time savings, which take into account congestion of existing roads. Even without congestion, a road deficit of $8 billion presents a very different picture from the road 'rip offs' frequently alleged by motoring clubs and truck lobby groups.

Australia's road deficit for 2000–01 will significantly increase as a result of the decisions by the Howard Government in introducing the New Tax System. This is due mainly to the reduction of diesel excise from about 43 cents per litre to 20 cents a litre for all heavy trucks with a Gross Vehicle Mass (GVM) exceeding 20 tonnes (some heavy rigid trucks, and almost all articulated trucks). In addition there are further concessions to medium-weight trucks (from 4.5 to 20 tonnes GVM) operating in rural and regional Australia, and some petrol concessions. With the introduction of the GST, cars became cheaper while public transport became more expensive. Also, some employees can continue to claim cars as a tax concession but cannot claim public transport costs.

TABLE 4.3
AUSTRALIA'S ROAD DEFICIT

	$ billion
Road system costs	7.0
Total cost of road crash costs	15.0
Other health impacts	3.0
Net tax refunds for motor vehicle use	2.8
Queensland fuel subsidy	0.5
Total	28.3
Federal fuel excises from road vehicles	8.5
Annual registration fees etc	3.8
Insurance premiums for road crashes	8.0
Total	20.3
Net road deficit — without congestion	**8.0**
Road congestion in major cities	11.0
Net road deficit — with congestion	**19.0**

SOURCE See text for estimates of road system and related costs, plus government and other revenues in Australia for recent financial years

As traffic levels grow, 'road deficits' increase. They have now reached a point where Government action is warranted. The 'road deficits' do not include the cost of operation, maintenance and capital servicing of motor vehicles. As noted before, the total costs of road transport were broadly estimated at some $80 billion in 1992–93 (Allen Consulting Group, 1993, p 13).

ROAD FREIGHT DEFICITS

The question of what road system costs are attributable to the operation of heavy trucks is a contentious one. At the end of the day, any cost allocation procedure is assumption-sensitive and subject to severe data limitations. Thus, if a Government agency produces a report showing that there are large hidden subsidies to the operations of heavy trucks, it is equally possible for another Government agency to produce a report that shows existing taxes and charges and track operations cover all road system costs.

Indeed, such a situation occurred in the late 1980s. In 1988, the respected Bureau of Transport Economics published a Review of Road Cost Recovery that found during 1985–86, articulated truck operations had a resultant under-recovery of road system costs of $1283 million. Yet, in the same year, a Royal Commission into Grain Storage, Handling and Transport (1988), in recommending that all road transport 'restrictions and impediments' be immediately removed, found that '... sufficient revenues are generated by the various taxes and charges on road transport to cover the costs of any additional road damage'.

Some balance was restored by an Inter-State Commission (1990) report and a high level Over-Arching Group of officials recommended increased charges for the heavier long-distance trucks in 1991. However, as we shall see in Chapter 5, these higher charges were rejected. In brief, a Special Premiers' Conference chaired by Mr Bob Hawke in July 1991 agreed that a new National Road Transport Commission (NRTC) would determine charges for heavy trucks. Then, in 1992, the NRTC determined 'user friendly' charges for heavy trucks. A critique of the NRTC charges is given in Appendix D which shows that the NRTC charges that prevailed in the 1990s resulted in appreciable under-recovery of road system costs from semitrailers, B-Doubles and road trains. As seen by the Industry Commission (1992):

> ... Annual fixed charges are not efficient because costs vary with the distance travelled and the mass of the vehicle. The result is that some vehicles — the heaviest travelling long annual distances — will meet less than 20 per cent of their attributed costs ... The charges, as recommended, will therefore potentially distort the long-haul freight market as rail reforms take effect ...

The NRTC determined new annual registration charges for 1 July 2000. However, the new NRTC charges retain many of the deficiencies of the old NRTC charges, and continue to result in significant under-recovery of road system costs from the heavier articulated trucks that haul long annual distances.

Road transport lobby groups relentlessly argue that the taxes and charges that they pay far outweigh the outlay by Government on roads. On the other hand, as outlined in Appendix D, a succession of Government inquiries has found significant under-recovery from road system costs from heavy trucks. Appendix D also gives details of recent estimates of road system costs attributable to articulated trucks, and, rigid trucks, and the offset road user charges using NRTC (1998) data. The results are summarised in Table 4.4, which shows a shortfall of road system costs in 1997–98 of some $1235 million for all articulated trucks and about $50 million for rigid trucks.

We have already noted the unit cost of road crashes involving articulated trucks as 0.5 cents per net tkm. Appendix D considers the cost of noise and air pollution. Including these external costs suggests a road freight deficit for articulated trucks in the order of $2 billion, which excludes congestion costs. Whilst questions can be raised about the accuracy of such estimates, it is difficult to argue against a succession of government reports that have found large unintended subsidies to the operation of the heavier long-distance trucks, and the desirability of reducing these hidden subsidies.

TABLE 4.4
AUSTRALIA'S ROAD FREIGHT DEFICIT

	Articulated trucks	$ million Rigid trucks	All trucks
Attributable road system costs	1955	545	2500
Road user charges (NRTC)	720	495	1215
Net road system costs	**1235**	**50**	**1285**
Road crash involvement costs	450	*	450
Environmental costs	282	157	439
Hidden subsidies	**2017**	**207**	**2224**

SOURCE Appendix D. Note rigid trucks include truck trailers
*Not known

As of 1 July 2000, the Federal diesel excise was lowered from about 43 cents a litre to 20 cents a litre, with 20 cents a litre nominated as a road user charge. The cost to the nation, based on articulated trucks using about 2.7 billion litres of diesel a year in the late 1990s (ABS, 2000b) of this concession, is some $620 million per year. Although excise was removed from diesel used in rail operations, as rail is about three times more fuel efficient than road for line haul freight, the change further distorts competitive neutrality (BTE, 1999d).

In other words, more loads on roads, in trucks driven by over-worked drivers.

We have already noted that road freight has experienced sustained high growth in Australia, and, that Australia now has the highest road freight per capita in the world. Although one would expect that Government would move towards more equitable and economically efficient charges for heavy vehicles to introduce some demand management, the reality is that both sides of politics have shown a remarkable reluctance to deal with the issue.

A series of recent Government reports in Australia concerning competition policy and transport reform, have effectively side-stepped the issue of road cost recovery as it relates to rail in Australia. These reports include Hilmer et al (1993), NTPT (1995), BIE (1995), the Australian Transport Council (1995) and the Productivity Commission (1996). Moreover, the Howard Government firmly rejected in April 2000 a recommendation of the Productivity Commission for an inquiry into road provision, funding and pricing.

By way of contrast, New Zealand has had, since 1978, a system of road user charges for heavy trucks that is based on mass-distance charging. This system was introduced as a considered decision to put into place full road cost recovery from heavy trucks before lifting rail protection. The NZ road user charges are a necessary condition for rail freight profitability of New Zealand's railways.

RAIL DEFICITS

In contrast to large hidden 'road deficits', rail deficits often receive much government and media attention in Australia. Yet, the reality is that the much-vaunted rail deficits, having peaked at some $1.7 billion in 1985–86 dropped to $1.4 billion in 1993–94, and have generally been decreasing.

Moreover, Government rail freight deficits, which were broadly estimated at about $525 million in 1989–90, have during the 1990s been turned into aggregate rail freight profits. The aggregate operating profit in 1997–98 of the three Government rail operations of Queensland Rail, FreightCorp (NSW) and Westrail (WA) was nearly $300 million. This far outweighed freight Community Service Obligations and operating losses for freight for all rail systems.

Thus, by the end of the 1990s, most government operating subsidies for rail were for passenger transport. Moreover, most of these subsidies were payments for clearly defined Community Service Obligations (CSOs). The NSW Government has also paid track CSOs to help maintain the interstate track and regional tracks with light traffic. However, at some $177 million in 1997–98, this is small when compared with NSW rail passenger CSOs or, the Roads and Traffic Authority net cash flows from Government at $1695 million for 1997–98.

In New Zealand, the contrast between road deficits and rail deficits is even more marked — rail deficits were virtually unknown during the 1990s. One reason for this is relatively good intercity track compared with basic intercity highways, and reasonable road cost recovery from heavy vehicles with mass-distance charging. As well, long distance rail passenger services in New Zealand were able to operate without government subsidy, although questions were raised by TranzRail in 2000 about their future.

SOME GLOBAL REASONS FOR CHANGE

There are three major global factors that will require governments in Australia and New Zealand to radically change their transport policy. These are as follows:

1   The adverse impact of the total cost of vehicle ownership and use on international competitiveness and balance of payments;

2   Obligations to reduce Greenhouse gas emissions by the years 2008 to 2012 to no more than 8 per cent more than 1990 levels for Australia, whilst capping at the 1990 level in New Zealand; and,

3   The inevitable end of cheap oil — either in the near future, or at some later date.

We will look at each factor in turn. The current Australian road deficit is maintained at the cost of Governments and all people. Australia's Gross Domestic Product (GDP) was estimated at some $557 billion in 1997–98 (2000 Year Book, p 374). Of this, $33.5 billion of industry gross value added, or 6 per cent, was attributed to transport and storage. There is also significant household consumption expenditure in transport. Although some gains have been made through the 1990s to reduce the cost of transport services, we are still paying too high a price for the way we move ourselves, and our freight, around Australia.

In terms of balance of payments, the net cost to Australia for all fuel and transport in 1998–99, from ABS data (2000 Year Book, p 767–8), was about $12.8 billion (b). This net debit results from imports of $4.47 b for fuels and lubricants and $16.17 b for transport equipment (excluding civil aircraft) in 1998–99 offset by exports of about $4.46 b for 'other mineral fuels' and $3.35 b for transport equipment.

TRANSPORT AND OIL

The need to conserve oil use in transport was well appreciated during the 1970s as shown, for example, by government reports such as that of the Australian Transport Advisory Council (1979). During the 1980s and 1990s, government was effectively 'out to lunch' on the issue. In 1998–99 Australia used some 16.1 billion litres of petrol (12.9 billion litres unleaded, 3.2 billion litres leaded) plus 5.8 billion litres of diesel and the equivalent of 2.0 billion litres of LPG and CNG to move their road vehicles. This energy use far exceeds the use of about 0.5 billion litres of diesel plus electricity use by the rail systems to perform a significant passenger task, and a freight task that was of similar size to the road freight task. This is because when it comes to moving people in urban areas, efficient public transport — be it bus or rail — is at least twice as energy efficient as people driving cars. Fully loaded electric trains are five times as energy efficient as compared to cars (Newman and Kenworthy, 1999). When people move between cities, bus or rail are much more energy efficient than using cars and planes. For line haul freight, rail is generally three times more energy efficient than trucks.

The mandatory energy labelling of all new cars in Australia which belatedly started on 1 January 2001 is just one of many measures needed to conserve transport energy. Energy labelling will allow prospective car buyers to see up front the expected fuel use (urban and non-urban) for the car, and how this performs, using a star rating, with other vehicles.

More details of transport energy use and efficiency are given in Appendix A. The energy story has been told many times in Australia in the past 20 years with the main policy conclusion being that we must improve the technology of our vehicles. However this policy has been a dismal failure in Australia. The fuel use of cars, measured in litres per 100 kilometres, has changed very little over the last 35 years, as shown by Figure 4.1.

FIGURE 4.1
THE FUEL CONSUMPTION RATE OF THE AUSTRALIAN CAR FLEET SINCE THE 1960s. SOURCE: MOTOR VEHICLE USAGE SURVEYS.

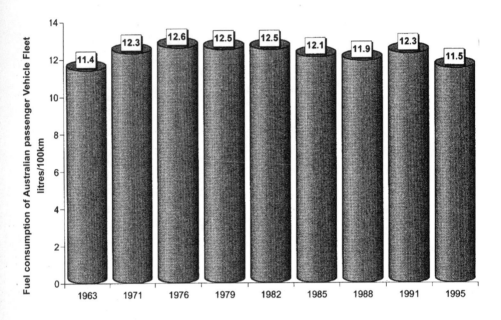

SOURCE MEES 2000

This dismal performance is due to the aging vehicle fleet that continues to wash out any improvements derived from new vehicles, and the growth in the Four Wheel Drive market, which has shown that consumers can always choose to move away from technological efficiency.

The failure of the policy to improve energy use in transport through vehicle technology does not mean that this should not be seen as an important part of the future. The issue is critical enough to need policy options to be pursued at many levels, including the need to facilitate changes in mode and to reduce the need to travel. This is critical due to increasing clarity about the end of the era of cheap oil and also the need to reduce Greenhouse gases.

The world has been exposed to two major oil price shocks, in 1973 and in the late 1970s, as well as a temporary price rise in 1990–91. However, these have always been seen as short-term issues and with 'normal' conditions to return. As the new millennium began the oil price was back to $US30 or more per barrel but the reasons for the price rises were becoming less obvious.

Increasing clarity on the geophysical data concerning oil now show that the world is consuming around four times as much oil as it is finding. Furthermore, the peak in discoveries occurred in the 1960s and the expected peak in oil production is looming (Fleay, 1995). There is more and more acceptance of this view from the International Energy Agency and oil companies like Shell and BP which have diversified into renewable fuels and gas as the transition fuel. Even a conservative body like the Chartered Institute of Transport in Australia found that the oil situation required a sternly worded statement at their 1998 national Symposium in order to warn the government, industry and the general public (see Box 4.2).

The response of the Howard Government to these concerns was to make cars and diesel much cheaper as part of the GST package. The reality is that it is not only the 'road deficit' that fails to be an issue in

---

BOX 4.2

THE END OF CHEAP OIL?

Our greatest ever source of cheap energy may soon contract and the 'Petroleum Age' in which we live now can be seen to be approaching an eventual end.

The Symposium heard that a clear consensus is emerging that cheap oil production outside the Middle East will begin permanent decline around the year 2000, to be followed by permanent world decline within 15 years.

We have reached a crucial stage in the development of our local, national and international transport services. Our present path is leading us into potentially serious economic, social and environmental problems. New directions are needed for our future transport fuels and vehicles.

'More of the same' in our current transport plans and ways of thinking is no longer tenable. A shrinking supply of cheap oil will characterise the next century and confront us with one of the greatest transformations of human affairs. The signs are already there. Risks of chaos, disorder and conflict will arise unless we face up to this great challenge and make the difficult decisions essential to the future wellbeing of us all. These decisions must be based on the care of people and of the environment if we are to proceed down the path of constructive change.

Congestion, pollution and diminishing oil supplies are the central drivers of this change. Communities across the world will increasingly be faced with the need to revise their transport systems in response to these drivers. Congestion and pollution are already major factors in some cities — the diminishing fuel supplies will become increasingly apparent as the next century progresses.

Should self-interest predominate, we could become locked in conflict, unable to adapt and with the likelihood that we will dissipate unproductively the scarce high quality petroleum fuels so essential to a safe transformation to a world 'beyond oil'.

Canberra, but that the looming oil crisis was only placed on the agenda after a sustained increase in domestic petrol prices. The final issue, greenhouse gas emissions, is on the agenda but its transport implications are not.

A further expression of concern from a conservative group was given by the Institution of Engineers, Australia (1999). The broad recommendations from this report on Sustainable Transport were as follows:

1 Taxation and fiscal policy instruments should encourage sustainable transport. At present, these measures encourage car and truck use.

2 There is a strong case for increased investment in transport infrastructure that is more sustainable and less greenhouse gas intensive. Where market forces fail, government should intervene.

3 More holistic approaches that integrate considerations of impacts on health, sustainability and greenhouse gas emissions into transport decisions are needed.

4   There is a need for research to support cleaner transport fuels and technologies, along with transport pricing, economics and demand management technologies.

THE NEED TO REDUCE GREENHOUSE GASES

International concern about climate change has led to an ongoing global process that is forcing constraints on the global market for fossil fuels. A new market is emerging for renewable fuels, natural gas is emerging as the transition fuel, carbon sequestration through plantations is proceeding through new market mechanisms, and energy efficiency is once again at centre stage. This new market is rapidly becoming part of the fifth cycle economy (see Chapter 1), as nations see it not so much as a threat to their economies but as the issue which defines the new agenda and which will determine who will be competitive in the new era.

The difference over this issue is that international pressure through UN-based processes are forcing recalcitrant governments like Australia to take this process seriously. Thus, a new group of public servants in Canberra in the Australian Greenhouse Office (AGO) are developing the options and are providing mechanisms for these to be facilitated. Some of their conclusions to date on transport in Australia are listed below (AGO, 2000, p A–12).

'Domestic transport produced an estimated 72.6 million tonnes of carbon dioxide equivalent emissions, or 15.9 per cent of total net emissions in 1998. Some 89.3 per cent of this was from road transportation.'

Greenhouse gas emissions from the transport sector are also the fastest growing emissions of any sector. They had increased by 18.1 per cent from 1990 to 1998. As noted in a 1999 statement by the AGO:

Under the Kyoto Protocol to the United Nations Framework Convention on Climate Change, Australia is committed to a target for national greenhouse gas emissions of 8 per cent above 1990 levels by 2008–12. This represents about a 30 per cent reduction against current business-as-usual projections of greenhouse gas emissions for 2008–12.

The Government has introduced a range of initiatives, including funding of $10.1 million, to help reduce greenhouse gas emissions from the transport sector. These are outlined in the Prime Minister's statement: Safeguarding the Future announced in 1997. The Sustainable Transport Team of the Australian Greenhouse Office (AGO) is delivering the following initiatives: Compressed Natural Gas Infrastructure Program, and Environmental Strategy for the Motor Vehicle Industry.

These measures were complemented by a number of new initiatives announced as part of the Government's A New Tax System (ANTS) in May 1999. These include: Alternative Fuel Conversion Program, and Alternative Fuel Grant Scheme.

However, the options being provided so far are as limited as those suggested during the past twenty years of coping with the oil issue. They are merely trying to improve the technology of vehicles or to try and switch fuels (minimally). As noted above, this has failed dismally to date. Serious policy changes are beginning to be addressed in electricity (eg the 2 per cent renewable energy target is a significant boost to creating a renewable energy industry in Australia) and in carbon sequestration. But in transport there is only a shrugging of the shoulders and a sense that it is just too hard.

The difficulties of change were highlighted in an inquiry of the Senate Environment, Communications, Information Technology and the Arts Reference Committee (2000). Of the 106 recommendations made by the majority of the Committee, no fewer than 21 addressed transport Greenhouse gas emissions and solutions. However, these 21 transport recommendations were all but dismissed by the two Government members on the Committee, with only two recommendations gaining their support. The other 19 recommendations were considered to be 'already being dealt with through existing Government measures and processes and as such are superfluous', or, 'not supported by evidence, ill conceived, impractical or are premature'.

It needs a new approach to address the heavy bias towards oil-based road transport in Australia. A whole new program is also required to shift passengers from road to rail in our cities and regions, and, to shift freight from road to rail. We suggest that government should commit to reduce transport greenhouse gas emissions by 2010 to their 1990 levels, which in Australia's case will require a reduction of 17 per cent on 1998 levels.

WHERE TO START?

We address this question in the final chapter. However, it is helpful to first examine in the next chapter the 'policy paralysis' of the 1990s that has surrounded all levels of Government in Australia, and also in New Zealand, in real transport reform. We also examine in Chapter 6 the role of the road transport lobby groups in Australia that have helped to continue 'business as usual', and a 'keep on trucking' type of approach.

5

THE INSTITUTIONAL PROBLEM: POLICY PARALYSIS

PHILIP LAIRD

> If we are serious about rail being able to compete with modern road transport, if we are serious about the efficient distribution of bulk commodities, if we are serious about our commitments to the environment, if we are serious about road safety and if we are serious about the economic efficiency of Australia, the Australian rail system must be addressed.
>
> Paul Neville MP (House of Representatives, 8 February 1999)

We have seen in Chapter 2 how Australian and New Zealand intercity passenger and road freight transport has grown, and continues to grow, in a manner that is simply unsustainable. In Chapter 3, we have seen how our major cities are choking with traffic. The high economic, environmental and social cost of present car and truck dependence outlined in Chapter 4 shows us that 'something must be done'.

Throughout the 1990s, Governments at all levels in Australia and New Zealand have recognised a need for change in transport policy. In many ways, as shown in Chapter 2, the 1990s has been a decade of change to improve operational efficiency. This includes the privatisation of Air New Zealand and QANTAS along with the privatisation of New Zealand Railways followed by various Australian rail systems. Competition Policy has also been actively pursued in both countries. However, at the beginning of the 21st century, Australia and New Zealand both have major land transport issues to address.

This chapter briefly outlines the failure by governments to develop transport systems with good economic and social outcomes and less environmental impact. The goal of 'integrated transport' which means integration between transport modes and consideration of land use is yet to be achieved. This is simply because of a lack of political will, and the fact that government funding decisions have been divorced from reform recommendations.

SYDNEY AND ITS PROBLEMS

Even in Sydney, where the adverse impact of too much traffic is most keenly felt, the Federal Government has encouraged traffic growth through generous tax incentives for company cars, lower truck registration fees, and the removal of Federal funds for urban public transport. Moreover, the New Tax System, as of 1 July 2000, introduced cheaper cars, cheaper diesel for trucks, and placed a Goods and Services Tax (GST) on all public transport. At a State level, the NSW Government's approach has been mixed. On the one hand, it has funded modest improvements to public transport, introduced a CBD parking charge, and put in place world-class transport arrangements for the Sydney 2000 Olympic Games. On the other hand, the NSW Government has favoured roads and vehicle use. The general situation was aptly summarised by John Laird writing in the Consumers' Transport Council (CTC) *Newsletter* of June 1991.

Sydney, as we well know, has growing pains. Our unique combination of private enterprise, a multitude of local governments, the NSW State Government, Quangos (quasi-autonomous government organisations) and a remote Federal Government (together hereinafter called 'The System') have created over the years the monster megalopolis by the simple practice of lurching from crisis to crisis.

Every now and again, the chronic sickness becomes acute by the eruption of one symptom or another, and acute pain draws attention to the problem. Rarely, however, is there a good doctor to be found — and too often, when the problem is diagnosed, the patient flatly refuses to take the medicine prescribed.

Often, the patient's relatives (you and me) and 'The System' just simply refuse the good doctor's advice in terms such as 'it costs too much', 'the cure will take too long', and 'the operation is too painful'. Or, 'if we talk about it for long enough we will get used to the pain and the operation won't be necessary'.

With few exceptions, such as Bradfield's plans for the early 20th century, this is the kind of thinking that has since dominated the growth of Sydney. Indeed this approach is also destroying the economic and social health of most other Australian cities.

The response to date of 'The System' has been the creation of further suburbs on the periphery of an already swollen city with more roads, more cars, and more shopping centres — indeed more everything. All of this is at the expense of our health and quality of life with air pollution, congestion, family isolation, and loss of countryside. The distances we are required to travel reduce our opportunities for sport and leisure, and place on many working people the burden of high travel costs in terms of time and money.

The cures to these problems for cities approaching four million people are well researched and documented. The first prescription, historically tested and demonstrated in many European and Asian cities, is focused development of the inner city. This makes possible full economic use of the infrastructure of the city at the same time freeing chosen areas to provide parks — even forest enclaves — along with increased inner city population.

Restraint on suburban sprawl is effected by similar controlled development in satellite cities — each equipped with modern social facilities interlinked with equally modern light rail transit systems.

Such regional development can be shown to give enormous savings to the community. The number of motor cars could be reduced dramatically. With such a reduction, the amount of parking space, road construction and maintenance, pollution, noise and road crashes would be reduced for the benefit of all.

'The System' in Sydney must do better and receive more help from Canberra.

AUSTRALIA'S FEDERAL GOVERNMENT

The Commonwealth, or Federal government, has most of its Civil Service located in Canberra. The City of Canberra now has one of the world's ten most automobile-dependent populations (Kenworthy et al, 1999). Canberra residents have been encouraged to drive by an ever-expanding system of urban arterial freeways with no tollways and completion of a dual carriageway freeway (four lanes, no tolls) between Canberra and Sydney. This ease of car use for people living in Canberra is happily accompanied by relatively good air quality. Thus, for the most part, the Federal bureaucracy is not forcefully reminded of Sydney's air pollution problem that is due to too much car use.

Federal parliamentarians, who almost always arrived in Canberra by train when the Parliament was moved there from Melbourne in 1927, would now rarely use a train to get to Canberra. Most ministers, members and senators, and their influential staff and out-of-town lobbyists, now arrive by plane. Some, however, will drive from Sydney or southern NSW. Few such people would use public transport in their State capital city.

In 1991, a detailed report from an Ecologically Sustainable Development (ESD) Working Group on Transport was released. This report was one of nine reports on ESD sponsored by the Federal Government. The ESD transport final report gave a careful examination of the issues, and made some 30 recommendations. These addressed concerns about concessions within the Fringe Benefits Tax system that encouraged the provision of company cars, the need to encourage the use of public transport as part of salary packages, better vehicle pollution control measures, effective schemes to improve fuel efficiency with labelling, the removal of subsidies to encourage greenfield suburbanisation, road pricing mechanisms, priority for high-occupancy vehicles, bicycling etc. Most of these recommendations were ignored by Government when formulating budgets, although some influenced 1992 Government policies on ESD, and a National Greenhouse Reduction Strategy. These 1992 recommendations included reducing '... total energy consumption in transport through improved technical and economic efficiency of urban and non-urban transportation and switching to alternative transport technologies or modes where this reduces greenhouse emissions per passenger or unit of freight'.

Fine as these sentiments are, they were given only limited Government support in Australia. Throughout the 1990s, the annual reports of the Federal Department of Transport made little or no reference to energy efficiency. In contrast, annual reports from this Department in the late 1970s did address the issue. Moreover, the 'Vision Statement and Objectives' of the Australian Transport Council (ATC) released in 1994 did not even bother to mention energy efficiency. This was in marked contrast to one goal of the United States Intermodal Surface Transportation Efficiency Act 1991. This was to: '... develop a National Intermodal Transportation System which is economically efficient and environmentally sound, provides the foundation for the nation to compete in the global economy and will move people and goods in an energy efficient manner.'

Road pricing mechanisms to induce modal shifts were also ignored during the 1990s, despite the advice of the Federal Department of Energy (1986) of '... potential energy savings from more use of the less energy intensive sea and rail freight transport modes, and, that such greater use would be more likely with improved road cost recovery from heavy truck operations'.

In a further bid to address growing recognition within Government back benches that 'business as usual' in transport would not be viable over time, in 1993 the Keating Government established a National Transport Planning Taskforce (NTPT). The aim was '... to develop a truly nationally integrated transport system'. Three Taskforce members were appointed with a small staff and a budget of about $1 million. The main conclusion of the summary NTPT (1994) report was that 'Significant changes are needed in the way Australia makes and implements transport decisions'.

The NTPT report gave 16 recommendations, including the following:

• 'Commonwealth, State and Territory Governments negotiate and seek endorsements of the Council of Australian Governments to establish a framework for national strategic transport planning in Australia — a National Transport Infrastructure Network ...'

- 'That road, rail, port and airport infrastructure investments and their funding arrangements should be considered within a framework that allows intermodal, network and corridor considerations to be evaluated transparently.' The rationale was that '... more flexible funding mechanisms should be negotiated so funds can be channelled into corridors and modes of highest priority'.

- 'All governments ensure transparency in setting of taxes and charges on freight transport. In setting taxes, governments should consider the consequences for competition between modes ...'

- 'All governments ensure development mechanisms for pricing for the use of transport infrastructure which reflects the costs of efficient provision of that infrastructure and take into account congestion and environmental factors in a transparent way.'

The first NTPT recommendation was yet another call for integrated transport planning whilst the second one urged a more balanced approach to transport infrastructure investments. This echoed the 1991 ESD transport working group recommendation that:

> ... Government funding of interurban road and rail infrastructure development, including the National Highway system and the National Rail Corporation's network, should be brought onto an even-handed basis that incorporates ESD principles, by assessing both road and rail projects according to a single set of criteria covering national and local economic, social and environmental benefits and costs.

The NTPT recommendation regarding transparency in taxes and charges was a discreet acknowledgment that Australian road pricing for heavy trucks could be distorting modal competition. The last recommendation cited was in recognition (NTPT, 1994, p52) that: '... Investing in better roads will not necessarily achieve reduced congestion; in fact, it could prove counter productive in some circumstances, attracting more users onto the roads as travel times temporarily decrease.'

The NTPT reports provided a strategy to improve Australia's transport network and to assist international competitiveness. As a package, the 16 NTPT recommendations were in part designed to try and make transport less subject to political intervention, and to put more emphasis on economic measures whilst also taking into account environmental factors. However, the ALP Federal Minister for Transport of the day, the Hon. L. Brereton MP showed a marked reluctance to release the three detailed NTPT reports. One possible reason was that one of these reports (NTPT, 1995) clearly indicated that Sydney's airport capacity would be adequate until about 2015. This was at a time Mr Brereton, representing angry electors near Kingsford Smith Airport, was anxious to secure more Government funding for a second Sydney Airport at Badgerys Creek. In addition, the same report had identified major deficiencies in the mainline inter-capital city rail track and found that about $3 billion of investment in this track was economically warranted. Eventually, Mr Brereton was moved to release the three reports in the quiet media time just before Easter 1995.

Although the Keating Government had supported the NTPT work, it did not make any response to its 16 recommendations. Nor did the new Coalition Government elected in 1996. The Howard Government indicated (Hansard, 2 June 1997) that it did not intend to make a formal response to the reports and recommendations of the NTPT.

THE INDUSTRY COMMISSION TACKLES RAIL AND URBAN TRANSPORT REFORM

Other efforts by the Federal Government in the early 1990s towards land transport reform included two inquiries conducted by the Industry Commission (1991, 1994). The first inquiry was into rail and the final report made 27 recommendations, some of which urged a more commercial focus by the rail industry, and others that indicated where Government action would be helpful. By the end of the 1990s, as shown by a Productivity Commission (1999) Inquiry, rail reform had been advanced by the rail industry.

The second inquiry into land transport led to the Industry Commission's 1994 final report on Urban Transport. Some quotes follow:

> Australia's urban transport systems are falling far short of their potential contribution to the economic and social wellbeing of our cities. There are no 'quick fixes' available: rather a mutually reinforcing package of policies is needed. This chapter develops a program for reform which attempts to balance practicalities, equity concerns, and transition costs with the imperatives for change. While the approach entails some potentially difficult and far-reaching changes, avoiding these decisions will fail to secure the transport systems needed for the next century.

> Transport is vital to making our cities work. Many believe that the financial, economic, social, and environmental consequences of the way we build and operate our urban transport systems cannot be sustained.

> In Australia in recent years, significant reform has occurred in other areas of transport such as long distance road transport, and domestic and international aviation. Urban transport lags behind, although there have been some notable improvements in several States in recent times ...

> There are no easy answers to the many problems facing urban transport in Australia today. In part, this reflects the complex interlinkages between urban transport and the city. As a result, many of the recommendations in this report are interdependent ...

Given the need for a phased approach, the IC mapped out a timetable for reform. '... The key action is to start the process.'

The IC also noted that the process may well change over time and is influenced by changes in technology. An IC priority was to begin introducing competition into those areas where it was largely absent, in the expectation that competition would drive other necessary reforms. For example, governments could ensure service coordination and integrated ticketing arrangements are in place, together with a framework for delivering community service obligations such as transport concessions and non-commercial services.

Although the absence of comprehensive direct road pricing limits the degree to which road authorities can pursue commercial objectives, the IC considered that there was scope for improving the performance of road provision and maintenance with more private sector involvement.

Initial steps should be taken towards direct road pricing. The IC recommended an incremental approach, starting in Sydney and Melbourne with tolls (preferably electronic) on certain new or upgraded urban arterial roads, bridges and tunnels. In due course this should lead to public acceptance of more sophisticated approaches. Meanwhile, parking restrictions, parking taxes and traffic management measures should continue to form part of demand management strategies implemented on an area-wide basis.

Public transport fares should be restructured to create a greater difference between peak and off-peak fares, and to increase with the distance travelled. Any fare increases should be phased in over several years and should be accompanied, if not preceded, by improvements in service quality. As well, early reform of the taxi and hire-car industry and improving accessibility for the transport disadvantaged was called for. The needs of cyclists and pedestrians should be given higher priority in transport planning, with a national bicycle strategy adopted. This would go a long way to enhancing the role of what are, after all, the only non-polluting modes.

The IC also considered that a number of initiatives aimed specifically at addressing environmental concerns should be commenced or continued. Emission standards for vehicles are playing a role in ameliorating pollution and should continue to do so. A system of emission tests, with fines or loss of registration for 'dirty' vehicles, should be introduced as a means of reducing pollution in those cities where pollution problems are most severe. Should these measures fail to achieve pollution standards which governments consider acceptable, further measures such as differential fuel franchise fees and surcharges on road pricing charges in particular areas should be considered.

The broad thrust of the recommendations put forward by the IC in its 1994 Report on Urban Transport received Commonwealth Government support (Joint Ministerial Statement cited IC 1993–94 Annual Report, p394). It was then stated that the Federal Government had decided to request the IC to report on progress on urban transport in 1997. This did not happen.

As noted in the 1994 IC report on urban transport, the lack of a simple solution is reflected in the number of recommendations, and a staged approach. The trouble is that the limited gains Australia has made towards sustainable urban passenger transport during the 1990s have been far outweighed by robust road-building programs with virtually no congestion pricing for car commuters.

Although some progress had been made on some of the IC recommendations in the late 1990s, none was made on road pricing, with the sole exception of Melbourne's new ring road with electronic tolling that started in 1999. Meantime, the Bureau of Transport Economics (1996) had found five 'no-regrets' measures for transport reform to reduce liquid fuel use. These reform proposals comprised four urban transport measures, plus transferring some inter-capital city road freight onto rail. This was followed by an inquiry into urban air pollution by the Australian Academy of Technological Sciences and Engineering (AATSE, 1997). This report recommended that land transport reform on several familiar fronts be undertaken.

INTEGRATED TRANSPORT PLANNING REVISITED

The need for integrated transport planning was again reiterated by the House of Representatives Standing Committee on Communications, Transport and Microeconomic Reform (1997, 1998). The Committee, chaired by Mr Paul Neville MP, in its 1997 report on roads recommended, '… that the Commonwealth consult widely, develop and publish an integrated national transport strategic plan by 1 July 1999'.

Needless to say, the first of July 1999 came and went without any integrated strategic plan from Canberra. By then, further support for integrated transport planning had been given by the Neville Committee's August 1998 report on rail, and, in a report called 'Revitalising Rail' by a Rail Projects Task Force (1999) established by the Prime Minister. This Task Force found that the lack of an integrated national transport strategy and 'substandard national track' were the two major barriers to improved rail performance. Their first recommendation was that: 'The Commonwealth Government takes the lead in developing an economically driven National Transport Strategy that will secure a seamless domestic transport system embracing road, rail, sea and air transport, and provide for the entry and exit of people and goods by sea and air at world competitive standards.'

This recommendation of the Rail Projects Task Force was yet another variation of the long sought after National Transport Strategy recommended in 1991 by the ESD Working Party, the NTPT report in 1994, and the two Neville Committee reports of 1997 and 1998. The move to more integrated national transport planning was to be delayed, with proposals for a National Land Transport Commission (NLTC) abandoned as shown below.

THE FATE OF THE NATIONAL LAND TRANSPORT COMMISSION

In an effort to develop '… an effective integrated approach to national transport' the Neville Committee (1998, p133) had recommended '… that the Commonwealth establish a National Land Transport Commission to provide:

- advice to the Government on a national transport plan

- recommendations to the Government on the allocation of funds for rail and road projects on the strict basis of highest benefit-cost ratios, which address all relevant externalities, such as accidents, congestion, pollution, greenhouse gas emissions and noise.

Further, the Commonwealth give higher priority to land transport infrastructure investment within total budget outlays than is currently the case'.

The proposal for a National Land Transport Commission (NLTC) had also received strong support from the Australian Transport Council (comprising Australia's Transport Ministers) at its meeting of April 1998 which 'agreed on the need for an integrated approach to road and rail freight operational and regulatory issues. They therefore requested [a report to their] November meeting on the options for achieving this, including the feasibility of incorporating rail within the responsibilities of the National Road Transport Commission thus creating a Land Transport Commission'.

This approach was favoured at the November 1998 ATC meeting. However, the Road Transport Forum strongly opposed the concept, which could have meant a NLTC taking over the role of the National Road Transport Commission. The Federal Department of Transport failed to give strong support to a NLTC. Eventually, the Australian Transport Council agreed to support a National Transport Secretariat (NTS) with more limited functions. The NTS commenced work in 2000. It should be no surprise to the reader that road pricing is not specifically on their agenda.

By the end of the year 2000, no fewer than twelve reports produced during the 1990s had called for land transport reform. These calls for transport reform, were supplemented by reports from the Inter-State Commission (1990), and, the Senate Committee (2000) examining greenhouse gas emissions.

Despite these numerous reports, the Federal Government has continued to fund roads at the expense of rail and urban public transport. Federal funding for rail projects was effectively suspended from 1995 to 1999, whilst funding for new urban public transport projects was all but terminated in the mid-1990s. Perhaps most damagingly, NRTC heavy vehicle charges were not indexed for inflation throughout the 1990s, the price of petrol and diesel was allowed to fall in real terms after the mid-1990s, and the diesel excise was reduced on 1 July 2000 for heavy trucks.

DATA DEFICIENCIES

A major requirement for good public transport policy is adequate and accurate transport data. Limitations on transport data were noted as acute as far back as 1980 by the NSW Commission of Inquiry into the Road Freight Industry (McDonell, 1980). The situation regarding timely and accurate transport data available for the public record did not improve during the 1980s, and became steadily worse as the 1990s progressed.

In other words, the situation for Australian transport data went from bad to worse.

Transport data is an important area in which the Australian Bureau of Statistics (ABS) is struggling with other demands on its resources. The ABS ceased its publications *Rail Transport* in the mid-1980s and *Interstate Freight Statistics* in the mid 1990s. Other Government agencies with experience in analysing land transport data have been merged with other agencies with a resulting loss of expertise. These include the Inter-State Commission in 1990, the Bureau of Industry Economics in 1996, and the Energy Research and Development Corporation in 1997. Still other agencies such as the Bureau of Transport Economics, along with Australian universities, have been downsized.

Against this trend, some helpful work was carried out during the 1990s by a Steering Committee on National Performance Monitoring of Government Trading Enterprises. However, even this Committee was disbanded after it had analysed data for the 1996–97 fiscal year.

As one of many examples of the need for better rail data, two significant errors in rail freight tasks appeared in the *Australian Year Book* 1997 (page 532) published by the ABS. The first error was that the freight task for public rail systems in net tonne-kms was overstated by some 25 per cent. The second error was that non-Government rail for one year was understated by 25 per cent. Although these errors were corrected in the *Australian Year Book 1998* (page 532) non-Government rail data was significantly understated for other reasons. This, in part, reflected the lack of a robust mechanism in place to ensure full and accurate reporting of all rail freight data — both tonnages and tonne-kilometres (tkms) — and Government and non-Government, as Government systems fragment, and are privatised. Indeed, after decades of *Australian Year Books* giving details of rail freight tasks, the 2000 *Year Book* simply omitted all reference to rail tkms.

The ABS also had severe problems with its 1995 Survey of Motor Vehicle Usage (SMVU), which resulted in the usual Preliminary Report being issued, but a failure to produce a Final Report. Instead, the ABS (2000a) had to advise that significant 'recall bias factors' required a revision of some estimates, including a reduction of the estimated total distance driven by all motor vehicles by 7 per cent down to some 156 billion kilometres. There was also a problem with the estimates of the road freight task in 1994–95, with the preliminary ABS estimate taken to task by Apelbaum (1997), who proposed a lower estimate. Despite efforts by ABS (2000a) to improve the 1997–98 SMVU, publication was delayed to February 2000, with an unduly low estimate of the road freight task. Fortunately, the situation improved for ABS (2000b) with their road freight estimates for 1998–99.

Clearly, better land transport data is needed in Australia. Aviation and maritime statistics are much better than road and rail statistics. There is a good case that the resources to publish up-to-date and accurate Australian land transport data should be provided by the Commonwealth. Here, the US Bureau of Transportation Statistics is a good model. This was established as a result of the United States Intermodal Surface Transportation Efficiency Act 1991. Funding for the United States BTS was continued in the Transportation Equity Act signed into law by President Clinton in 1998.

THE FAILURE TO BRING INTERSTATE RAIL TRACK UP TO SPEED

In the early 1990s, it was clear that if the new National Rail Corporation was to win back line haul intercapital city land freight that had been lost to the road freight industry in the 1970s and 1980s, then the interstate rail track had to be upgraded. Indeed, the former Inter-State Commission (1987) had argued that reduction of transit times should be a priority for the rail systems.

However, the reality is that during the 1990s, despite Adelaide–Melbourne gauge standardisation and deferred maintenance undertaken as part of the Keating Government's 1992–95 'One Nation' capital works program, the average terminal to terminal speeds of intermodal freight trains in 1999 were woefully slow. They included about 50 km per hour on the Sydney–Brisbane corridor, and 70 km per hour on the Melbourne–Sydney corridor. Melbourne–Adelaide–Perth average speeds have shown some improvement due to the work of an Australian Rail Track Corporation (ARTC, 2000) formed by the Federal Government in 1998.

At an historic 'Rail Summit' in September 1997, the Australian Transport Council (ATC) agreed to adopt certain measures with a view to making '… dramatic improvements in the performance of interstate rail' in order to overcome the present situation where rail has '… failed to compete effectively with road transport'. The measures included lifting the average speed of intermodal freight trains to 80 kilometres per hour as a five-year goal, and 100 km per hour as a 'longer term' goal.

To attain the average ATC speed goals for the track linking Australia's three largest cities will require some track straightening, along with other upgrading. These goals were carefully formulated in 1994 for the NTPT, and an investment of $3 billion to bring the interstate track 'up to speed' was found by the BTE to be economically warranted. In addition, the ATC speed goals were endorsed in 1998 by the Neville Committee, which had also identified a need for an integrated national transport plan. Moreover, the Neville Committee found that if the existing mainline interstate track was not upgraded, '... *rail will continue to deteriorate*' to the point that the loss for intercity rail will become '*irretrievable*'.

Sydney–Melbourne is the most important intercity transport corridor in Australia. **Between Australia's Bicentennial in 1988, and 2000, no fewer than 20 major studies have proposed improvements in the Sydney–Melbourne rail track** (Laird and Adorni-

---

BOX 5.1
SYDNEY–MELBOURNE RAIL STUDIES

The following 20 reports deal fully, or in part, with Sydney–Melbourne rail track

1988	V/Line Fast Freight Train (FFT) Proposal
1988	State Rail study re Main South Line: Reduced Transit Times
1989	High Speed Rail Engineers (HSRE) Fast Freight Train
1989	McLennan Magasanik Market Feasibility study for the FFT
1990	State Rail study re Curve Straightening on Main South
1991	National Rail Freight Initiative (NRFI)
1991	Jacana Study
1993	Energy R and D Corporation project report
1993	BTCE economic evaluation
1994	NRC Railway Infrastructure Plan
1994	Examination of the 'Wentworth Route' for State Rail
1995	BTCE Report for the NTPT
1995	Sydney–Canberra Rail Corridor: Infrastructure Study (for SRA and NSW DOT)
1995	Bureau of Industry Economics, International Benchmarking, Rail Freight 1995
1996	Intercity land freight transport in Eastern Australia
1998	Maunsell report on Operational Standards
1998	Neville Committee inquiry and report
1988	NSW Public Works Committee inquiry into tilt trains
1998	Booz, Allen and Hamilton, report re interstate rail track capital program
2000	Project 11 report for ARTC and the Rail Access Corporation

Braccesi, 1993, Laird, 1998 and ARTC, 2000) all without implementation. There has been no shortage of work identifying necessary
upgrading to increase the efficiency of rail on the Sydney–Melbourne
corridor and its competitiveness against trucks operating over a
reconstructed Hume Highway. These studies are listed in Box 5.3
and are in addition to the reports on the Very Fast Train (VFT) from
1984 to 1991, plus extensive studies on the more recent Speedrail
proposal.

Sydney–Melbourne track upgrading continues to be studied.
However, the reality is that no track straightening has been undertaken for decades, and the high-powered diesel electric locomotives

BOX 5.2
COMMENTS ON RAIL TRACK TO THE PRODUCTIVITY COMMISSION

The following quotes on rail track deficiencies are from submissions to
the Productivity Commission's inquiry into progress in rail reform (PC,
2000, p 238):

> Many of the vital transport networks ... [including the standard gauge
> network], both interstate and intercity, are in dire need of considerable
> upgrading ...
> *The Australian Shipping Federation*

> At an infrastructure level, the lack of investment on track and signals
> constitutes one of the main factors which has resulted in slow track
> speeds and low axle load capacities.
> *The Australian Wheat Board*

> The poor quality of interstate rail infrastructure is a legacy of many
> decades of neglect by State governments, and has many aspects ...
> [including obsolete alignments, obsolete signalling and communications
> equipment, short crossing loops, inadequate height clearances, inade-
> quate track strength and poor quality track structure].
> *National Rail Corporation*

> Most operators have expressed their concerns regarding ... the poor
> track condition, the lack of long passing loops, inconsistent and prohibi-
> tive speed limits, the inability to double stack containers from
> Melbourne and the far from world's best practice maximum axle
> weights.
> *Specialised Container Transport*

> ... the network has numerous speed-weight restrictions due to: wooden
> sleepers in Victoria; light weight rail on the Melbourne to Albury stan-
> dard gauge track; a curve for every kilometre plus steep ruling grades
> from Albury to Sydney; poor alignment from Sydney to Brisbane ...
> *Railway Technical Society of Australasia*

continue to be stuck with 'steam age' track. As observed by Ross Gittins (*Sydney Morning Herald*, August 25, 1999) '... Governments fantasise about glamorous high-speed trains. Yet spending on straightening out the Sydney to Melbourne rail line has been put off for 50 years, even though it would pay big dividends in reduced pollution, greenhouse gas emissions, road congestion and accidents'.

Turning now to the Sydney–Brisbane railway, for much of its length, the track is a series of old branch lines with numerous speed restrictions due to excessive curvature. There is no doubt that the viability of this track in its present condition is in grave doubt. Indeed, an NTPT (1995, p 63) report found that 'Transit times, reliability and costs are so poor that the corridor may not survive as a commercial freight alternative unless improvements are implemented'. The Neville Committee endorsed this view in 1998. Large-scale upgrading of the Pacific Highway now under way without rail track upgrading will exacerbate this situation.

Rail operations on the East–West rail corridor linking Melbourne, Adelaide and Perth are much better than the Melbourne–Sydney–Brisbane corridor. The better rail freight performance of the East–West track for the most part reflects a $500 million investment by Australian National from 1978 to 1994, and, its double-stacked container capability between Adelaide and Perth. This capability could usefully be extended to Melbourne, along with some grade and curve easing on the eastern side of the Adelaide Hills. More comments on 'substandard national track' are given in Box 5.2.

As we have seen in Chapter 2, Queensland has shown that mainline track straightening is an effective way to bring trains up to speed. It is also much less expensive than building four-lane highways. Had the Commonwealth and/or the NSW Government matched the Queensland Government's mainline upgrading programs during the 1990s, and had the Interstate Commission's 1990 recommendations for mass distance charging of heavy long-distance trucks been implemented, interstate rail freight would have been more competitive with line haul road freight. As a result, by 1999, Australia would have been saving about 100 million litres of diesel fuel a year and highway maintenance costs (IC, 1991b). Undoubtedly, on the basis that some 36 per cent of fatalities in road crashes on the NSW sections of the NHS outside of cities involve interstate truck operations (Laird, 1996), some lives would also have been saved.

The delays by the Howard Government to deal with the issue of substandard national track came at a time when three large rail projects (Alice Springs to Darwin, Melbourne to Darwin and Speedrail) were being encouraged by the Federal Government. These delays were accompanied by increasing unrest amongst the backbenches of the House of Representatives, as noted below.

BACKBENCHERS' RUMBLINGS ON RAIL

The report, 'Tracking Australia', was considered by the House of Representatives on 8 February 1999. There were six speakers and Mr Paul Neville MP moved a motion, in part to request that a Government commitment of $250 million to rail infrastructure be expanded. He noted 'The most neglected mode of Australian transport is unquestionably rail. As we approach the 21st century we expect it to make a significant contribution to the efficiency of the Australian economy, but for the most part we restrict it to a 19th century capability. Little wonder then that industry, business and tourism ask: is government serious about rail?'

Mr Neville also said that '… when you consider that Queensland Rail will have spent nearly a billion dollars between Brisbane and Townsville in less than a decade on just one line it is not a big ask that, for a national system that links the five mainland capitals, we spend $2.75 billion over 12 or 13 years. What is important about it is that we have a bipartisan will to make it happen. The benefits are immeasurable. I again refer you to Queensland Rail, which has done some very innovative things over recent years. They have recently opened the tilt train between Brisbane and Rockhampton. As recently as the 1980s, the train took 14 hours for that journey. The tilt train takes seven'.

The motion was seconded by Mr Colin Hollis MP who noted an urgent need for '… the upgrading of the safe-working arrangements between Casino and Brisbane' [which had featured on the ABC 7.*30 Report* on 6 November 1998], and observed that '… the current upgrading of the Pacific Highway to a near four-lane standard by 2005 may prove to be in vain if all it achieves is taking more and more freight off rail and putting it onto B-doubles'. Also, he argued that we need to '… compare the national benefits of spending $1000 million on facilitating road trains on the Newell and Goulburn Valley Highways, or to spend about the same amount in developing a basic inland standard gauge railway from Melbourne to Brisbane via Parkes that would be capable of carrying double-stacked containers'.

Mr Macarthur MP noted the iron ore railways in the Pilbara region operating at world's best practice, which '… proves that we can do it here in Australia if we are prepared to invest … I would advocate to members of this House that we get our current railway system in order. Let us make the investment. Let us make the rolling stock better. Let us get the track in order. Then we can start looking at new investments such as Alice Springs–Darwin'.

Throughout 1999, Parliament and the rail industry waited for a Government response to the Neville Report. This response was put off until April 2000, a delay of 20 months. By then, there was the report of the Rail Projects Task Force (1999) and the final report of an inquiry into progress in rail reform by the Productivity Commission

(2000). The release of the final Productivity Commission (PC) report was almost six months after a statutory requirement to table it in Parliament within 25 sitting days of receipt by the Treasurer, Peter Costello, in August 1999.

A summary of the response to these three rail reports, plus the 1997 Parliamentary Report on roads, is given in Box 5.3. The waiting time of 30 months to respond to the Neville Report on roads was probably the longest time in the history of Federation for a Government response to a House of Representatives Committee report.

The reply of Shadow Transport Minister Mr Ferguson MP on 13 April to the Government response was also very limited. It gave no hint of how an ALP Government might have responded to the reports. Meanwhile, National Rail and other interstate freight operators continue to do the best they can on substandard track.

By way of contrast to major track upgrades, the Federal Government continued to pressure the States into accepting heavier trucks operating on the National Highway System. Such market distortions were put clearly into perspective by the Chief Executive, Mr Vince O'Rourke of Queensland Rail (1997 *Annual Report*. p 18):

> The cutthroat nature of competition in the transport and logistics industry is a very real challenge. Road, shipping and air transporters — like

---

BOX 5.3

GOVERNMENT RESPONDS TO FOUR TRANSPORT REPORTS

In April 2000, the Federal Minister for Transport, John Anderson finally released a formal response to four land transport reports. The response of the Federal Government to the 98 recommendations in the four reports was very limited.

Both national integrated transport planning and a National Land Transport Commission were further delayed — the latter until at least 2004. Long overdue investment to upgrade 'substandard national track' was further delayed on the pretext that some States are still to comply with rail reform requirements. However, the ARTC was to undertake yet another study of national track upgrading requirements. There was a National Transport Secretariat with limited functions and there may be a new National Rail Transport Commission formed in 2001 to advance harmonisation of rail operations between the States.

The PC and Treasury approach to funding much-needed mainline interstate track appeared to be to commercialise roads to remove impediments to private sector investment in rail. However, the trucking lobby, the Federal Department of Transport, and the Coalition Government did not want major road projects evaluated on the same basis as major intercity track projects. Accordingly, a PC recommendation for an inquiry into roads was rejected by the Government on the flimsy pretext that there are no problems in road funding project evaluation. This conveniently ignores the fact that the PC call for a roads inquiry was a step towards competitive neutrality. Thus, the tilted playing field must continue with a low allocation of $250 million to upgrade substandard national track.

Queensland Rail — continue to improve performance levels and fight for business. Equally, the issue of competitive neutrality is of major concern to Queensland Rail and the rail industry generally. The road transport industry, for example, is being given heavier and heavier load limits with imposing B-Double and B-Triple trucks. Heavy trucks aren't paying their way for the roads they use and damage, let alone the associated community costs of crashes, congestion and pollution.

THE SPEEDRAIL PROPOSAL AND AN AFFORDABLE ALTERNATIVE

As noted in Chapter 2, the concept of using existing French TGV technology was initially proposed in 1984 by CSIRO for use between Sydney, Canberra and Melbourne. By 1991, it was decided that the

---

BOX 5.4
BOOSTING THE SPEEDRAIL PROPOSAL

The Prime Minister, John Howard, addressing an audience of hundreds at Parliament House in Canberra, on 8 August 1998 cleared the way 'for a new era in transport in Australia'. This was with the selection of 'SPEEDRAIL' — on merit ahead of strong competition — as the successful proponent to build and operate a very high-speed train service between Sydney and Canberra.

'SPEEDRAIL' will use the commercially proven and leading edge TGV technology now used to link major capitals throughout Europe, and deliver 15 thousand new jobs during three years of construction — due to commence in the year 2000.

Based on current information — fast trains will operate between Sydney and Canberra by the end of 2003 — with billions of dollars injected into the regional economy in the interim.

Nine TGV trains, each of eight cars, will travel up to 320 kph to provide a world class train experience every 45 minutes each way — taking just 81 minutes to make the journey.

'SPEEDRAIL' will build, own, and operate the Sydney to Canberra Very High Speed Train before transferring the railway to public ownership after 30 years.

Mr Howard said the very fast train would rival airline flight as the preferred means of travel for countless millions of Australians for decades to come.

'Our national transport vision is one free of State boundaries and differences where passengers and freight can move at lightning speed in complete safety.

'This nation-building project is concrete proof of my Government's determination to harness the latest proven transport technology and Australian ingenuity to deliver ourselves — and our children — a visionary new transport system of which we can all be proud ...'

project would not proceed, and in 1995 the Speedrail proposal between Sydney and Canberra was announced. After expressions of interest being formally invited in March 1997 by the Commonwealth, New South Wales and ACT Governments, Prime Minister John Howard announced in August 1998 with much fanfare (see Box 5.4) that the preferred option was Speedrail. This was on the understanding that if the project were to proceed, it would be '… at no net cost to the taxpayer'.

Exciting as the prospect was, it did not meet the test of '… at no net cost to the taxpayer' as interpreted to mean 'at no cost to budget'. By June 2000, there had been calls for the Government to re-open tenders so that the more affordable tilt train options could be properly considered. The proposal was finally set aside by the Federal Government in December 2000, when dealing with Sydney's airport problems, with the promise of yet another major study of fast train options for the East Coast.

As noted in Chapter 2, NSW people have had little other than the prospect of a VFT on new tracks ever since 1984, whilst Queensland has had a tilt train since 1998. The State of NSW has twice as many people as Queensland. Thus, by standards such as relative population and wealth, NSW should have had track straightening during the

BOX 5.5
THE GOULBURN–YASS BICENTENNIAL RAIL PROPOSAL

In 1981 the Institution of Engineers, Australia published a 'Bicentennial High Speed Rail Proposal' report. The proposal was for a new 'T-Line' railway from Goulburn to Yass with a spur to North Canberra. The cost of the new track was a modest $127 million. The benefits included faster rail freight services along with a three-hour Sydney–Canberra XPT service and a 6.5 hour Melbourne–Canberra XPT service.

The response from the NSW Government and State Rail to the proposal was negative. However, the State Road Commissioners were quick to see that Australia had a Bicentennial Road Development Program. As well, a new Goulburn–Yass four-lane dual carriageway, with town bypasses, was built by the mid-1990s at a cost of more than $500 million.

The negative reaction from Government to rail upgrading proposals, and the slow speeds of modern XPT trains over the 'steam age' Sydney–Canberra rail track alignment, were undoubtedly factors in prompting CSIRO Chief Dr Paul Wild to devote resources to a proposal for a Sydney–Canberra–Melbourne Very Fast Train or VFT in 1984.

Construction of the T-Line track would give significant reduction in freight train transit times, plus give savings in fuel use when compared to the current poorly aligned track between Goulburn and Yass. A new T-Line would also be ideal for tilt trains that could link not only Canberra and Sydney, but also Canberra to Yass, Cootamundra, Wagga and Albury.

1990s to improve freight train efficiency along with tilt trains. Instead, they have only had ongoing speculation about TGVs.

One option is that the mainline track linking Melbourne and Sydney and Brisbane could be upgraded by Government, with a Canberra connection being built from near Goulburn. This could be a public private partnership that could also operate tilt trains between Sydney and Canberra. Track improvements could include a Menangle–Mittagong direct route near the Hume Highway as proposed by the Hon. Bill Wentworth in 1991, and new track near Goulburn (as shown in Box 5.5), along with other track straightening.

The rejection in December 2000 of the Speedrail proposal suggests that it is time to revisit the 'T-Line' rail proposal. It remains to be seen how quickly the Federal Government's commissioning of even more rail studies is translated into actual track upgrading for faster trains.

NATIONAL COMPETITION POLICY — A CLAYTON'S REFORM?

In Australia, the Competition Principle Agreements (CPAs) signed by Heads of Governments at the April 1995 Council of Australian Governments (COAG) meeting have driven much 'reform' in Australia. These agreements required the States to implement various reforms and work to implement National Competition Policy (NCP). As a result, NCP has been pursued with far more vigour than Ecologically Sustainable Development (ESD). We have already noted that use of NCP as it relates to road transport was to induce New South Wales to adopt the deficient NRTC charges. For rail transport, it has led to pressure for 'vertical separation' of rail systems, and 'open access'.

The concept of vertical separation of rail systems basically means at least one authority to own and maintain the track and a separate authority or authorities to be responsible for the train operations. Although this model was introduced to Sweden in 1988, and found favour with European bureaucrats, it was rejected during the 1990s in the United States, Canada and New Zealand. It was also tried and found wanting in the United Kingdom in the mid-19th century and again in the late 20th century. However, this did not prevent its adoption in Australia. Thus, whilst in 1989 when a House of Representatives Committee in its report *Rail: Five Systems — One Solution* suggested that five rail systems were too many to be involved in interstate rail freight, there are now many more, as shown in Box 5.6.

It is worth noting that the entire Australian rail freight task, approaching 130 billion tonne km (btkm) in 1998–99 (Laird 2001), and performed by 20 private and publicly owned rail organisations, is less than the rail freight task of approximately 160 btkm performed each year in the late 1990s by one company, Canadian Pacific, in

BOX 5.6
THE GROWING NUMBER OF RAIL SYSTEMS

Public providers as at 31 December 2000

National Rail Corporation, interstate freight
Australian Rail Track Corp, interstate track
State Rail Authority, NSW passengers
FreightCorp, NSW freight
Rail Access Corporation, NSW track
Rail Services Australia, NSW track
Queensland Rail
TransAdelaide, Adelaide

Private providers

Australia Southern Railroad, SA freight
Austrac, NSW freight
Bayside Trains, Melbourne
BHP, WA, SA, NSW freight
Freight Australia
Great Northern Rail Services, Vic freight
Great Southern Railway, interstate passenger
Hamersley Iron, WA iron ore
Hillside Trains, Melbourne
Northern Rivers Railroad, NSW
Patrick, interstate freight
Robe River Railroad, WA iron ore
Silverton, NSW freight
Skitube, NSW passengers
Specialised Container Transport, interstate freight
Australian Transport Network, Tasmania freight
Toll Rail, Interstate freight
V-Line Passenger, Vic.
VicTrack, Vic.
West Coast Railway, Vic
Westrail, WA

SOURCE Productivity Commission (1999, p10) as updated. Excludes separate private maintenance and construction providers and tourist train operators, along with the numerous owners and operators of sugar cane railways. Note Australian National (AN) was still in existence between 1998 and 2000, but with no track and no operation of trains.

Canada. In turn, Canadian Pacific's rail freight task is less than Canadian National's rail freight task. Thus, it is likely that the next decade in Australia will see a series of rail freight company mergers.

When National Rail was formed under a 1991 Inter-governmental Agreement, it was intended that it would take up the control of the interstate mainline track away from the State capital cities. However, National Rail was slow to act in this regard, and lost this opportunity in 1995 when the Federal Government announced its intention to form a new track authority and allow competition for interstate rail freight. The first 'private' operator (using government locomotives and rolling stock), Specialised Container Transport (SCT), started Melbourne–Perth operations in July 1995. This was followed by Toll (initially TNT) in 1997. An Australian Rail Track Corporation, with the Federal Government as sole shareholder, was formed in 1998 to take over AN's interstate track, and manage access to interstate track in other States.

In July 1996, the NSW State Rail Authority was restructured to operate only passenger rail services, whilst the Rail Access Corporation was created to own the track, a Rail Services Authority created to maintain the track, and a Freight Corporation also formed. By the end of 2000, following consideration of a tragic fatal rail crash at Glenbrook, NSW, in December 1999, the NSW Government had introduced legislation to reduce the number of rail authorities from four to three. Vertical separation of track and train operations was considered by the Victorian Government, but later passed over for horizontal separation of train operations with privatisation of V-Line Freight in 1999 to Freight Victoria. Instead, a lease over the track was granted along with the formation of three passenger rail companies. As well, the Federal Government, when privatising Australian National's freight operations inside each of South Australia and Tasmania in 1997 effectively opted for vertical integration. The privatisation of Westrail's profitable freight operations in 2000 also opted for effective vertical integration, with questions over access to the interstate track in WA resolved in early 2001.

Queensland Rail, or QR, is by far the most successful and largest integrated system in Australia offering freight and passenger services. QR resolved, despite Government pressure, to remain as an integrated system. As seen by Mr Vince O'Rourke, the Chief Executive of QR (*Annual Report*, 1995–96, p60), 'Unlike other rail experiments, Queensland Rail believes it can be a great railway without being fragmented. I am firmly committed to a unified "one QR" with the ability to facilitate third party access within its integrated structure'. This assessment was supported by a study by Mercer (1996) that found from a study of rail operations around the world that the integrated ones tended to perform better.

The concept of 'open access' in Australia appears to go back to the Industry Commission, whose 1991 report on rail was concerned at monopoly profits, claimed to be some $400 million, being exacted by the Queensland and NSW Governments for the haulage of export coal. The IC approach was enthusiastically embraced by Hilmer et al (1993) in a definitive report on competition policy. However, whereas the Hilmer report was sensitive to road–rail competition, the CPA and NCP were not.

As a consequence of the 1995 CPA, a National Competition Council (NCC) was formed. Soon, the NCC was dealing with rail matters. Some applications to the NCC affecting access to rail track under Part III A of the *Trade Practices Act* 1974 (as amended) have been subject to review. The first rail application was by Carpentaria Transport Pty Ltd (then a subsidiary of TNT) in 1996 to recommend the formal declaration of certain Brisbane–Cairns rail freight services. This included not only the track, but also rolling stock and terminals. The NCC invited submissions. Here, a major private freight forwarder, FCL, which also operated in North Queensland had bluntly stated: 'This application should be treated with the respect it deserves and consigned straight to the garbage bin.'

Queensland Rail's public comment was more diplomatic, finding that the application was 'intriguing' since the applicant was seeking access to facilities and services that they had used for more than 20 years. In 1997 the NCC reported with a recommendation that the Queensland Premier do not formally declare the QR Services sought. This was done in August 1997 and the applicant then unsuccessfully applied for a review of this decision.

The NCC, amidst inquiries on gas, electricity and other matters, also dealt with further rail matters. These included those lodged by SCT for rail services and access in both NSW and WA, and the NSW Minerals Council regarding the Hunter Valley coal lines. A further inquiry was held in 1999 to consider access to the Tarcoola–Alice Springs, and Alice Springs–Darwin rail track. The irony of applying for access to a then non-existent rail track was hopefully not lost on the participants.

Perhaps the most interesting recent case was the application indicating a desire on the part of Robe River Iron Ore to gain access to the Hamersley Iron rail track in the Pilbara. This commenced with an application to the NCC, and was then subject to proceedings in the Federal Court which effectively found that as the Hamersley Iron ore railway was part of the mine production process, access should not be granted. This decision was appealed in July 1999.

The main problem affecting rail freight, raised in a submission regarding Carpentaria by one writer (Laird), was as follows:

Rather than giving significant attention to increasing intrastate competition between rail operators in Queensland, and other parts of Australia, genuine efforts should be made by Government at a national level to ensure true competitive neutrality between road freight and rail freight. Under the present NRTC charges and extensive 'highway subsidisation' it is a nonsense to talk of fair competition between road and rail for land freight. The proper addressing of these issues, on a national basis, would result in economic, social and environmental benefits.

The NCC response to this was simply to note it. Here, perhaps the last word in this section should go to Professor Hilmer (at the William Fraser Commemorative Address, Chartered Institute of Transport, Sydney, 29 September 1995) regarding the road freight industry. 'The road sector does not fully pay for the road damage and externality costs (Inter-State Commission 1990) and this may affect potential inter-modal competition with rail especially.'

Thus, whilst government in Australia continues to conduct its giant experiment in rail–rail competition, it is certainly taking its time to sort out rail–road competition for freight. This is despite the ATC meeting on 14 November 1997 at which it was agreed that competitive neutrality should be investigated 'without delay'. The NCC did not see this as part of their function although the NCC 2000 *Annual Report* considered they could take more of a role in rail reform.

In February 2000, the Senate Select Committee examining National Competition Policy recommended, inter alia, that '... the NCC address the matter of road–rail competition for freight as a matter of urgency'. The Howard Government in August 2000 rejected this recommendation on the grounds that the issue was a matter for Government and not the NCC.

At present, we have a Clayton's land transport reform agenda.

THE NEW SOUTH WALES GOVERNMENT

During the 1990s, the NSW Government has taken a keen interest in land transport problems. One initiative in the early 1990s by the NSW Roads and Traffic Authority (RTA) was to commission consultants, Sinclair Knight and Partners, to undertake a major study 'Road Transport — Future Directions'. The findings were stark. As seen by an official RTA brochure, the study found that air pollution could increase by 50 per cent and road congestion could increase by 600 per cent. The brochure candidly asked, 'Is this the world YOU want to live in?' It then stated that 'we believe, in New South Wales, that it is time to take a long, hard look at our transport options and develop a plan for the future'.

'The policies and ideas of current road planning are not necessarily appropriate for the long-term future. Transport does impact on our social and economic lives and we need a plan that takes into account the many competing demands of transport. The plan must address the transport of people, goods and services, as well as land use and development, the environment, increased population and funding to name a few of the issues.'

The detailed report *Road Transport — Future Directions* was later accompanied by a report (Commeignes, 1991) that then estimated the cost of road congestion in Sydney at some $1 billion each year. It was later estimated by the BTE (1999b) to be $6 billion each year. The NSW reports of the early 1990s were followed in 1993 by an 'Integrated Transport Strategy' that made many suggestions for Policy and Strategic Action. However, these suggestions did not clearly indicate a need for improved road pricing for either Sydney car commuters, or heavy vehicles.

The State Labor Government elected in March 1995 actually made road pricing worse, along with increasing funds for road works and constraining funds for rail and urban public transport. The setback in NSW road pricing occurred on two fronts. Firstly, in response to a pre-election promise to remove tolls on the M4 and M5 Motorways, a scheme was introduced to pay toll rebates to private car owners using these motorways. This was accompanied by the lifting of tolls on the Waterfall–Bulli motorway in 1996. Secondly, on 1 July 1996, NSW gave in to pressure from the Road Transport Forum and the Commonwealth to lower heavy truck registration fees as determined by the NRTC. The result was to halve the annual registration and permit fee for heavy six-axle semi-trailers (loaded to 42.5 tonnes), and to more than halve NSW annual fees for all B-Doubles. This cost the State of NSW an estimated $60 million in 1996–97, the first year of operation of the NRTC charges in NSW.

A further report on Integrated Transport Strategy for the Greater Metropolitan Region was released in January 1995. Better rail and public transport was also proposed. One action (#22) was to '... Develop methods to incorporate environmental costs and benefits, including effects on air, noise and water, into the evaluation process for transport infrastructure investment'. However, this strategy was again light on road pricing.

In November 1998, a report on tilt trains was released by the Public Works Committee of the NSW Legislative Assembly. This report gave particular emphasis to NSW mainline track. Whilst the NSW report refrained from commenting on the Speedrail proposal, it took the view that the use of tilt trains without a track upgrade would not be appropriate and recommended, in part:

> That the NSW sections of the Sydney–Melbourne and Sydney–Brisbane railway line should be aerial-surveyed, mapped, and computer formatted to improve knowledge of existing track alignments and to allow for proper planning of track deviations.

Such an insight is not beyond the obvious and one wonders what rail managers and planners have been doing for the past 40 years of computerised civil engineering; certainly the road planners would not need such a suggestion to be made to them.

In December 1998, the NSW Premier, the Hon. Bob Carr MP, released *Action for Transport 2010* statements for both Sydney and NSW. This comprised the usual statements about the need for reducing traffic congestion and increasing public transport use, but was coy on road pricing. The statement also made commitments for a $4 billion transport upgrade package. This included recycled promises for a Parramatta–Epping–Chatswood railway and a new Waterfall–Thirroul tunnel. There was also a new commitment for a $790 million track upgrade of the Hornsby–Warnervale railway, but no firm mention of any work on the Main South line south of Sydney

Thus, whilst the proposed work by 2010 is welcome, it should have gone further. *Action for Transport 2010* could also be regarded as a statement of NSW rail and public transport upgrading that should have been done during the 1990s.

In December 2000, a NSW Legislative Council General Purposes Committee released a report on the Government's plan to privatise its Freight Rail Corporation, or FreightCorp. The Committee's 15 recommendations included a proposal that half of the proceeds of the FreightCorp sale should be applied to upgrading track in regional NSW, and that the NSW Government should release a detailed Freight Strategy by mid-2001. A NSW Freight Strategy document was foreshadowed in the 1998 *Action for Transport 2010* documents. The failure to produce a Freight Strategy in two years, or to make a response to the 1998 Public Works Committee recommendations regarding a tilt train and track upgrading is indicative of transport policy paralysis at a State level.

OTHER STATES

Other States have also worked towards the Holy Grail of Integrated Transport. For example, Queensland produced a South-East Queensland (SEQ) Passenger Transport Study in 1991, an SEQ Transport Policy in 1993, a Draft Integrated Regional Transport Plan for SEQ in 1996, and then also under the Borbidge Government, an Integrated Regional Transport Plan (IRTP) for SEQ. Although the latest plan notes the need for the IRTP '... to moderate rather than strive to satisfy unrestrained traffic growth ... with targets for increased use of public transport, ride sharing, walking and cycling,' it is again light on road pricing.

Meantime, as noted in Chapter 4, Queensland has continued to grant a 'fuel subsidy'. The NSW Treasurer estimated this subsidy in 1998 to cost NSW some $35 million each year from the need for 'shadow' pricing in NSW near the NSW–Queensland border.

A further setback to road pricing in Queensland was the lifting of modest tolls on the Sunshine Coast motorways. These motorways had been built in the early 1990s as toll roads, but following local political agitation, tolls were lifted in the mid-1990s.

As also noted in Chapter 4, the 1994 Victorian Transport Externalities Study found that, although it is difficult to estimate external costs, these costs are significant. Notwithstanding this, Victoria has embarked on a robust urban arterial construction program, complete with some eight-lane highways west of the CBD. The most redeeming feature of this road augmentation is a privately operated toll road with peak and off-peak pricing.

Both South Australia and Western Australia have pursued 'travel blending' and 'travel smart' programs in an effort to encourage people to think twice before they jump into their cars. Here again, these commendable efforts are thwarted by the failure of government to price roads properly, and powerful State road construction agencies securing scarce public land transport funds at the expense of rail and urban public transport.

NEW ZEALAND TRANSPORT PLANNING

New Zealand transport planning has a mixed record. On the one hand, progress was made during the 1990s on a number of fronts and mass-distance charges were maintained for heavy vehicles. This progress includes the production of detailed regional transport plans with local input, and a drive in the late 1990s towards the commercialisation of roads. This involved a major Land Transport Pricing Study with extensive consultation and a string of reports (New Zealand Ministry of Transport, 1994, 1995, 1996, 1997) leading to a *Road Reform Report* endorsed by the New Zealand Prime Minister (1997).

However, at the end of the day, real road pricing reform was stalled, and New Zealand's significant car dependence remains. Moreover, New Zealand's largest city, Auckland, has a major road traffic problem. The 1990s must be seen as a lost decade to provide Auckland with a good urban rail system along the lines proposed by New Zealand Rail in 1990. This included a modest extension of the rail network, and the use of light rail transit. The proposed system was based on an extensive study and would have been less ambitious than the successful systems now operating in cities such as Calgary and Edmonton in Canada.

As in Australia, the 1990s saw almost total policy paralysis in New Zealand achieving a more integrated and sustainable transport system.

6
THE POLITICAL PROBLEM: THE ROAD LOBBY

PHILIP LAIRD

Australian roads do not cost taxpayers — they benefit them.

Deputy Prime Minister John Anderson MP relaying the message of the roads lobby
in a 1999 Federal Budget statement

Chapter 5 demonstrated the difficulty of achieving real land transport reform in Australia and New Zealand. We have also seen that it is all too easy for Governments to set to one side the high economic, environmental and social costs of excessive automobile dependence along with over-use of heavy trucks. When public concern does rise to a point at which it can no longer be ignored, then some minor measures can be introduced, or an inquiry can be held. As we have seen, there have been no fewer than 14 national land transport inquiries in Australia held during the 1990s along with numerous state government reports.

The question that is asked in this chapter is whether the lack of action in the policy arena is due to a political problem. Despite endless analysis that shows the need for reduced subsidies to roads and the crying need to rehabilitate and expand the rail system, nothing seems to happen. It suggests that politicians and public servants, particularly at the Federal level, are captive to the road lobby.

This chapter will mainly be concerned with *Australian* road-related lobby groups. The basic reason for this is that there are over 60 of these groups in Australia, as compared with only a few in New Zealand such as the Automobile Association and the Road Transport Forum.

The impact of the ability of industry associations, along with hired consultants, to influence either a Government Department or a political party in Australia is unknown. However, what is known is that there are numerous industry associations operating at a Federal and/or a State level that have interests in motor vehicles, roads, road transport, and petroleum. A list follows (List 6.1).

Motor vehicles in Australia now use about 22 billion litres of liquid fuel each year. The Australian Petroleum Institute mostly represents the interests of the petroleum industry. The word 'mostly' refers to the fact that the interests of retailers of liquid fuel do not always align with those involved in the production, refining or importing of refined fuel.

Perhaps the best known road lobby groups are the so-called 'motor associations', like the National Roads and Motorists Association (NRMA) that operates in NSW and the ACT and now offers insurance services interstate, the Royal Automobile Club of Victoria (RACV), and similar clubs in other States and the Northern Territory. These clubs provide valuable road service to members, take an interest in the price and supply of motor vehicles and in road safety, and offer a wide range of insurance services to members. However, the overriding message these clubs send, either directly or through the Australian Automobile Association (AAA) in Canberra, is that motorists are over-taxed, and that the Government should outlay more and more money for better roads. This message far outweighs the occasional suggestion that heavy trucks should pay more for the road wear and tear they cause, or, that there is a role for upgraded rail and public transport in reducing road congestion and improving road safety.

The attitude of the motoring clubs to problems caused by large numbers of semitrailers, or the growth in numbers of B-Doubles and road trains, is often hard to predict.

On the one hand, the NRMA and other motoring clubs took an active interest in heavy vehicle safety during the 1980s. The NRMA was also concerned during the mid-1980s about hidden subsidies to truck operations. One such expression of concern was a hard hitting NRMA media release on 28 November 1986 that stated, inter alia, that 'the present situation of cost recovery from the road transport industry is inadequate, in fact each motorist is now cross-subsidising that industry by about $100 a year'. The NRMA statement also said that a Government proposal to increase truck load limits could cost NSW motorists $100 million. These NRMA estimates were based on the rule accepted by most road construction authorities that a fully loaded truck can cause 10 000 times as much damage to a section of road as a car, and the heavier loads proposed would increase the damage inflicted to roads by 30 per cent.

On the other hand, the NRMA was relatively quiet during the 1990s on the question of road pricing for heavy trucks. By the late 1990s, there did not appear to be too much concern from motoring clubs for proposals for extensions for highways on which B-Doubles

LIST 6.1
ROAD-RELATED LOBBY GROUPS IN AUSTRALIA

1   Australian Automobile Association

Constituent Members
   National Roads and Motorist Association
   Royal Automobile Club of Australia
   Royal Automobile Club of Queensland
   Royal Automobile Club of Tasmania
   Royal Automobile Club of Victoria
   Royal Automobile Club of Western Australia
   Royal Automobile Association of South Australia
   Automobile Association of Northern Territory Inc.

2   Motor Trades Association of Australia

Constituent members
   The Australian Automobile Dealers Association
   The Motor Trades Association of the ACT
   The Motor Traders Association of NSW
   The Motor Trades Association of the Northern Territory
   The Motor Trade Association of South Australia
   The Motor Trades Association of Queensland
   The Motor Trade Association of Western Australia
   The Service Station Association Limited
   The Victorian Automobile Chamber of Commerce
   [incorporating the Tasmanian Automobile Chamber of Commerce]

Affiliated Trade Associations
   Australian Service Station Association
   Australia Motor Body Repairs Association
   Australian Motorcycle Industry Association
   Australian National Towing Association
   Australian Tyre Dealers and Retreaders Association
   Automotive Transmission Association of Australia
   Engine Reconditioners Association of Australia
   Farm Machinery Dealers Association of Australia
   National Brake Specialists Association
   National Radiator Repairers Association of Australia
   National Steering and Suspension Association

3   Australian Trucking Association (formerly Road Transport Forum, etc)

Constituent members
   Australian Livestock Transport Association
   Natroads Ltd
   NSW Road Transport Association
   Queensland Road Transport Association
   South Australian Road Transport Association
   Transport Workers Union
   West Australian Road Transport Association
   Victorian Road Transport Association

4   Other Truck and Bus Related Associations
   Bus and Coach Association
   Commercial Vehicle Industry Association of QLD
   Tasmanian Transport Association

5   Government Road Related Organisations
   AUSTROADS Incorporated
   Australian Local Government Association

Constituent members
   Local Government and Shires Association of NSW
   Local Government Association of Queensland Inc.
   Local Government Association of Tasmania
   Local Government Association of the Northern Territory
   Municipal Association of Victoria
   Western Australian Municipal Association

6   Other Road and Vehicle Related Organisations

   Australian Asphalt Pavement Association
   Australian Concrete Pavement Association
   Australian Constructors Association
   Australian Petroleum Institute
   Calder Highway Improvement Committee
   Cement and Concrete Association of Australia
   Civil Contractors Federation
   Driver Education Centre of Australia
   Eastern Ring Road Steering Committee
   Fix Australia, Fix the Roads
   Highway Safety Action Group of NSW Inc.
   Mid Murray Regional Development Organisation
   Institute of Municipal Engineering Australia

SOURCES House of Representatives Standing Committee on Communications, Transport and Microeconomic Reform (1997), MTAA Annual Report 2000, Australian Automobile Association, 1998, Australian Trucking Association Web Site, Feb 2000. Various issues: Australian Transport News, Truck and Bus could operate, or trials for even longer articulated trucks with three trailers called B-Triples. Moreover, whilst in the 1980s the NRMA believed trucks should pay more before any increase in road vehicle weight limit was allowed, the NRMA was virtually silent in the late 1990s when the road transport industry was seeking further mass limit increases.

One area where NRMA lobbying has coincided with Federal Government action on roads has been the substantial upgrading of intercity highways. This lobbying has followed NRMA research and publication of a series of reports on each major intercity highway in NSW (NRMA 1975, 1991, 1994 are just some examples of 49 NRMA Highway surveys). In turn, and with large amounts of Federal funding, the Hume Highway, the Sydney–Newcastle Freeway, the New England Highway, other interstate highways and now the Pacific Highway in NSW, have been progressively upgraded. This road upgrading has in turn been accompanied by substantial increases in truck numbers hauling more interstate freight. Whilst upgraded intercity highways are welcomed by all road users, the extra numbers of heavy trucks — often driven by drivers under pressure — do not make motoring more pleasant. Indeed, the gains from such highway upgrades in the United States have been questioned by Noland (2001). Regrettably, from time to time, heavy trucks are involved in fatal road crashes. Most NRMA members, and indeed the national interest, would have been better served if upgrading intercity rail links had been given some priority.

The second major area where NRMA and AAA lobbying has been successful has been to maintain the public perception that motorists, and hence all road users, pay taxes and charges far in excess of Government outlays on roads. The common, but incorrect inference, that road user taxes and charges exceed the total cost of motor vehicle operations to Government is not dispelled. The slowness of Government to act on such issues in Australia must then, in part, be attributed to the motoring clubs.

The supply to Australia of over 750 000 new cars each year since 1997, and the repair of the nation's passenger vehicle fleet (about 9.6 million as of August 1999), is a major industry. This industry has been well represented in Canberra since 1988 by the Motor Trade Association of Australia (MTAA). The MTAA is a federation of more than 10 members of the Motor Trade Associations in each State and Territory. In addition, there were no fewer than 11 Allied Trade Associations in 1999. At the time of the formation of the MTAA the 1988–89 turnover of motor vehicles, repairs and services, was some $52.5 billion and the industry employed over 200 000 people. By 1998–99 this turnover had grown to more than $83 billion, and employed over 230 000 Australians. An insight into the MTAA is given in Box 6.2.

BOX 6.2

ROAD LOBBY GROUP AT WORK IN CANBERRA

The modus operandi of the MTAA and similar groups were outlined by long-term MTAA Executive Director, Mr Michael Delaney, in an interview with the *Canberra Times* (8 January 2000) Some excerpts follow:

'It is inconceivable our members would think we could get by without a presence in Canberra now, even though it is a very expensive process,' said Mr Delaney.

'We have operating costs of $1.4 million a year which they have to pay, but they know full well that one false step, a couple of wrong decisions by government, and they could be up for a great deal more.' He says his role with government in Canberra revolves around two simple tasks. 'A large part of our work involves trying to stop processes happening which would be inimical to the interests of our members; the rest is about trying to create or direct favourable processes.

'It is a fact of public policy-making that things can go wrong for all sorts of reasons, and we have to work to get those wrong things ironed out before it is too late.

'We spent $12 million on building our headquarters here. We occupy only a small part of it, but the rest is fully let,' said Mr Delaney.

'Then there is our $1 billion superannuation fund which has its headquarters in Canberra and is a large investor in the city.

'And our association is not unusual. Others have similar set-ups and make similar contributions to Canberra.'

THE ALL-POWERFUL TRUCK LOBBY

The road freight transport industry is also well represented in Canberra. The Road Transport Forum (RTF) was launched in 1992 to more effectively represent in Canberra the interests of a multitude of road transport groups at a State and national level. This was following the formation of a Road Transport Industry Forum (RTIF) that was prompted by the adverse publicity from the 1989 Grafton truck and bus crash. The RTIF included the Australian Road Transport Federation, and the Long Distance Road Transport Association. The RTIF had a significant role behind the scenes in the establishment of a National Road Transport Commission in 1991, and, it would appear, in its subsequent operations including low annual charges for heavy trucks. The new charges included one round of effective relaxation of mass limits for heavy trucks in NSW and Victoria. In the late 1990s, there was a successful push for a further round of conditional relaxation of limits for heavy trucks.

It is instructive to see the truck lobby groups at work in several campaigns. The first campaign we shall examine was mounted to persuade governments at both Federal and State levels that tachographs should not be made compulsory. This campaign was successful, despite the need for action and well founded arguments for tachographs as outlined below.

The second campaign was to effectively persuade Government that it was overtaxed, and to ensure that changes to registration fees in the 1990s were 'revenue neutral'. Other successful campaigns include ensuring generous Federal funding of the National Highway System, and the ongoing relaxation of mass and dimension limits of heavy trucks.

During the late 1980s, the Parliament of NSW Joint Standing Committee on Road Safety (STAYSAFE) held an inquiry into heavy vehicle safety. The release of the STAYSAFE report entitled *Alert drivers, and safe speeds, for heavy vehicles* in September 1989 noted that both State and Federal Governments had bowed to the pressure of the road freight industry to approve measures for faster and heavier trucks, whilst safety measures recommended by the NSW and National inquiries were not being implemented. At a time when NSW road crashes involving heavy trucks had recently claimed over 250 lives in a year, the STAYSAFE report set the scene for NSW Government action on tachographs.

THE BATTLE AGAINST TACHOGRAPHS

Compulsory tachographs were recommended for most articulated trucks by the National Road Freight Industry Inquiry in 1984. Tachographs had been noted by the House of Representatives Standing Committee on Road Safety (1977) as a type of 'in flight' recorder that can provide supervisors with information such as engine speed, vehicle speed, and time, and '… therefore enable a close watch to be kept on the way a vehicle has been driven'. However, tachographs are unpopular with some truck drivers.

In 1986, regulations of the Council of the European Communities (EEC) required the installation of equipment that clearly records distance travelled, speed and time of heavy trucks used in road transport.

Australian legal speed limits for heavy trucks were relaxed in 1987, and again in 1988. As noted by the STAYSAFE report #15, there was a marked increase in fatal crashes involving articulated trucks. By July 1989, following more fatal road crashes involving semitrailers, the NSW Minister for Transport, Mr Bruce Baird was reported (*Sydney Morning Herald* 8 July 1989) as seeking Cabinet approval 'within the next few weeks' for tough new measures, including the automatic cancellation of licences for speeding an amount in excess of the new 100 km per hour limit, and the 'likely mandatory installation' of tachographs in large trucks. However, the road transport industry strongly resisted compulsory tachographs. Instead it urged the use of speed limiters only. This road transport view was supported by the then Federal Minister for Transport who announced that a new Australian Design

Rule would require speed limiters for all new trucks as of 31 July 1991.

At a crucial NSW State Cabinet meeting held in Cootamundra on 26 September 1989, tachographs were deferred. This was despite the strong support for tachographs in NSW that had come from the NSW Minister for Transport, Bruce Baird, and hence the Roads and Traffic Authority, the NSW Police, the NRMA, and the NSW Parliamentary Road Safety Committee.

Following this meeting of the NSW State Cabinet, various media reports occurred. One report was that the Cabinet passed up NSW 'going it alone' in requiring tachographs by one vote (*Illawarra Mercury* 30 September1989). This was after the Ministers had been lobbied before at dinner by '... no less than 20 burly members of the truck drivers' lobby group, the Road Transport Association, who sat on every table of the Cootamundra dinner to nag the ministers on this issue'.

The *Daily Telegraph* noted (30 September 1989) how during the dinner, trucking industry lobbyists secured strategic seats at tables so they could earbash ministers about the evils of tachographs. 'By the end of the dinner, the trucking lobby was openly boasting that it had the numbers in Cabinet to defeat any proposal for compulsory tachographs.'

After the Cabinet meeting, Premier Greiner and Mr Baird emerged with a road safety package, with increased penalties for excessive speeding and speed limiters for heavy trucks and buses. Tachographs were deferred pending more information as well as support from other States and the Commonwealth before a decision was made (*Sydney Morning Herald* 27 September 1989). This was seen by some commentators as 'Baird rolled by truckies' and a win for the road freight industry.

However, the ongoing fatal road crashes involving semitrailers surely prompted a rethink by both the Federal and NSW Government on tachographs. Here, much community feeling was reflected in an Editorial by Dr Rob Cortis-Jones from the November 1989 *CTC Newsletter*.

ROAD TRANSPORT NEEDS REGULATION

On Friday, 20 October 1989, the worst road crash in Australian history took place near Grafton. Twenty people were killed in a collision between a semitrailer and a long-distance coach.

If tragedies like this are to be avoided in the future there must be an honest examination of the present state of affairs on Australian roads. The comments (as reported in the Australian 21 October 1989) of then NSW Transport Minister, Mr Bruce Baird sum it up: 'A large section of the (heavy vehicle) industry is out of control ... We have tried self-policing and it does not work.'

Our roads should not be like a battlefield, calling for extremes of human endurance. Let's be honest and admit that over 70 hours work driving each week is too much and that truck drivers' hours should be reduced, not increased. Truck speed limits have been increased. There is no excuse for drivers who risk safety by travelling still faster.

Many NSW highways are inadequate for the large vehicles that now use them. But it is unrealistic to call for better roads without asking large trucks and coaches to contribute their fair share of the costs of road upgrading.

The issues have often been raised before, with several major Government inquiries being held. It is clear that the road freight industry has been slow to assume its responsibilities. At the present rate of progress it will be many years before full road cost recovery is achieved.

One important step in improving road safety and public confidence in the industry could be taken quickly. That step is the fitting of tacho-graphs. Many owners of vehicle fleets already use them, and one was reportedly fitted to the ill-fated coach in the Grafton crash. Honest dri-vers and honest companies have nothing to fear from their use. Indeed they can exonerate drivers from allegations of speeding, just as the loco-motive speed recorder ruled out excess speed as the cause of the Granville rail disaster.

Tachographs would both discourage speeding and help prevent drivers from spending too many hours behind the wheel. If in the future they are also used for a fair system of road charges, to fund better and safer roads, the road freight industry would benefit. The rapid growth of the indus-try suggests that it could well afford reasonable charges.

Since the industry has not agreed to adopt tachographs voluntarily, then Governments must make them compulsory. The Federal Government, having encouraged the States to permit heavier and faster trucks on our roads, must accept its responsibilities for road safety and not leave the hard road safety options up to the States alone.

Despite the weight of evidence, the use of compulsory tachographs was again found by Government to be too hard. So also was quality licensing. Instead, as agreed by the Australian Transport Council at its meeting of October 1994, an inter-governmental agreement was reached for the introduction of a national accreditation system for heavy vehicles. The National Road Transport Commission (NRTC: *Annual Report* 1994–95) noted the concept of alternative compliance to increase compliance with legal requirements and national consisten-cy. However, national uniformity has not always served NSW well. As we have seen, national increases to 100 km per hour for the heavy vehicle open speed limit in 1988 had to be reviewed in NSW — a year when fatal road crashes involving trucks saw a loss of 250 lives in NSW. They were then reduced to 90 km per hour, with permission for trucks fitted with speed limiters to move at 100 km per hour on certain roads.

However, in the late 1990s, the heavy truck open road speed limit was lifted to 100 km per hour. It is now common to see semitrailers exceeding 110 km per hour on the Hume and other Highways. Whatever happened to the setting of speed limiters at 100 km per hour?

The second major campaign the trucking lobby ran was during the early 1990s — in which it argued that it was subject to an unfair and high level of road-user charges and taxes. There appeared to be two phases to the vigorous campaign. The first phase is best explained by quoting a spokesman, Mr Ron Finemore (1992) for the influential Road Transport Forum (RTF), when talking about charges for six-axle articulated trucks:

> Progress has been made with charges over the last few years. Recommendations — in 1988 the BTCE recommended the registration charge of $44 000. In 1990 the ISC ... made a recommendation of $21 400 to be implemented by July 1992. In 1991 the Over-Arching Group recommended $14 000 to be implemented by January 1993. And now we have the NRTC recommending $4000 for implementation by 1 July 1995. A lot of difference in the figures, and we still don't have, of course, a surety of the bottom recommendation being implemented.
>
> We now have a reform agenda for a national registration scheme; sensible charging, a truly independent National Road Transport Commission, efficient road construction and maintenance, taxation and regulation reform, effective industry and government consultation and industry professionalism. However, the registration charge issue has dominated our time lately. The recent vote by the Ministerial Council to accept the NRTC's recommended national registration charge, required a lot of lobbying by all responsible parties ...
>
> **But it wasn't achieved without a lot of lobbying of the various state governments by all parties associated with the RTF.** The success of the RTF in this area is particularly strong, because the majority of state and federal Ministers who voted in favour of the NRTC's recommended charges are up for re-election in the near future.

Mr Finemore in his 1992 speech then paid particular attention to the opposition of the NSW Government to the new NRTC charges, naming both the then leader of the National Party in NSW, the Minister for Roads, The Hon. Wal Murray MP, and the Chief Executive of the Roads and Traffic Authority, Mr Bernard Fisk, who had the audacity to propose an additional environmental levy for heavy trucks. 'The RTF will use its efforts to ensure that common sense prevails and we're able to get either Mr Murray or if not, the New South Wales government, to fall into line ...'

Eventually, with the help of one of the clauses of the 1995 Competition Principles Agreement, New South Wales did 'fall into line'. This was at a cost of some $60 million per year to the NSW taxpayer.

The second phase of the campaign was to persuade Government to accept that even the NRTC charges, which were generous to the trucking industry, and diesel fuel excise indexed to inflation, were too high. A 1994 report prepared by Swan Consultants for the Road Transport Forum found that the fuel excise and vehicle registration fee paid by heavy trucks in Australia amounted in 1990–91 to $2.4 billion, of which only one half was a road user charge. It was claimed that the other half was a tax; moreover, if this was removed and replaced by higher income taxes, the Australian economy would be boosted by $600 million a year. This report, accompanied by effective lobbying, was very successful. In this case, the finding of a $1.3 billion hidden subsidy to articulated truck operations by the Bureau of Transport Economics (1988) along with recommendations for mass-distance charges of the former Inter-State Commission (1990) for the heavier long distance charge were completely set aside throughout the entire 1990s.

Moreover, the low NRTC charges were not indexed for inflation or adjusted until 2000, and, no explicit charges were made for externalities. In addition, the Coalition government reduced the diesel excise on 1 July 2000 as part of the New Tax System.

A further demonstration of the strength of the RTF is the ongoing high level of funding for the National Highway System at about $800 million a year and, the acceleration of upgrading the Pacific Highway without the imposition of tolls. As seen by Swan Consultants, retained by the RTF in 1996 '… Australia has under-invested in its road network and that increased expenditure is required in the near future. However, funding this expenditure via increased road user charges and tolls would substantially reduce the benefits of any road investments undertaken'.

The most pressing need was seen as construction of dual carriageways in the Pacific Highway between Hexham and Tweed Heads so as to save over two hours of truck haulage time. The NSW Government's proposal in the early 1990s was to construct 'Motorway Pacific' with a series of toll roads. The RTF must have hardly believed their luck when the Commonwealth and NSW Government agreed in 1996 to outlay $2.2 billion jointly over ten years between Hexham and Tweed Heads with no tolls. This left most of the cost to be borne by NSW taxpayers. A further $850 million was also outlaid for upgrading the Pacific Highway in Queensland.

Supporting the efforts of the major road lobby groups outlined above are other privately funded groups such as 'Nat Roads' and 'Fix the Roads'. In addition, as per Box 6.3, road transport interests were very capably represented in the 1980s to the NSW Labor Government by the Transport Workers Union or TWU and its NSW Assistant Secretary Mr Harry Quinn.

BOX 6.3
AN EFFECTIVE PRESSURE GROUP

During the 1980s, the NSW branch of the Transport Workers Union was effective as a pressure group on the NSW Government. This was recognised by the *Sydney Morning Herald* (SMH) in a well informed article 'Coal not bound for Botany Bay' (SMH, 17 August 1983) which observed in part: 'The Government's policy of maximising the use of rail for transporting coal is in tatters. A substantial investment in rail infrastructure for this purpose now has little prospect of getting an effective return. Surprisingly, the rail unions have been remarkably quiet about the inroads the TWU has made into the Government's rail policy.'

Later, an article entitled 'The Influence of Harry Quinn' (SMH, 5 October 1983) concluded:

But the TWU's clout with the Government is not only a product of its industrial strength and its militancy. It has been a generous donor to the Labor Party's campaign funds.

According to the Election Funding Authority's report, it donated $14 000 to the ALP before the last NSW election. According to Harry Quinn, the union gave $28 000 earlier this year for the Federal election campaign.

That sort of money buys a lot of influence for a union. Judging from Harry Quinn's list of achievements, a transport worker would regard it as money well spent.

But people living in Port Kembla, with six tonnes of coal dust descending on them each day; or in Botany, Campsie, Marrickville and other suburbs, suffering the problems of big lorries delivering containers; or residents of the Blue Mountains and other centres along the Great Western Highway, having to cope with large coal trucks carrying some 1100 tonnes of coal each day; they would have another word for it.

In October 1999, the RTF was relaunched by Prime Minister John Howard as the Australian Trucking Association (ATA). The effectiveness of the ATA was demonstrated by the Prime Minister's attendance and speech where he praised the industry and confirmed lower diesel excise for truck operators. He was also able to state what a good advocate around the Cabinet table the road freight industry had in the Deputy Prime Minister and Minister for Transport, the Hon. John Anderson.

It should be noted that the interests of the road transport industry are well represented in each State, and, are supplemented by numerous specialist groups.

THE GOVERNMENT ROAD LOBBY GROUPS

'Austroads' is the national association of road transport and traffic authorities in Australia and was formerly the National Association of Australian State Road Authorities (NAASRA). Austroads has eleven member organisations, comprising the six Australian State and two Territory road authorities, the Federal Department of Transport, the Australian Local Government Association and Transit New Zealand. According to their 1998–99 *Annual Report*, the income of Austroads that year was about $3.6 million.

There is no doubt that Austroads performs a valuable role in information transfer between the different State and Territory road authorities, the Federal Department of Transport, local government, along with harmonisation of road construction and maintenance standards. However, Austroads is not backward in promoting more Government outlays on roads through publications such as *Australia at the Cross Roads* (Austroads, 1999). Regrettably, although road pricing may be raised in such reports, it is lost in the thrust in the need for ever more road funding.

The Government-funded NRTC may be seen by some as a Government-funded road lobby group in view of its truck-friendly road user charges and advocacy for heavier mass. The reality is that the NRTC generally puts its responsibilities to the nation ahead of those of the trucking industry. The 1998–99 government contributions to the NRTC was $3.54 million, of which nearly $1.24 million was from the Commonwealth. Since its formation in 1991, the Federal Government has allocated over $10 million to the NRTC.

One may question whether the Australian Local Government Association (ALGA) should be regarded as a Government roads lobby group. However, at the end of the day, the ALGA and its constituent organisations are funded by ratepayers. Its liking for roads was shown, for example, by proposals (*Lloyd's List Daily Commercial News*, 25 September 2000) for a $2 million Better Roads campaign. This was designed to help intensify electoral pressure during 2001 on the Federal government for increased road funding. As seem by ALGA President Mr John Ross, 'When electors go to the ballot box next year, we will have ensured that the need for a boost in funding for Australia's roads is one of the most prominent public issues'.

Austroads, the NRTC, and ALGA, as government-funded groups work with the three major lobby groups located in Canberra, the AAA, ATA and MTAA. The result is that all six organisations work together to develop a view within the Federal Government that more money for roads is a good thing. However, not all people were reassured by the Deputy Prime Minister and Minister for Transport, the Hon. John Anderson who on budget night, 11 May 1999, found more funds for roads but no extra for rail, and none for urban public transport. He also noted that 'Australian roads do not cost taxpayers — they benefit them. On average, one dollar spent improving the National Highway Network generates $2.50 for the Australian community.'

The same budget was one of a succession with much money for roads, little for rail, and none for structured urban public transport programs. Indeed, in the five Howard–Costello budgets delivered between 1996 and 2000, and the November 2000 roads statement, no less than $8 billion has been allocated to national, State and local roads. This is about 100 times the amount that has been allocated to rail works by the Howard Government to date. It is hard to see why the United States allocates nearly 20 per cent of its Federal land transport funds to rail and mass transit and Australia only allocates 1 per cent of such funds to this important area.

Australia needs a more balanced approach. It needs to get 'back on track'.

AUSTRALIAN RAIL AND PUBLIC TRANSPORT LOBBY GROUPS

In Australia, lobby groups representing the rail and urban public transport interests are very few and far between, and with limited resources. Indeed, some newspapers have given more coverage to the views of community groups such as the Sydney-based Action for Public Transport and Total Environment Centre, or the Melbourne Public Transport Users Association.

The peak rail industry group is the Australasian Railway Association Inc (ARA). The ARA was formed as recently as 1995 from the former Railways of Australia (ROA). The ROA was a longstanding organisation that provided for information exchange between the various State and Commonwealth rail systems. To some observers, ROA was regarded as a 'Commissioner's Club'. The ARA has within five years made significant progress to broadening its membership to over 135 members, with most members coming from the private sector. However, like the former ROA, the ARA has only a small staff based in Melbourne, with no permanent staff in Canberra.

Other rail industry groups include the Australian Rail Industry Association with over 100 private and public sector members, and the Rail Track Association of Australia. Along with promoting technical aspects of railway engineering, the Railway Technical Society of Australasia has also made representations to Government to upgrade rail track and published, in 1999 and 2000, a series of six *Fix the Rails* brochures.

The interests of urban rail passenger operations are also represented by the International Association of Public Transport Australia/New

Zealand, which has a small office in Canberra.

Until recently the Bus and Coach Association has aligned itself with the road lobby. A change in administration has led to it becoming a more transport-oriented group seeking an integrated role with rail.

OTHER INFLUENCES

The establishment of lobby groups is just one way of putting a point of view to Government. Other ways are to make donations to political parties. Some of the 1998–99 donations, as listed on the Australian Electoral Commission web site, and noted by Hoyle (2000) are of interest. Donations include:

Road haulier, Finemores	$31 250 to NSW Liberals, $10 000 to NSW ALP;
Hills Motorway Pty Ltd	$10 000 to NSW Liberals;
Stillwell Ford	$10 000 to SA Liberals;
Toyota	$17 350 to Victorian Liberals, $6000 to Qld Liberals and $3000 to Australian Democrats;
City Ford (Sydney)	$10 880 to NSW Liberals; along with
Bus and Coach Association (NSW)	$35 750 to NSW Liberals, $53 500 to NSW ALP.

In 1997–98 the Victorian Automobile Chamber of Commerce donated $34 000 to the Victorian Liberals, Highway Construction Pty Ltd gave $17 500 to the WA Liberals, Brambles donated $45 000 to the Federal Liberals, RACV gave $5000 to the Federal Liberals and the Victorian Liberals benefited from a $10 000 donation from car manufacturer Nissan.

Road construction companies, which sometimes do rail work or other construction projects, were also generous donors. Transfield — $48 800 to various Liberal Party branches and $23 700 to the ALP; Leighton Contractors — $35 000 to Liberals, $40 000 to the ALP and $15 000 to the Nationals were examples. Rail was not completely left out with Evans Deakin Industries donating $10 000 each to the Queensland ALP, Liberals and Nationals and the Victorian Liberals. Goninan gave $2000 to the NSW ALP. The rail donations are small when compared with those of the road transport lobby. The Australian Trucking Association (ATA) also paid John Laws and Sydney radio station 2UE $163 224 between January and June 1998 for 'getting the message across' as an ATA spokesman explained in 1999 to an Australian Broadcasting Authority inquiry into 'cash for comment' arrangements.

AUSTRALIA'S TRUCKING CULTURE

Australians have shown considerable innovation and drive in building up a large road freight industry. Undoubtedly, this development has been assisted by the need to transport freight over large distances in areas not served by rail, and road transport's flexibility in door-to-door urban deliveries.

The development of larger and heavier trucks in Australia has been a mixed advance. On the one hand, increased road freight productivity has led to lower transport costs, which are vital for international competitiveness. On the other hand, encouraging road freight through hidden subsidies takes freight away from other potentially efficient transport modes. These include rail, sea, pipelines, or conveyors. A further effect of artificially low land-freight transport costs is to encourage more land freight, as opposed to optimal distribution and manufacturing arrangements. Here, there is an old story about large numbers of tomatoes that used to pass each other in trucks crossing the Nullarbor.

Governments, when allowing larger and heavier trucks, sometimes repeat industry propaganda that there will be fewer trucks on the roads. Both the Federal and NSW Governments produced glossy brochures to promote the use of B-Doubles in the late 1980s when there was notable community and local Government opposition to their use. The Victorian Government also shared this opposition, and the *Age* in its editorial of 4 July 1988 'Let us say no to the Juggernauts'. This editorial rejected claims that the larger B-Doubles would lead to fewer trucks on the roads, and felt the State Government should confront problems in the railways and road pricing.

The reality is that relaxation of mass and dimension limits have gone hand in hand with more articulated trucks being registered and each class of articulated truck driving, on average, more kilometres. The net result has been a high rate of growth in the articulated freight task, to the point where Australia has excessive road freight. Continuing such a high growth rate for another decade is simply unsustainable. However, trying to manage demand for road freight, like demand management for cars, is a major challenge for government. This challenge will be difficult in Australia due to a dominant trucking culture created by a powerful and persistent road lobby.

7

CITIES BACK ON TRACK: USING A SYSTEMS APPROACH FOR SUSTAINABLE CITY POLICY

MARK BACHELS AND PETER NEWMAN

If the business heart of the city becomes strangled by traffic congestion on its streets as well as along the access routes to it, the whole structure of the urban area and its circulatory system will be drastically altered: the cost to the community is almost beyond calculation.

W.B. Johnston (1965)

INTRODUCTION

Not only do we have a trucking culture, we have a car culture — especially in our cities. This has been shown in Chapter 6 to be a political objective of the road lobby. However, there are many good public servants and consultants giving advice to local, State and national government who do not in any sense see themselves as working for the car or road lobby. Yet in reality they provide advice that is heavily biased towards the same objectives as those building the bitumen — advice which gives greater priority to projects and policies that favour car dependence.

How does this happen? This chapter suggests that in cities, transport professionals have for too long been seeking solutions that do not optimise the city. Their approaches are narrow and linear in concept whereas they should be more holistic.

Unfortunately, and typically, planning policies use a linear relationship (eg, congestion leads to the need to increase road capacity) and thus miss consequences and complexities of feedback mechanisms affecting our transport system and car use. If examined more holistically a different perspective and a more sustainable outcome can be generated. In technical terms, the required approach is called a 'systems approach.' The use of a systems approach reveals the complexity of these urban systems, and more importantly, reveals how unintended consequences are occurring because feedback is not being considered. Thus, new policy approaches are required if we intend to make our cities more sustainable.

This chapter is divided into three sections. Section one provides the results of a systems analysis approach to give some substance to the conclusions that transport policy has (inadvertently) become captive to increasing car use, road building and the road lobby. Section two explores what new policy approaches are needed, and section three identifies some specific city policy changes that are required in our main Australian and New Zealand cities in order to achieve more sustainable transport outcomes.

A LINEAR APPROACH VERSUS A SYSTEMS APPROACH

A LINEAR APPROACH

Five examples will be given of approaches to transport that have been influential in shaping the present predicament we face in Australian and New Zealand cities. The contentious and currently practised linear policy approaches are:

- Building roads is merely to ease congestion; it does not create increases in car use. Indeed, easing traffic congestion can help us save fuel and reduce emissions.

- Land use patterns, the physical form of cities, especially the density of development, does not have much impact on transport patterns.

- Public transport needs to be efficient, so reducing services will save money and enable reinvestment to occur.

- Increasing the speed and efficiency of traffic has no impact on cycling and walking modes.

- There is little you can do to get people out of their cars; thus traffic levels will rise inevitably.

A SYSTEMS APPROACH

These five approaches are examined by assessing data on land use, transport, economic and environmental indicators from 49 international cities (including cities in the USA, Australia–New Zealand, Europe and Asia) to evaluate transport and land use system interactions. Using this approach feedback from linear policy decisions are identified which appear to be increasing car dependence and reducing the sustainability of our cities. The model for developing a systems approach is set out in Appendix E showing the 5 sub sets of transport interactions and the sub sets of how urban form links to transport. The detailed approaches are in Bachels, Peet and Newman (1999). The results address each of the five linear approaches identified above and show the following.

INCREASING ROAD PROVISION LEADS DIRECTLY AND INDIRECTLY TO INCREASES IN TRAFFIC

Rather than solving traffic congestion, the addition of new roads (extra large capacity at higher speeds) just feeds the process that creates traffic. As shown in Figure 7.1 below, a 'vicious cycle' is created through a system feedback, where the strength of association between variables is shown by the width of the arrow (refer to Appendix E for details). Essentially the traditional linear approach of traffic/transport planning fails to take into account the feedback on our daily travel pattern from planning decisions which increase traffic flow and overall average speeds. Nor does such a linear approach take into account future mode split decisions — that is, how our decisions to take the car, rail, bus or bike are likely to change once improvements in vehicle speeds and traffic flow are made. Thus, as cars are given greater priority in our 'linear' transport planning approach, this directly leads to both more car travel and less use of alternatives. This in turn leads to more congestion and a greater need to improve the free flow of traffic and increase traffic speeds — a truly vicious cycle of road-building and car-based improvements.

The key to this feedback cycle is the Marchetti constant or 'constant travel time budget' whereby every city in the world adjusts to an average half-hour journey to work. By increasing traffic speeds the city adjusts by people moving further out, resulting in people driving more, further and faster. The extra traffic is sometimes called 'induced traffic'.

There are two key traditional transport-planning approaches that are challenged in using this systems understanding:

TIME SAVINGS CANNOT BE USED TO PROVIDE THE BENEFIT FOR NEW ROADS IN COST-BENEFIT ANALYSIS
Every major highway is justified on the basis of a cost-benefit analysis where most of the major benefits are from time savings due to congestion relief. These benefits are illusory, as explained above, due to the constant travel time budget, and the ensuing result of actually driving further and faster. It is time that the justification for building roads using this analytical basis be significantly altered or

FIGURE 7.1
ROAD BUILDING AND CAR USE

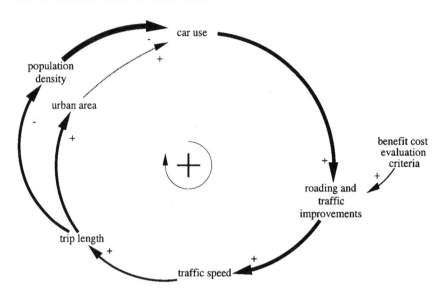

abandoned, as it has no rational basis for addressing (and in fact directly contributes to) the automobile-dependence facing all of our Australian and New Zealand cities.

FUEL SAVINGS (& EMISSION REDUCTIONS) CANNOT BE ANTICIPATED FROM FREEING UP CONGESTION IF EXTRA ROAD CAPACITY IS THE MECHANISM

Another way of justifying major roads is even more insidious, as it claims to provide all kinds of environmental benefits. The arguments, first developed from the General Motors Laboratory in the 1960s, suggests that by freeing up congestion there will be fuel savings and emission reductions as vehicles work better in smooth driving conditions rather than stop-start congested conditions. We have shown this not to be a true relationship, for the same reason as outlined above — savings in time are illusory as people will just drive faster and further. As shown in the diagram below (Figure 7.2) when congestion is reduced and feedback assumptions are included, there is more fuel used due to greater car dependence and reductions in other transport modes. Data to prove this was published by Newman and Kenworthy (1988) but the practice continues in Australia. The justification is no longer used in most European and nearly all US transport discussions. On the other hand, by shifting to other modes through an integrated transport strategy it is possible to make considerable fuel and emission savings as it reinforces the feedback toward lower car use.

The same principles can be applied to accidents as well as to fuel and emissions. The more road building is done (often justified on the basis that it will reduce accidents) the more car use increases and the higher the likelihood of accidents. This is confirmed by our data in Chapter 3. It is also confirmed in a recent study by Noland (2001) which showed that improvements in United States highway infrastructure that occurred between 1984 and 1997 have not reduced traffic fatalities and injuries but rather have had the effect of increasing total fatalities and injuries. This conclusion conflicts with conventional engineering wisdom on the benefits of 'improving' highway facilities and achieving higher standards of design.

LAND USE PATTERNS ARE CRITICAL TO DETERMINING TRANSPORT PATTERNS

The urban area and its close association with population density strongly influence the amount of car use in a city. A systems analysis of the 49 cities referred to above suggests that as the city sprawls and as population density declines, both the average trip length and overall car travel increase, with less use of alternatives. Increasing use of cars is associated with increases in the size of the urban area, and overall a vicious cycle of urban sprawl and increasing car dependence is created.

In response to pressure from developers, cities often tend to zone far too much greenfield land for residential and commercial development, instead of ensuring efficient use of the existing built-up urban area. Combine this linear land zoning approach with the self-supporting road building system and the result is an ever-increasing pre-determination of urban sprawl and car dependence. Policies to provide an urban growth boundary and to facilitate density increase will lead to less car use, more public transport and more walking / cycling.

THE VICIOUS CYCLE OF PUBLIC TRANSPORT DECLINES DUE TO SERVICE CUTS CAN BE REVERSED IF A SIGNIFICANTLY BETTER SERVICE TO THAT PROVIDED BY CARS IS IMPLEMENTED

Increases in public transport service quality relate to increases in use of public transport and increases in fare box returns, which enables a reinvestment in service delivery. This is known as a 'virtuous cycle'; however, this virtuous cycle can and has over the past 20 years turned to a vicious cycle as increasing car use and the subsequent decrease in patronage levels have led to decreasing service delivery and decreasing fare box returns. These all lock together resulting in less system reinvestment. Another feature of declining services is that the private sector is then less likely to invest in land improvements around the service, further reducing public transport's viability. Improved services will

FIGURE 7.2
LINEAR APPROACHES AND CAR USE FEEDBACK APPROACHES TO
THE LINK BETWEEN TRAFFIC CONGESTION, FUEL AND EMISSIONS

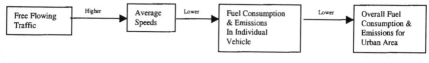

Model 1: Linear Assumptions

(a)

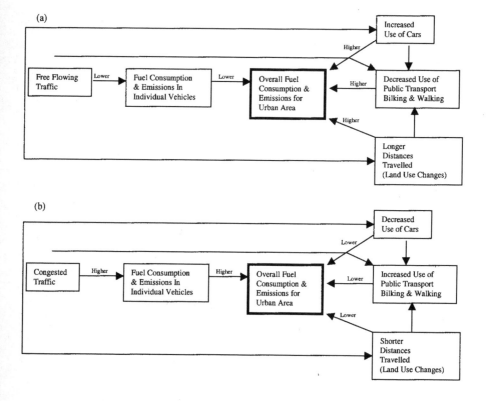

(b)

induce increasing use and improved investment, and therefore more usage of the service as the virtuous cycle feeds back with land use reinforcement.

INCREASING THE SPEED OF TRAFFIC WILL INCREASE CAR USE AS WELL AS REDUCING CYCLING AND WALKING

In this case study the slow modes of cycling and walking, and slow mode safety, were found to decrease with increasing traffic speeds and traffic volumes. Thus, as traditional traffic engineering has improved vehicle speeds and increased traffic volumes, the 49 cities' data suggest there is a direct statistical relationship to decreasing use of cycling and walking, which in turn is related to an increasing trip modal share by cars. Conversely, a more sustainable and holistic approach would require that all proposed traffic engineering projects include a thorough assessment of the impacts to cycling and pedestrians and ensure that these slower modes are catered for with appropriate footpath, cycle lanes and intersection priority.

SIMPLE TRAFFIC DEMAND MANAGEMENT AT LOCAL LEVEL CAN REDUCE TRAFFIC AND CAR USE

The use of traffic demand management policies across the 49-cities data set showed direct statistical feedback for decreasing car use. The traffic demand management policies tested showed that car use decreases (and walking, cycling and public transport use increases) as central city parking supply is reduced, public transport speeds are improved with respect to private traffic speeds, and the price of vehicle use is increased (eg, registration taxes, petrol taxes, etc.).

There is a lot that can be done through simple traffic calming at a local level. Traffic will fill every available niche if given a chance so when streets are narrowed and landscaped, roundabouts installed and lots of priority given to pedestrians, cyclists and public transport, the traffic will be reduced. Many communities are calling for a more holistic approach to traffic management and local government traffic engineers play a critical role. These engineers need to see this as their responsibility and not to continue applying outdated traffic engineering paradigms like the inevitability of traffic growth, and building wider and faster roads, but instead to apply more holistic and creative solutions to meeting new community visions to reduce car dependence.

NEW POLICY APPROACHES ARE NEEDED

The results of each of these case studies suggest that feedback interactions are indeed occurring between transport and land use planning and policy decisions, and a more holistic approach in policy formulation is required. Essentially, traditional planning approaches are overly simplistic and relatively linear, and thus miss many important feedback mechanisms affecting urban transport choices. In fact, the results suggest that these feedback mechanisms appear to be producing unintended increases in car use.

Specifically, the system studies reveal some important insights into policies for reducing car dependence. They show that:

- Increases in road building directly relate to unintended increases in car use;

- Increasing urban areas and decreasing population density directly relates to unintended increases in car use;
- Decreases in public transport service quality directly relate to decreases in use, and unintended increases in car use;
- Increases in traffic speed and traffic volumes result in unintended decreases to cyclist and pedestrian safety, which in turn leads to increasing car use;
- Traffic demand management policies such as decreasing parking supply, improving public transport speeds, and increasing the cost of car travel can all lead to decreasing car use.

On the other hand if a city were to restructure its transport decisions to favour a 'back on track' approach — eg. upgraded and extended rail systems along with associated land use and traffic demand management — most of the negative problems due to growth in car use would be overcome. The systems approach indicates the need for complementary policies that:

- build quality transit infrastructure;
- prevent further growth in urban sprawl;
- increase densities;
- improve all non-car modes;
- implement traffic calming;
- restrict parking; and
- have better vehicle taxes.

Thus it is necessary to examine how cities can make packages of strategic policy with regard to transport, land use and financing. Some suggestions are made below and then applied to ANZ cities in section three.

PLANNING POLICY STRATEGIES FOR REDUCING CAR DEPENDENCE

In general, three planning policy approaches need to be considered for reducing automobile dependence in modern cities:

- Strategies for integrated transport and land use;
- Strategies for improving alternatives — public transport, cycling and walking;
- Strategies for reducing travel demand.
  Each of these is addressed below.

STRATEGIES FOR INTEGRATED TRANSPORT AND LAND USE

As the results indicate, transport and land use policies are integrated — changes in land-use policies affect transport choices, and changes in transport policies affect land use. Unfortunately, transport and land-use planning policies are often developed separately, without taking into account such feedback effects.

To reduce the effects of automobile dependence, transport and land-use integration requires policies (and infrastructure provisions) which will:

- reduce vehicle trip lengths; and

- enable more viable transport alternatives (public transport, cycling and walking).

To achieve this an integrated transport and land-use approach is recommended which utilises an urban form of nodal sub-centres along well defined corridors, like 'beads on a necklace', to reduce travel in general as well as increase use of non-auto modes. In turn, transport policies and infrastructure development should support this 'nodes and corridors' approach for the full benefit of integration to occur. Figure 7.3 depicts such a nodes and corridors approach.

FIGURE 7.3
INTEGRATED TRANSPORT AND LAND USE — NODES AND CORRIDORS (SOURCE ZEIBOTS, 1994)

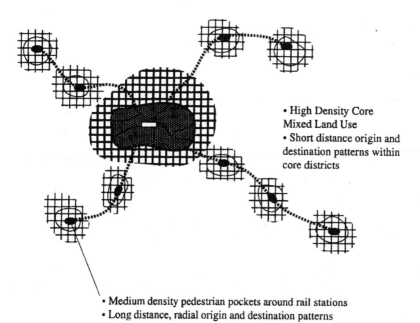

- High Density Core Mixed Land Use
- Short distance origin and destination patterns within core districts

- Medium density pedestrian pockets around rail stations
- Long distance, radial origin and destination patterns

STRATEGIES FOR IMPROVING PUBLIC TRANS-PORT, CYCLING AND WALKING

Unless alternatives to private vehicle travel are significantly improved, no measure of encouragement will induce people to use anything but the car for most trips. Thus, a concerted effort to improve public transport, cycling and walking is needed.

Integrated transport and land use requires excellent public transport services. Each city should develop a public transport strategy that supports its integrated transport and land use goals. To support the recommendation of a nodes and corridors approach, fast efficient and reliable public transport services should be developed. Again, integration is the key: public transport services need to become part of, not apart from, all transport and land use development plans — developments should be designed to support excellent public transport access, ease of use and recognition (with particular emphasis on the identified nodes and corridors). In most cities this inevitably means that cities must develop good rail options. There are several debates that this immediately raises.

BUILDING RAIL IN LOW-DENSITY CORRIDORS

Many low-density car-based corridors developed in the automobile era have communities that want a better public transport service than the all-too-common infrequent bus service. In the past few decades they invariably have been advised by transport policy makers that they cannot have a rail service, as the population density is too low. The Northern Beaches corridor of Sydney was told it must double its densities before it deserved a rail service. Similar arguments have recently occurred in Auckland and Christchurch. In all these cities, the political reaction was predictably to ditch the rail idea. But the traffic has continued to grow.

It is possible to see now that many low-density corridors in cities in the US, Canada and Australia have indeed been provided with rail services and they have been successful. Cities like Calgary, San Diego, Portland, Los Angeles (the Blue Line in particular) and Perth have all shown that rail can work in car-dependent suburbs. Now the low-density cities like Atlanta, Phoenix, Houston and Denver are all building rail. How does this work in cities that were always thought never to need or deserve rail? There are two reasons:

THERE IS NO REAL ALTERNATIVE TO RAIL AS THE CAR-BASED INFRASTRUCTURE HAS ALWAYS FILLED TO CAPACITY AND IS NOT ABLE TO COPE IN A POLITICALLY ACCEPTABLE WAY.

The limits to solving the transport problems of a low-density area depend on whether cities choose to either dilute the traffic further by spreading the city further out or to expand road capacity.

The first solution (to disperse land use even further) means that cities soon run out of land and it becomes politically difficult to sprawl into good agricultural or scenic land. This is the basis of the 'smart growth' movement in the US where 26 per cent of Americans now say urban sprawl is their biggest political issue (*Christian Science Monitor*, 2000). In Denver the figure is 40 per cent and this is feeding the movement in that city to build rail and contain growth around the new stations. The *Smart Growth America* web site sets out a survey which shows 78 per cent of people in the US now want to see an urban growth boundary to stop further urban sprawl.

The second solution (to create more road capacity) invariably requires the widening of already large freeway systems. Double decking of freeways is the only alternative left in many cities to increase car-based capacity. Yet in the cities which have built the most road capacity (California) only 18 per cent of people believe that freeways will do anything to solve the traffic problem (Franz, 1989). This is confirmed by the Texas Transportation Institute which found in a study of US cities over the past 30 years that there was no difference in the levels of congestion between those cities that invested heavily in new roads and those that did not (Surface Transport Policy Project, 1998). The reason for this is easily explained by the UK's SACTRA (1994) report; it conclusively showed that increases in road capacity lead to increasing traffic. These findings suggest that the traditional project improvement approach of 'predict future traffic flow and provide additional lane capacity' is no longer working and communities know it. When the *Smart Growth America* survey asked people in the US how they would like to see traffic congestion addressed only 21 per cent said they wanted more roads, 47 per cent said better public transport and 28 per cent said develop communities so there was less need to travel. In Perth a similar survey found that only 9 per cent want to see new or extended roads, and over 90 per cent wanted transport funding to be spent on public transport (WA DOT, 2000). These figures are so dramatic in Perth because the public have seen how a new rail line has been built successfully into the low-density northern suburbs. Political reality then meant that a similar system should be built to the southern suburbs and this was announced in November 2000. Similar results were obtained in Christchurch during consultation on the development of transport strategies there. In a random phone survey 74 per cent of respondents were concerned about traffic growth, and 58 per cent called for improvements to public transport, with only 25 per cent requesting continued roading improvements.

The reality of the new rail lines in car-based cities and corridors is that for the price of one extra lane of traffic capacity the city can build a rail system with the capacity of six lanes of traffic. This is the political basis of why even the most car-dependent cities in the US are now voting to build rail systems. Denver is building three new rail lines,

Houston is going for rail, and in early 2000 Phoenix (the city which was born and raised with the car) has voted two to one for a sales tax that will build a $2 billion rail-based transit system.

There is another reason why rail systems in low-density corridors can work.

THE RAIL SYSTEM IS BASED NOT ONLY ON A WALK-ON SYSTEM AS IN DENSE CORRIDORS BUT UTILISES A RANGE OF INTEGRATED FEED-IN SERVICES BY BUS, CAR AND BIKE.

The idea of integration of bus feeders into a rail station is very obvious but has not always happened because of silly rivalries between the two modes. With a rail station as a major community centre the local bus service can flexibly move around a community providing the links needed to reach many local destinations including the station. Then when services are coming in from both sides of a station it is possible to use the station as a hub for cross-suburban services. In Canada the 'time-pulse' system is used to coordinate the buses so they come in together and leave together; thus transfers from bus-to-bus and bus-to-rail are seamless.

Local buses that feed into a rail system and provide local services need to be very clear about how they communicate their routes. Boulder has a very transparent set of different bus types for their HOP, SKIP, JUMP and DASH services. These are all paid for by their Eco Pass which are given to students and employees and particular neighbourhoods who have the annual price of the Eco Pass negotiated for them with the city council which runs the buses. On-demand local buses are likely to be a growing part of any new integrated transit system. Shared use by passengers with similar but not exact origins and destinations can be coordinated by new technology using real-time tracking of vehicles and dynamic passenger matching capability in despatch systems. GPS technology allows for vehicle identification and continuous tracking. Evolving computer software will enable the real-time matching of demands and dynamic routing of vehicles. Experimental systems are now being developed and many central city free bus services are able to use GPS to display the time at bus stops when the next bus is due to the nearest 20 seconds. For example, Christchurch, a city of about 350 000, is currently installing the first stage of a city-wide bus real-time information system to provide passengers with up-to-the-minute information on where and when their bus will arrive. This approach will undoubtedly become common for many cities on all local services and thus free people up to better manage their time and coordinate their trips.

Bike parking and park n'ride services are also important at stations though it is important not to sterilise important land around a station with too much park n'ride. The intensive, people-oriented functions of a station need to have priority, with park n'ride areas further away.

Japanese stations have multi storey bike parking facilities but in Australian and New Zealand cities the need is for a modest but secure bicycle storage area.

Taxis are an important resource, which can also be better integrated into station areas. Transit passes should have a certain number of low-cost taxi rides as part of their benefit.

CYCLISTS AND PEDESTRIANS

Over the past few decades, transport planning has often neglected the needs of cyclists and pedestrians. However, improving access and safety for cyclists and pedestrians can contribute to reducing vehicle travel, especially for short trips. Evidence suggests increasing traffic volumes and traffic speeds is increasingly marginalising these slow transport modes. Efforts should be increased to determine what design elements and infrastructure best meet cyclist and pedestrian needs, both in urban mixed-use settings as well as suburban–residential settings. As a recent study found, areas with continuous footpaths and short blocks have far higher pedestrian counts (by almost three to one) than areas with long blocks and discontinuous footpaths (see Moudon et al, 1997). In addition, recent trends show that more and more parents are driving their children to school (and for other trips) due to the real and perceived danger that streets are no longer traffic safe for young cyclists and pedestrians (see Whitelegg, 1993). A new set of ideas from David Engwicht (1999) shows how each neighbourhood can reclaim their streets. The manual includes a technique for streets to develop temporary traffic calming devices with their local council which can help manage traffic and create more aesthetic street environments.

STRATEGIES FOR REDUCING TRAVEL DEMAND

A number of transport planning policies can also reduce the demand for travel. Generally these strategies are identified as traffic or travel demand management (TDM) strategies and include such elements as:

- traffic calming (slowing or 'calming' vehicle traffic movements);
- parking policies that put a cap on total parking space capacity, introductions of appropriate prices and ration usage based on user pays;
- traffic priority for alternative modes including public transport, pedestrian and cycle priority at intersections and during road upgrades;
- educational processes such as 'travel blending' or 'travel smart' which provide people with motivation and the knowledge of alternative options available to them. (For example, the travel smart process in South Perth found a 15 per cent reduction in car travel through this technique, see WA DOT, 2000.);

- pricing mechanisms that ensure road users pay for what they use (see next chapter);

- recognising induced traffic in road construction, where longer term forecasts need to consider the increase in traffic from the new road as a 'disbenefit' or cost against the proposal (eg. see Cairns et al 1998); and

- requiring integrated transport and land-use plans in regional and local design.

CONCLUSIONS TO A SYSTEMS APPROACH TO URBAN POLICIES

Cities are under increasing pressure from traffic and urban sprawl, which are now clearly linked in the public mind. However, solutions to them are not always being provided as the policies to ease traffic and manage land are not always understood in their full systems implications.

Many of our urban 'systems' are not taking into account the need to integrate transport and land-use policies.

Decision-making in cities is influenced by many agencies at local, state and national level. Decision-makers do not always think of the urban implications in their policies, eg the Australian government's policy to make truck freight and cars cheaper and public transport more expensive as part of the GST package was done for rural reasons and the city impacts do not seem to have been considered. Only if the cities make a clear statement of their policy directions with regard to transport will these agencies think of them. This chapter shows how many cherished policies are impacting negatively on Australian and New Zealand cities and they need to be reconsidered.

Finally, the chapter presents some strategies to integrate transport and land use better to achieve more sustainable outcomes for our cities.

KEY POLICY RECOMMENDATIONS FOR AUSTRALIAN AND NEW ZEALAND CITIES

This section identifies some of the key findings that the authors believe are appropriate for each city to consider in improving its respective transport and land-use patterns to reduce car dependence.

AUSTRALIAN CITIES

Sydney

INTEGRATED LAND USE AND TRANSPORT: NODES AND CORRIDORS FACILITATING INTENSIFICATION, AND URBAN GROWTH MANAGEMENT

- Sydney is Australia's most intensively developed city with nodes and corridors following its rail system. It is also rapidly re-urbanising around these nodes and corridors and this has subsequently led to growth in the transit system. Reactions to infill are also apparent and design guidelines seem to be needed to ensure redevelopment has public support.

- Fringe development is still occurring and the establishment of a growth boundary to the west similar to those in the north and south could assist intensification of development.

- There has been significant growth in long-distance commuting of 80–100 kilometres to Sydney from areas such as Gosford, Wollongong, the Blue Mountains, Wyong and Shellharbour. A strategy needs to be developed which reduces automobile dependence for these longer trips including public transport, park 'n ride and car-pooling.

IMPROVING ALTERNATIVES — PUBLIC TRANSPORT, CYCLING AND WALKING

- Sydney's rail system has shown it is able to cope with major events like the Olympics but has not yet shown it can become such a major player in transport on a daily basis. The traffic in Sydney is the worst in Australia and the poorly serviced, unintegrated private buses are not competitive in outlying suburbs. The obvious solution is to expand the rail system. But achieving extensions to the rail system has been painfully slow. The Eastern Suburbs line was over a hundred years in the planning and once built it was hard to see how the city could have worked without it. The new line to the airport has experienced teething problems but will eventually be just as indispensable as other major city airport links. The planned $1 billion busway in the western suburbs is unlikely to be a major competitor to the car in these areas, judging by overseas experience — Only the Ottawa and Curitiba busways have had much success and these are in highly dense corridors, whereas the low-density western suburbs will need high-speed connections. The planned Parramatta to Chatswood rail link is a $1.4 billion investment that is not fully funded; the government may need to seek private investment to achieve the capital required and to build the intensive rail-oriented villages along its stations. Heavy rail extensions to Bondi and to the University of NSW seem to be required.

- The biggest potential for growth is the light rail system. The new Light Rail line has now been successfully extended to Lilyfield but needs to be fully part of the CBD, as in Melbourne.The extension of light rail along Anzac Parade seems an obvious route due to the heavy bus use there, and the Northern Beaches area is another region where light rail is needed. The southern suburbs 'Bay Light Express' concept for a southern light rail line is gathering strong popular support.

- Integrated ticketing, where one ticket is valid for a bus trip as well as a train trip, would assist people using public transport in Sydney. Integrated ticketing has been used in Perth for many years.

- Cycle facilities in Sydney are the worst in Australia and there is not much attention to walkability in the historic centre of Sydney, though it has been improving.

REDUCING TRAVEL DEMAND

- No travel demand program is in place apart from road congestion and heavily restricted parking availability in the CBD, along with CBD parking taxes.

Melbourne

INTEGRATED LAND USE AND TRANSPORT: NODES AND CORRIDORS FACILITATING INTENSIFICATION, AND URBAN GROWTH MANAGEMENT

- Melbourne, more than most Australian cities, is two cities. One part of the city has highly integrated land development around its tram system and corridors of development along its train system. The other part consists of some of the worst kind of car-dependent suburbs with extremely poor bus services that are worse than in any of the other cities. The need to rebuild its middle and outer suburbs with more intensive, focused centres and better transit is obvious. However, most urban development is now focusing on the inner area which offers one of the highest qualities of urban life in the world, with the tram system central to that. Further intensification of development is now much more difficult due to an effective campaign to stop infill by the 'Save our Suburbs' movement. This seems to be a result of inadequate urban design guidelines and is now so complex to do that re-urbanisation is effectively stifled and much more urban sprawl will result.

- No growth boundary is in place to prevent sprawl. Despite a new planning strategy 'to build a more sustainable Melbourne' there seems to be little being contemplated to achieve this — such as its 'Urban Villages' strategy which was released about ten years ago. This strategy has since been sidelined.

IMPROVING ALTERNATIVES — PUBLIC TRANSPORT, CYCLING AND WALKING

- The provision of rail-based public transport is good in the older parts of Melbourne though it is not integrated with private bus services. The extension of tram and rail lines to new areas is still needed. Upgrading of some lines is being done to provide more effective regional rail services. The promise of large-scale freeway building continues to hang over the city where the road lobby agenda seems to have been superimposed over the new ALP government transport policy.

REDUCING TRAVEL DEMAND

- No travel demand program is in place but one should be pursued.

Perth

INTEGRATED LAND USE AND TRANSPORT: NODES AND CORRIDORS FACILITATING INTENSIFICATION, AND URBAN GROWTH MANAGEMENT

- Perth is a very low-density city by any standards but is highly planned around nodes and corridors. Continuing development at the urban fringe has a large component of subsidised housing as around 40 per cent of all new housing has either a WA government loan or is state housing and the majority of this is on the fringe. The majority of social housing now needs to be sprinkled into the popular inner suburbs.

- Re-urbanisation has been occurring without state assistance or planning guidance despite it being more sustainable. Design guidelines created for New Urbanist style development have been successful at guiding some new fringe development into innovative, community-oriented centres and denser development known as the 'Fremantle style', though often this is without a good transit base. This style of guidance needs to be applied to redevelopment and infill in older suburbs near the transit system, to avoid problems with those offended by re-urbanisation.

- No urban growth boundary exists at present. The Planning Minister in the Coalition government elected in 1992 immediately rezoned sufficient land on the fringe for 40 years of urban development. Problems with negative equity (where the value of a house has fallen below the loan value) now confront such areas, especially those places without good public transport. A green belt and an urban growth boundary are now an opportunity to improve all aspects of urban development.

IMPROVING ALTERNATIVES — PUBLIC TRANSPORT, CYCLING AND WALKING

- Perth's rail system has been revived after one line was closed in 1979; public reaction has since been heavily supportive for upgrading and extending the railways. The latest stage in the extension was an announcement by the Court government in November 2000 to build a $1 billion southern rail network to Rockingham and Mandurah. The route follows a freight line to Kenwick, thus adding a further 14 minutes to a rail trip compared to going straight down the freeway as the northern line does. This more direct line needs to be built and a branch line to Fremantle as well. Further extensions can be envisioned around the city to the airport and then out to the new north-east corridor.

- A light rail system could be phased in to some of the important bus lines such as the Circle Route, which goes around the middle suburbs and links the universities. This line has been made like a rail service with separate livery, longer distances between stops and direct service without the need for a timetable. Its success has shown why fixed services rather than flexible ones are fundamental to providing good transit. The possibility of linking new light rail into new urban development through joint public–private ventures needs to be facilitated.

- Cycling in Perth has a strong future as the city is reasonably flat and the climate good but the provision of cycleways has been much less than promised. The walkability of central Perth and Fremantle have been much improved over the past ten years as well as traffic calming in all main street shopping areas (now considerably more popular in terms of floor-space value than new shopping centres). Traffic calming needs more commitment from the state and a new funding regime to allow local priorities to be given better consideration.

REDUCING TRAVEL DEMAND

- CBD parking provision in Perth is very high but has recently been linked to public transport provision through a parking tax that pays for the successful CAT bus in the city centre.
- Travel Smart has illustrated how effective is direct education of households about non-car options and the $1 million commitment from the WA government was easily justified by a benefit-cost ratio far higher than any other part of transport.

Adelaide

INTEGRATED LAND USE AND TRANSPORT: NODES AND CORRIDORS, FACILITATING INTENSIFICATION, AND URBAN GROWTH MANAGEMENT

- Adelaide has been a planned city from its beginning with nodes and corridors. Like Perth it has built substantial car dependence into its post war development though often this was subsidised with the provision of innovative state housing.

- Little development is occurring in Adelaide compared to other Australian cities, which means that opportunities to shape development in more sustainable ways are not available. It means that a growth boundary is not as necessary as in other cities but the spread of the city due to unsustainable hobby farms with their almost total car dependence, needs to be avoided.

IMPROVING ALTERNATIVES — PUBLIC TRANSPORT, CYCLING AND WALKING

- Adelaide's rail service is just a little better than that of Auckland, which means that it is one of the worst cities in the developed world. Despite several hundred millions of dollars being spent on stations and livery the basic diesel rail system is just not competitive enough with the car. Unless it is electrified and extended as in Perth it will continue to be largely irrelevant. The O-Bahn is Adelaide's contribution to transit innovation. The lack of other cities following its example probably indicates that it is no cheaper than rail and still suffers from the problems of buses where the congestion in the city slows the system down considerably. The noise and fumes from buses do little to promote close integration with urban development.

- The Glenelg tram would benefit by extending the line in the city towards Rundle Mall.

- The inner city cycleway system and central area walkability are attractive features of Adelaide, as are the parklands that were to be freeways.

REDUCING TRAVEL DEMAND

- Travel Blending is the South Australia Governments attempt to reduce travel demand in Adelaide. Early results are not as encouraging as in Perth but show that this more subtle kind of intervention is likely to be more politically successful than heavier taxing approaches.

Brisbane

INTEGRATED LAND USE AND TRANSPORT: NODES AND CORRIDORS, FACILITATING INTENSIFICATION, AND URBAN GROWTH MANAGEMENT

- Brisbane has one of the least integrated land use and transport systems, possibly because its electrified rail system has come late in the city's development. Its nodes and corridors are defined much more by car access than by transit. A well-developed plan for integrating future development has been created but little commitment to it seems to be obvious.

- Re-urbanisation in the inner area is occurring though again there is not enough attention to design that can avoid political processes causing the process to be stopped.

- No growth boundary is in place although population growth is reasonably strong with the potential for further car dependent sprawl.

IMPROVING ALTERNATIVES — PUBLIC TRANSPORT, CYCLING AND WALKING
- Extensions to the rail system occurred with Federal funds over several different eras (the last to the Gold Coast by Better Cities funds — the only major rail commitment by the Federal government in recent years and that not from the Department of Transport). The extension does not link the Gold Coast together which is ideally designed for rail as it is linear and dense (several recent rail proposals were stopped by road lobby intervention). The best rail commitment has come from a private consortium that built a rail link from the airport to the Queensland Rail system, with trains linking the Brisbane airport to the Gold Coast. The other success story in Brisbane is the new ferry service, which has been very popular.

- The proposed Brisbane light rail was axed in 2000 after receiving only lukewarm assistance from Brisbane City Council which runs the bus fleet. Busways are thus Brisbane's main investment from the 1990's and these expensive options (most have significant parts that are elevated) will be tested in the coming years.

- Cycling and walking facilities have received little commitment in Brisbane.

REDUCING TRAVEL DEMAND
- No travel demand plan is in place.

Canberra

INTEGRATED LAND USE AND TRANSPORT: NODES AND CORRIDORS, FACILITATING INTENSIFICATION, AND URBAN GROWTH MANAGEMENT
- Despite being one of the most planned cities in history with a strong commitment to nodes and corridors the planning of Canberra has been undermined by assumptions about car dependence and the inability to facilitate dense, mixed use areas. In recent years the popularity of development in Manuka and Kingston has undermined those who tried to stop any intensification of land use. However any attempt to develop more intensively in other parts of Canberra, including an innovative European style development option for Gunghalin, has been prevented by planners who found its density offensive. As a result the city sprawls more than any other Australian city and its car use is significantly higher as well.
No urban growth boundary is in place.

IMPROVING ALTERNATIVES — PUBLIC TRANSPORT, CYCLING AND WALKING
- A light rail plan for Canberra was part of the original concept and was re-planned in the early 1990's but was rejected after a campaign based on how it would bring a 'non-Australian' lifestyle. The result is now that a freeway is seen to be essential for the new car dependent suburbs. The possibility of building this with a rail system integrated into it (as in Perth) should be seriously considered as one step away from this American style car dependence.

- Canberra's cycleway system is the best in Australia and it has a few percentage points more than other Australian cities as a proportion of the journey to work. Walkability has declined in suburbs and sub centres as traffic has grown so that most children are now driven to work. Traffic calming needs to be a higher priority. Pedestrianisation of Civic has been successful.

REDUCING TRAVEL DEMAND
- No travel demand plan is in place.

REGIONAL AUSTRALIAN CITIES: OVERVIEW OF RECOMMENDED IMPROVEMENTS

GOLD COAST Extend rail line to Coolangatta and provide better integration with buses. A light rail along the main street would be worthwhile at some time, as the intense, linear form of the development is ideal for this mode.

NEWCASTLE Maintain rail line to city centre and better integration of Newcastle buses with rail. Build the Fassifern–Hexham rail freight bypass and straighten the main passenger rail line between Hornsby, Gosford and Newcastle as provided for in Action for Transport 2010. Further examine a light rail option for new suburbs in Newcastle. As suggested by Newcastle and Hunter Business Chamber (1998): upgrade of rail both to and within the port to reduce heavy transport from urban areas, new regional bus/rail interchange at Glendale to create a transport hub for western Newcastle/Lake Macquarie, relocation of rail line at Cardiff to improve access to a shopping centre and to speed up Newcastle—Sydney trains, new railway station at Kotara to serve the Garden City shopping centre and industrial area, and development of transitway links along former rail corridors linking various suburbs and the University of Newcastle to the city centre.

WOLLONGONG Better integration of private bus services and introduction of bus services to meet the main commuting trains, development of a new railway station at Oak Flats to serve the growing residential areas of Shellharbour City Council with a rail–bus interchange and parking areas for cars and bicycles. Construction of Waterfall–Thirroul railway tunnel to start immediately after Dapto–Kiama electrification (now under way) for faster passenger services and more efficient freight trains. Completion of the Maldon–Port Kembla railway to give better freight access to Port Kembla and to develop an Illawarra–Macarthur–Parramatta link for rail passengers. Introduction of parking charges in Wollongong's CBD — it is one of the few cities in the OECD of its size with no parking meters. Continued development of cycle-ways and commencement of a long overdue program to provide more footpaths on residential streets.

SUNSHINE COAST Begin to try and reduce heavy car dependence, commence work on the Sunshine Coast railway and advance Caboolture–Landsborough duplication. Improve bus services, and their integration with the nearby rail services to Brisbane.

HOBART Examine possibility of reinstating passenger rail system, perhaps by LRT.

MELBOURNE REGIONAL TOWNS Complete Bracks government's new fast rail services linking Melbourne and its regional centres, and ensure local bus services are fully integrated into the new services.

BUNBURY Examine long-term passenger rail plan for south-west of WA, including electrification and extension to Busselton, and provision of daily passenger/tourist services to forest towns. Plan for eventual return of passenger rail to Geraldton and Albany.

NEW ZEALAND CITIES

Auckland

INTEGRATED LAND USE AND TRANSPORT: NODES AND CORRIDORS, FACILITATING INTENSIFICATION, AND URBAN GROWTH MANAGEMENT

- Overall urban density in Auckland is reasonably low, though densities are now increasing. Facilitating this market-based density increase so that both population and job densities increase would reduce the need to travel and improve the viability of public transport, cycling and walking. Appropriate mixed use development at nodes and/or along corridors should be pursued as a means of both reducing local trip lengths and providing more viable concentrations of activities for public transport services.

- There is very clearly some concern in Auckland over the process of intensification. Improving the process of intensification may require a review of how other communities have successfully created attractive environments while increasing density in select areas (eg, Ministry for Planning, 1997).

- Auckland is experiencing the signs of sprawl including growing traffic congestion; to reduce car dependence and associated effects an urban growth limit as well as the overall urban growth strategy recently developed by the local authorities should be strongly supported.

- Reasonably low Gross Regional Product (GRP) in Auckland on an international scale suggests that transport investment decisions require careful consideration (either for future public transport or roading projects) and that a shift in priorities towards public transport would be better for the urban economy.

IMPROVING ALTERNATIVES — PUBLIC TRANSPORT, CYCLING AND WALKING

- Public transport service provision in Auckland is low. This is particularly true when comparing rail services, which are very low compared to a number of Australian cities. Significant increases in public transport require a revamped rail system. This policy has been discussed for over 50 years but Auckland never quite seems to be able to decide. Access to the commercially leased rail tracks is a serious barrier with some promising but not assured increases in service under discussion. A political resolution is required.

- Public transport speeds are low, especially in comparison to average road network speeds. If public transport is going to be more viable in Auckland, improving public transport speeds will be important. This will need a combination of bus priority and electric rail.

- Improving the provision of cycle and walk facilities, and motorist awareness of cyclist and pedestrian safety needs, should be addressed. In addition, increasing urban densities in appropriate locations (nodes) can decrease the number of required car trips and increase the share of cycling and walking.

REDUCING TRAVEL DEMAND
- To date very little attention has been paid to overall traffic demand management. Significant improvements in public transport combined with decreasing provision/priority for cars should be addressed and CBD parking pricing and management policies should support improvements to public transport like the recent bus priority and integrated bus/rail/ferry initiatives.

Wellington

INTEGRATED LAND USE AND TRANSPORT: NODES AND CORRIDORS, FACILITATING INTENSIFICATION, AND URBAN GROWTH MANAGEMENT
- Wellington's urban density is high by NZ standards. Re-urbanisation of the central and inner area is occurring rapidly but it is the only NZ city that showed declines in overall density, and specifically declines in outer area density; this suggests that some urban drift is occurring. Maintaining Wellington's strong 'nodes and corridors' urban form will be important for achieving reductions in car dependence and a review of urban area growth management is warranted.

- Although Wellington has the highest per capita gross regional product of the NZ cities, on an international scale it still spends a much higher amount on city-wide transport operating costs than most other cities in the Global City sample. Thus extensions of the rail system and integration of bus services and land use are still needed.

IMPROVING ALTERNATIVES — PUBLIC TRANSPORT, CYCLING AND WALKING
- Wellington is the only New Zealand city that achieved an increase in journey-to-work mode share for both public transport and cycling/walking between 1991 and 1996 (conversely Auckland and Christchurch showed declines in each). An assessment of why modal share increased for these modes would be valuable to determine what policies should continue to be pursued. It may partially be due to increasing CBD and inner area residential densities.

- Wellington currently has a reasonably high modal share of walking and cycling. Programs to improve cyclist and pedestrian accessibility and safety should be considered (eg, driver awareness programs to develop a 'culture of respect of slower modes', traffic engineering and site development design which meets cyclist/pedestrian needs, etc.).

- Investment in strategic public transport services and infrastructure should be pursued. These could include continuing the investments recently made in 'park n ride' facilities, public transport priority and particularly additional rail services to the southern region.

REDUCING TRAVEL DEMAND
- There is no overall travel demand strategy in place and CBD parking provision is high (although current pricing policies may reduce the effects of prospective over-provision).

Christchurch

INTEGRATED LAND USE AND TRANSPORT: NODES AND CORRIDORS, FACILITATING INTENSIFICATION, AND URBAN GROWTH MANAGEMENT
- A policy of urban area growth management should be pursued which encourages development in nodes and along corridors, and which discourages development in sprawling areas or areas difficult to service with quality, high frequency public transport, and facilities for cycling and walking.

- There is concern in Christchurch over the process of intensification and improving the process may require the facilitation of community-developer design guidelines to create more attractive environments while increasing population density.

  As with the other NZ cities, because Christchurch is not a 'wealthy' city, careful consideration should be given to transport investments to ensure that urban transport efficiencies are optimised, where a shift in priorities towards public transport is likely to be beneficial to the urban economy.

IMPROVING ALTERNATIVES — PUBLIC TRANSPORT, CYCLING AND WALKING
- Significant improvements in public transport should be pursued in Christchurch if improvements in urban transport system efficiency are to be attained. Changes are occurring with the new bus interchange integrated with retail, a new real time information system, introduction of a new ring-route 'orbiter' mall-to-mall service, significant increases in coverage of the central business district, introduction of limited stop services and a smart card ticketing system ordered for early 2001.

- Christchurch should improve the speeds of its existing slow bus system and investigate appropriate rail opportunities to improve the viability of public transport (especially for longer trips); there is obvious potential with a currently unused passenger rail line for services to link existing potential 'nodes' in the urban area.

- The rate of journey-to-work cycling and walking is high in Christchurch, although it declined between 1991 and 1996. Christchurch has a stated desire to improve its cycling; Amsterdam and Copenhagen would be worthwhile cities to investigate how improvements have been achieved.

REDUCING TRAVEL DEMAND
- No travel demand strategy is in place. Programs are needed to address parking management, traffic calming and public transport, cycling and pedestrian improvements. For example, CBD parking in Christchurch is the highest of the 49 international cities sample.

8

CONCLUSIONS: WHERE DO WE GO FROM HERE?

PHILIP LAIRD AND PETER NEWMAN

What this country is crying out for is a government, and especially a minister, with courage and foresight to accept that this country needs a national transport policy — and I do not care on what side of the House it is — that embraces all modes of transport: road, rail, sea and air, to give us an integrated program that will be for the benefit of all Australia instead of this piecemeal state-centric nonsense that passes for transport policy in this country.

Mr Colin Hollis MP (House of Representatives, 1 June 2000)

Earlier chapters have traced the development of Australian and New Zealand land transport systems and the increasingly heavy reliance on road transport. We have also seen how total urban car kilometres have doubled in the 27 years to 1999 while during this time, the urban road-freight task has tripled, and the non-urban road-freight task has quadrupled.

Such high levels of growth have been fuelled by massive hidden subsidies. As we have seen in Chapter 4, Australia now has a road deficit arguably exceeding $8 billion even when road congestion costs are excluded. This $8 billion road deficit far exceeds published rail deficits, which mostly arise from urban passenger transport, and have been decreasing during the 1990s.

Australia now has the highest road freight per capita, measured in tonne kilometres per person, in the world. The hidden road freight deficit has continued to grow and now exceeds $2 billion per year. In contrast, aggregate rail freight deficits, that were about $0.5 billion in 1990, were eliminated during the 1990s and replaced by aggregate rail freight profits.

The overseas experience has overwhelmingly demonstrated that in attempting to solve road traffic problems the way forward is not to build more and more roads, but to be selective in road works and develop alternatives to road vehicle use. It is also necessary to price road use to cover all costs in a fair manner. In Australia, the overall trend has been to pour ever more money into roads, while reducing road user charges in real terms. Better roads and low road pricing have led to more road congestion and increasing road deficits. And while Australians may have gained some comfort from falling numbers of loss of life from road crashes, for most but not all of the 1990s, increasing air pollution from motor vehicles in major cities has inflicted poor health on some people.

In New Zealand the traffic problems in cities are generally not as severe as those experienced in Australia's major cities. However, Auckland clearly has a problem and has arguably the most undeveloped passenger rail system in all OECD cities of a million people or more.

Australia's response to the problem of increasing road vehicle usage has been mixed. On the one hand, most State Governments have made some effort to improve urban public transport and to encourage people to occasionally leave their cars at home. On the other hand, all State Governments have poured ever more money into roads, while the Federal Government now puts almost all of its land transport funding into roads. Indeed, many Federal budgets during the 1990s have had little or no funds for rail and urban public transport, and the situation generally became worse as the 1990s advanced. This is in contrast to the United States where increasing Federal land transport funds have gone to urban public transport — now over 20 per cent.

Local government, with little control over car use or truck mass limits, has been obliged to put more ratepayers' funds into roads. They then plaintively ask the State and Federal Governments to outlay more money on roads.

Car ownership and usage has also been encouraged by the Federal Government's taxation policies to the extent that some 20 per cent of Australia's passenger vehicle fleet are registered in company ownership. The current Federal Treasurer, the Hon. Peter Costello MP, openly boasted that the New Tax System would make cars cheaper. This subsidy does not sit well when the Federal Government goes to international forums to plead a special case as to why reducing greenhouse gases in Australia will ruin its economy.

During recent decades, when Governments have been actively encouraging road vehicle use through underpriced roads, funds have been denied for even the most basic rail track upgrading. As a result, the mainline track linking Australia's three largest cities of Melbourne, Sydney and Brisbane retains 'steam-age' alignment that slows modern trains down. Such physical limitations seriously impede rail's ability to compete with trucks using reconstructed National

Highways. As a result, interstate trucking continues to grow.

On the important question of road pricing, Australian and New Zealand governments continue to make political and popular short-term decisions. Moreover, as we have seen in Chapter 5, this short-sightedness has been allowed to outweigh important economic and environmental factors.

With the steady growth of traffic on urban roads, and ever more 'loads on roads', even Government has reached the conclusion that 'something must be done'. The problem is what should be done that will not only not slow the economy, or upset the next election, but also not unduly offend a host of lobby groups associated with vehicles and road transport. As we have seen in Chapter 6, there are influential road lobby groups to promote their transport policies.

This book suggests a need for Australia and New Zealand to get 'back on track'. One start for governments would be to look again at the reports that they commissioned during the 1990s to deal with emerging traffic problems.

One can ask why governments in both Australia and New Zealand should implement measures in the new decades that they were not prepared to introduce in the 1990s. There are now many reasons for a change of heart. Many of the road traffic problems in the year 2000 are much worse than they were in 1990. Moreover, rail has during the 1990s demonstrated its potential to offer sustainable transport solutions in an efficient and low cost manner. Also, as road traffic grows, so does the cost of not fixing the problems.

We now have a much keener awareness of the need for government to address the problems, and more overseas experience to draw on than was the case in 1990. This includes advances in the United States discussed in this chapter, along with new integrated transport measures proposed for the United Kingdom by the Deputy Prime Minister (1998) Mr John Prescott in trying to persuade people '... to use their cars a little less'. There is the increasing likelihood that if Australia does not move to reduce energy use in transport, it will be unlikely to meet the Kyoto target for greenhouse gas reductions. It is quite possible then that if Australia does not move 'back on track' on its own initiative, it will come under increasing international pressure to do so.

There are three broad areas of change we would like to suggest as the conclusions to draw from this book:

- The need to change the charges for, and taxes on, transport;
- The need to change the funding system for transport; and
- The need to change the planning system for transport.

These three areas of change will be considered in terms of Australia's policies and then briefly considered in a New Zealand context.

CHANGING THE TAXATION AND CHARGING SYSTEM IN AUSTRALIA

The following four broad principles are suggested for reforming road pricing for cars and trucks operating in Australia.

1 Bring the perceived costs of urban car use closer into line with the actual total costs of car use by means of parking taxes and congestion tolls on major urban roads. A parking tax in each central business district or major outlying centre can be used to directly fund improved public transport. For example, Sydney parking fees have provided funds to build park-and-ride facilities at some major rail stations, and in Perth the very successful free Central Area Transit bus is paid for from parking fees. Sydney, Melbourne and Brisbane now have some toll roads. All States should ensure that their major cities use congestion tolling on at least one major urban arterial road. At least one major arterial road that is part of the National Highway System linking Australia's three largest cities to an outlying urban area should also have congestion tolling. The funds raised could go again into the high-profile quality transit options so urgently needed in these cities.

2 Reduce Federal taxation benefits for car ownership and usage and increase tax benefits for urban public transport use.

3 Increase in all States, Territories and the Commonwealth, the aggregate level of road cost recovery from heavy vehicles to at least 25 per cent of road system costs, with application of some mass-differentiation and distance-differentiation in annual charges. The New Zealand type of mass-distance charges for heavier trucks should then follow in Australia's populous zone.

4 Increase Federal fuel excise so as to recover external costs of road vehicle usage to maintain current levels of transport funding, and to improve the balance of funding between road, rail, urban public transport and provision of footpaths and cycleways and other innovative transport funding such as traffic reduction strategies (see later under funding).

These principles will be applied to the petrol price, the tax system and charges on heavy vehicles

PETROL PRICES

Many people's perception of the cost of driving a car is simply that of the cost of petrol. This cost of petrol is less than 10 cents a kilometre for most cars in Australia. Yet, the Australian Tax Office will allow in some cases, a tax concession of at least 50 cents a kilometre.

An increase in petrol and diesel taxes of 10 cents a litre would raise approximately $2 billion a year in Australia, about one-quarter of

Australia's 'road deficit'. This would be enough to reduce annual registration fees and third party insurance fees for Australia's smaller car
fleet, and in addition allow for capital upgrading for urban rail and
public transport. There is a good case that larger and heavier cars,
along with four-wheel drive vehicles, larger station wagons, camper-
vans, etc should pay higher registration and third party insurance
fees. Further increases in petrol prices would generate additional revenue that could also be used for better public hospital facilities
and/or equalisation of fuel prices between rural and urban Australia.

An increase in petrol pricing of 10 cents a litre would only lift the
marginal cost of most car use by one cent per kilometre. For the average Australian passenger vehicle, which drives some 14 400 kilometres a year at some 11.5 litres per 100 km this would amount to
about $160 a year. Most, but not all of this, could be off set in lower
annual registration and third party insurance fees for smaller cars.
Such an increase in petrol prices is unlikely to make a major difference in driving and car use habits, and should be followed with further annual increases in petrol and diesel prices. This was recent
policy in the United Kingdom, which was implementing a 5 per cent
per annum petrol price rise during the late 1990s.

Such a policy will not be politically feasible unless it is done in a
ratchet manner with a clear mechanism showing how the extra funds
are being used to improve conditions for motorists, as well as benefiting public transport and rail freight.

The recommended measures of higher fuel prices, parking taxes
and congestion tolls are commonplace in Western Europe, and were
recommended for wider adoption in 1996 by both the World Bank
and the United Nations Conference on Human Settlements (Habitat
II). We do not recommend that user-pays road pricing in urban areas
with full application of the 'polluter pays' principle is immediately
applied, but suggest that a start should be made by Government. We
would also suggest, with few reservations, that with an informed
debate and honest disclosure of all the relevant facts and figures, the
move towards user-pays urban road pricing will eventually win general public acceptance.

One Australian example that supports user-pays pricing is the
move in Perth and Sydney to user-pays pricing for water. Here, it was
observed by the *Sydney Morning Herald*, 20 May 1988, that the
manager of the Water Board had said, 'You can keep on building
dams forever, then you start to realise you might be better to modi-
fy people's use of water'. As a result of moving to user-pays pricing
for water, Sydney has been able to defer indefinitely the construction
of a new Welcome Reef dam on the Shoalhaven river (*National Parks
Journal*, December 2000, p15) '... due to a 20 per cent decline in
water consumption in Sydney over the past decade'.

A further example during the 1990s was the take-up of mobile phones with charging by the minute in the face of firm ongoing opposition to charging local calls in this way. However, in transport it seems that pricing changes need to be introduced with a simultaneous improvement in the quality of the transport — in this case we would suggest the improvements needed to bring our rail freight, public transport, cycling and walking systems up to world best practice.

TAX SYSTEM

The second broad area for reform in transport policy in Australia and New Zealand is that of taxation. Over the years, taxation concessions have led to incentives for some companies — both large and small — to provide employees or directors with 'a company car' as part of 'salary packaging'.

Although Australian tax benefits for company cars were trimmed in 1985 with the introduction of 'Fringe Benefit Taxation', the reality is that in 1997-98, concessions granted for motor vehicle expenses taxation exceeded $11 billion. This comprised about $2 billion for individuals as work-related expenses, approximately $6 billion for companies, and some $4 billion for partnerships and trucks. This massive overall concession was offset by about $1.5 billion in Fringe Benefit Taxes (FBT) for motor vehicles. Moreover, the FBT receipts were understood (ABC Radio National's *Background Briefing,* 3 September 2000) to have been about $800 million a year too low.

The situation has now reached the point, as seen by the Deputy Prime Minister and Minister for Transport, the Hon. John Anderson MP in a speech on 5 November 1999 to Ausrail, that '...all modes of transport will eventually face charges that more closely reflect their true economic and environmental costs. Logically, this would mean more commercial infrastructure provision with charges that reflect the benefits derived by users and the lifecycle costs of provision'.

Mr Anderson also acknowledged data deficiencies and envisaged '...a move over time towards transparent and explicit treatment of externalities through "charges" on behaviour with negative environmental and safety outcomes, as well as the payment of "Community Service Obligations" for desired regional development, and environmental outcomes'. However, he concluded his speech by noting that '...transport policies will seek to avoid unexpected changes to the relative competitive positions of different modes...'

In other words, as per St Augustine, 'Give me chastity, but do not give it to me yet'. Or, in the Australian transport context 'keep on trucking'.

CHARGES ON HEAVY VEHICLES

In respect of road pricing for heavy trucks, we have already noted in Chapter 4 the hidden road freight deficit of $2 billion, including road system costs and the cost of road crashes, noise and air pollution but excluding congestion costs. We have also noted that Australia has the highest level of road freight per capita in the world, and the relative ineffectiveness of Government to date in the face of determined and strong lobby groups.

As a first step to real reform of heavy vehicle charges in Australia, we suggest the simple expedient of mass-differentiation in annual charges for each type of truck (rigid or articulated) and a given number of axles, based on the Gross Vehicle Mass (GVM) at which the truck will be licensed to operate. Such a system operated in NSW until 1996, with variations in other States, and a two-stage system also operated under the Federal Interstate Registration Scheme (FIRS). Moreover, a simple three-stage system was recommended in the 1990s by a high level inter-governmental committee, called the Over-Arching Group or OAG. The fact that the OAG proposals were not taken up by the National Road Transport Commission (NRTC) during the 1990s for either the first or second generation of charges should not prevent their adoption at the next review.

The present inter-governmental agreements for the NRTC allow for two charging zones. Given the concentration of Australia's population in a coastal band from Townsville to Adelaide in a 'populous' zone, and the added dependence on road transport in the 'non-populous' zone, it would make sense for NRTC to impose mass differentiation with a higher level of charges for heavier trucks within the populous zone.

One may expect strenuous objection to such proposals, and reluctance by some State Governments to adopt more sophisticated and equitable charging regimes for heavy trucks. However, with some leadership from the Commonwealth, as opposed to capitulation to trucking industry demands, more equitable road pricing for heavy vehicles would follow.

Mass differentiation in annual charges for heavy trucks would simply be a first step. The second initial step would be to have distance differentiation in the populous zone. This means that an operator of an articulated truck hauling only say 20 000 kilometres a year in local work would pay a lower annual fee than, say, an interstate operator hauling 200 000 kilometres per year. With today's technologies, including the SAFE-T-CAM in successful use in NSW, and its recommended extension to all of Australia (HORSCCTA, 2000) or the vehicle tracking mechanism on trial in Tasmania since 1998, verification of claims for rebates would be quite possible.

Ultimately, a system like the New Zealand mass-distance charges is desirable for the heavier trucks operating in Australia's populous zone. In the meantime, Australia's long-distance semi-trailer operators enjoy better roads at one third of the road access fees than their New Zealand counterparts. For B-Doubles, Australian operators can pay as little as one quarter of the road access fees that would be paid in New Zealand.

However, the main challenge for governments is to ensure that appropriate charges are made to cover all external costs of all road vehicle usage, including the full cost of road crashes, noise and air pollution. This would require an increase in liquid fuel excise.

CHANGING THE FUNDING SYSTEM

Federal transport funding in Australia is unbalanced, with about $43 billion in 1999 terms going to roads since 1974, as against $1.3 billion for real capital works and $1.5 billion for urban public transport (Appendix C). Unable to respond to the market or to government, it has become an elitist, top-down, bureaucratic exercise that is never evaluated. It is also heavily influenced by the road lobby and has lost its original rationale.

Government does not speak with one voice in Australia on this issue. Most State governments, faced with growing road traffic problems in their capital cities, have tried to improve public transport, and sometimes even encourage people to think twice before making an urban car trip. We have also noted the warnings given by the NSW Environment Protection Authority about Sydney's air quality and how most of Sydney's air pollution is now mostly due to motor vehicle emission. However, these same State governments, with the notable exception of Queensland, have put most of their land transport dollars into roads. As we have seen above, the Federal Government is the worst offender in this area. This is despite recent warnings by the Federal Bureau of Transport Economics (1999b) that urban transport problems '…are likely to get much worse by 2015,' with the need for policies, including '…road pricing, travel blending, fuel excise … higher car occupancy, CBD parking restrictions' that directly affect car use.

With regard to Commonwealth investment in land transport, as we have seen, no fewer than 14 reports published during the 1990s have called for a more balanced approach. Yet, we have also noted the balance of Federal funding between road provision and the other land transport options at the end of the 1990s was worse than at the beginning of the decade.

This deterioration is due to several factors. In the early 1990s, the Federal Department of Transport had a structured program for urban public transport (about $216 million from 1989-90 to 1992-93), and contributed some $430 million for the 'One Nation' rail capital works program, plus $296 million towards the start up of National Rail. However, by the end of the 1990s, there was no structured funding for urban public transport, and less than $90 million had been outlaid of a $250 million rail track upgrading package promised in 1997. The paucity of Federal funds in Australia for urban public transport or mass transit is in marked contrast with the United States where the Transportation Equity Act, signed into law by President Clinton in 1998, will see around 20 per cent of all Federal land transport funds invested in approved mass transit projects.

Australia's obvious bias to roads may have some sense if it were based on a continuing rationale. This bias began as a means of providing a national highway system and in an era when rail was seen as a drain on the public purse. The need for a good road system dominated all other considerations. This rationale has now passed. There is an international acceptance of the need for a balanced transport system, for passengers and freight. Rail services are now seen as a vital rather than a passing mode, and public acceptance of new large roads (especially in cities) is very fragile. Indeed, over-promotion of a freeway has even removed a government, as shown in Queensland in the 1995 election resulting in a change in Government in early 1996.

There are serious questions as to whether continued funding with a bias towards roads is providing a clear benefit to the economy. The process for assessing benefits and costs in individual roads is flawed. The costs are usually understated (and are rarely evaluated afterwards) while the benefits are overstated. The models put far too much emphasis on travel time-savings which never actually eventuate and fuel, emissions and accident reductions which are illusory in an urban system that adjusts to accommodate increased speeds of traffic or longer journeys (see Chapter 7 and Newman and Kenworthy, 1988, 1999a).

At State government level the bias towards roads in the funding process continues. The biggest source of road funding comes from Federal Government grants that are tied to roads and are given to the Main Roads departments. The States also raise funds from vehicle registration and formerly from a dedicated fuel tax, which is now collected by the Commonwealth. These funds also go directly to State road agencies and are disbursed without rigorous financial assessment. Such funds are not available for other transport modes. But neither do all State governments seem to see that transport priorities may need to be more accountable.

An example of priorities is seen in the West Australian Government's $5 billion Transform WA program announced in 1998 which is to fund transport from 1998 to 2008 and consists of the following:

- $2558 million COUNTRY ROADS;
- $2145 million CITY ROADS;
- $84 million PUBLIC TRANSPORT (Bus only);
- $22 million BICYCLES;
- $273 million OTHER (safety, education, black spot removal etc.).

This $5 billion Transform WA program was heavily publicised using the very popular Northern Suburbs Railway but not one cent of the program was for rail. An extension of the rail system is planned, but this will require funds from the sale of the State gas company that occurred in 2000. Like the Northern Suburbs Railway in the early 1990s, there are no grants that can be tapped for rail infrastructure, and a State loan was required for this railway. However, the freeway alongside which it runs was built with a Federal grant.

How can the playing field be so un-level? How can such a process be allowed to continue?

When there are large quantities of money for roads in a guaranteed pot, the process for deciding transport priorities becomes extraordinarily distorted. The particular program in WA outlined above, Transform WA, was dreamed up by the Minister for Transport and two road engineers on one weekend and announced before any other agency had even heard of it. How can such expenditure processes be so lax? How can they be so totally separated from any serious market assessment or from the communities they are meant to benefit? No other area of government seems to be able to get away with such an appalling lack of accountability.

The problem is made worse when we reflect on the data we have collected on cities across the globe that we discussed in Chapter 3. This data shows that those cities putting their spending priorities on big roads are not as economically effective as those that are putting their priorities on good public transport. Apart from the direct costs of driving, fast roads feed urban sprawl, which is very expensive to service by governments and the market. The immediate benefits that are promised by these road developments are therefore highly illusory. They also make us more car-dependent when the challenge is to reduce the long-term impacts of the car in matters like smog and greenhouse emissions.

The same process seems to characterise local government in Australia. Apart from the city of Brisbane, local councils see little or no responsibility for public transport. Although they have limited responsibility for bicycles and pedestrians, almost all their transport focus is on roads. Local councils are now supplicants who ask for funds from the big pot of State and Federal funds dedicated only to roads. A good council is one that gets the most road funds. To say no to such funds would be unheard of. But no alternatives are ever presented for them to consider.

THE UNITED STATES EXPERIENCE

In order to ensure that alternatives are given a chance, there needs to be a wider process established involving broader government assessment and involving the local communities that the transport is meant to be benefiting, ie. the transport funding process needs to be democratised.

This kind of process has been set up in the US during the 1990s in a stunning reversal of transport policy. During the 1950s, the US invented the system for assigning transport funding from central taxes, distributed to States for highways only, based on simplistic engineering models. The system for doing this was automatically re-authorised every five years until a consortium of alternative transport groups called the Surface Transportation Policy Project in the 1980s decided that the system was no longer relevant or appropriate. In its place, it was determined that the system must be democratised and they were able to write an alternative transport funding act called the Intermodal Surface Transportation Efficiency Act (ISTEA) and have it adopted by Congress in 1991 — much to the chagrin of the road lobby.

The system no longer has guaranteed road funds but sets up a process where local cities and regions must evaluate options before the funds are assigned. Part of that process must be the fulfilment of clean air goals which recently led to the cessation of all highway funds to Atlanta until an alternative set of options was found. Each year of the process has seen a growth in funding for transit, bicycles, traffic calming, travel demand management and intermodal facilities.

As Don Chen from the Surface Transportation Policy Project has said: 'United States transportation policy changed from one that was engineering-driven, top-down, secretive, fiscally irresponsible, and almost entirely focused on highways, to one that is more planning-based, locally-controlled, open, fiscally constrained, and intermodal' (Chen, personal communication, 1999).

When the ISTEA legislation was up for re-authorisation in 1997 the road lobby appealed to Congress for a return to the old system. However the new act (TEA-21) which went even further in the democratisation of funding, was passed 96 to 4 in Congress.

We can learn from this transition which is now widely acknowledged as a success politically and on the ground (Camph, 1999; Gifford, 1999). In the period since ISTEA was begun there has been a slow but definite shift in spending priorities towards the more sustainable modes and away from big highways. It is mirrored in similar trends within the States and local funding systems. For example the most road-oriented cities in the US — Houston, Denver and Phoenix — are now all building new rail systems. In Milwaukee, the city voted to use Federal TEA-21 funds to dismantle a highway that they felt was not helping the city economically.

The system for funding transport in Australia needs to learn from this US democratisation process — it needs to open up. It is one of the last areas of secretive, top-down funding from Australian governments that is left and it is certainly beginning to look like Australia may be one of the last countries to leave such a system in place.

PROPOSED ALTERNATIVE FOR AUSTRALIAN AND NEW ZEALAND FUNDING

The following five characteristics need to be incorporated into the funding process for transport in Australia and New Zealand.

I   THERE SHOULD BE NO 'ROAD FUNDS', JUST 'TRANSPORT FUNDS'.
The need for flexibility, balance and local accountability in government argues against a process that picks winners before the evaluation process begins. The provision of a rail line along a busy corridor can be equivalent to the provision of a six- or eight-lane lane freeway; the process of weighing up which alternative is the most cost effective and acceptable cannot be done from Canberra. At the same time there may be much better ways to spend 'transport' funds on techniques such as traffic calming and travel demand management strategies. These do not create new infrastructure at all but may be the best way to solve traffic problems as well as broader environmental and economic problems. A market survey in 2000 of 400 households in Perth by the Department of Transport, found that their priorities for funding were all to do with better public transport, cycling and walking (only 9 per cent wanted new roads), and 87 per cent wanted road funds used for alternative modes.

2   THE FEDERAL GOVERNMENT SHOULD NOT ASSIGN TRANSPORT FUNDS TO PROJECTS; THEY SHOULD JUST ENSURE A PROCESS OF REGIONAL PLANNING HAS OCCURRED TO DETERMINE HOW BEST TRANSPORT PRIORITIES SHOULD BE ASSIGNED TO THEIR TRANSPORT FUNDS.
The virtual completion of the National Highway System means that the excessive focus on that priority can now be changed, just as the ISTEA legislation in the US could be enacted upon completion of the Interstate Highway System. Many urban roads have been added to the Federally-funded road program, which was meant to just link major rural roads into a national highway system. These have been given funding and planning rationales that are not real and have led to considerable public concern as no other options were considered. The re-authorisation of the US ISTEA legislation occurred against the wishes of a powerful road lobby who wanted a return to guaranteed road funds. This happened because the political agenda of a more flexible, locally sensitive process appeals to all sides of the political spectrum. There should be similar support in this country.

The focus should now shift to a new and more responsive process that involves more than just road agencies. In the US the Federal Government sets guidelines on where it thinks transport funds should go and has pushed the proportion going to public transport up to 20 per cent. However, local areas can utilise more of their 'transport' funds for transit if they wish. A similar goal for Australia would be a terrific start in rebuilding the non-road-based transport infrastructure in this country.

Performance criteria can be included to ensure a) the funds assist in achieving economic development, b) international goals on reducing carbon dioxide are met, and c) all national guidelines and standards are met such as accessibility for people with disabilities and air quality from transport emissions. Social criteria can also be included, as the process will be a community building exercise if it is able to assist communities achieve their goals and values.

3   STATE GOVERNMENTS SHOULD ABOLISH THE PLANNING POWERS, GUARANTEED FUNDING AND DIRECT ACCESS OF THEIR ROAD AGENCIES TO MINISTERS; THESE AGENCIES SHOULD BECOME ROAD-BUILDING AGENCIES ONLY, UNDER THE DIRECTION OF BROADER DEPARTMENTS SUCH AS TRANSPORT OR INFRASTRUCTURE.

This process has occurred in Queensland and it is perhaps the only state where there is a belief in an expanded role for freight rail, as well as having an integrated urban transport plan which they are implementing. Perhaps this transition was motivated by the process whereby the Queensland road agency, with guaranteed Federal funds, was able to almost single-handedly remove their state government when they wanted to build a major highway through a koala sanctuary.

The WA government elected in February 2001 has brought its Main Roads into the Planning and Infrastructure portfolio (with only one transport fund) after strong community reaction to the excessive road orientation of the Coalition government.

Road-building agencies have lost the trust of the community. They can no longer be left alone, as their single-minded objective of more tarmac no longer fits the more complex needs of our cities and regions.

4   TRANSPORT FUNDING SHOULD BE ASSIGNED ONLY AFTER A PROCESS OF PLANNING HAS OCCURRED IN CITIES AND REGIONS THAT IS BASED ON A FULL ANALYSIS OF ALL OPTIONS. THESE OPTIONS SHOULD BE BASED ON BOTH TECHNICAL ANALYSIS AND PROPER CONSIDERATION BY PLANNING BODIES IN CITIES AND REGIONS THAT ARE DEMOCRATIC (INVOLVING ELECTED OFFICIALS) AND INVOLVE CUSTOMER/STAKEHOLDER-ORIENTED GROUPS.

The technical assessment of all alternatives is not a well-developed process. The techniques are only beginning to be developed in the US now that the old models have been found to be no longer valid (Camph, 1999). The importance of a new approach is to concentrate on the broad set of outcomes required, not to be dominated by illusory time savings from highly discredited land use-transport computer models.

These broad outcomes are mostly being set by Departments of Transport or Planning which are looking at goals for modal split and indicators for a range of factors to do with urban sprawl, air quality, greenhouse gases, jobs–housing balance, sub-centre development, and the facilitation of communities through better urban design. Plans such as WA's *Metropolitan Transport Strategy* and the *Urban Design Community Code*, Sydney's *Shaping our Cities,* or Victoria's *Urban Villages Project,* would have some chance of being implemented if they were linked to the transport funding process. Transport demand management schemes can be given a serious assessment instead of being marginalised by engineers who like to build their way out of problems.

There are increasing signs that in trying to achieve the goals and ideals being set by our planning agencies, the present system of prioritising infrastructure is working against them. No city is saying they want to facilitate growth in traffic. In fact, all cities all are saying road traffic needs to be reduced. No region is saying they want more trucks on their highways. The best alternative to bring together the goals and the funding in many cities, including Brisbane, has been to say that there should be a moratorium on any increase in road capacity in the city and that all new infrastructure will build up public transport or high occupancy vehicle capacity. New roads can be built, but only if that capacity is transferred in such a way as to reduce capacity elsewhere. The same can be applied to regions.

The new process also needs to be more oriented to the communities that the infrastructure is meant to benefit. This is only bringing to transport what virtually every other area of government has had to do: join the post-Fordist management approach which seeks to find outcomes that meet real needs, not solutions imposed by experts from on high.

As Gifford (1999) says in reviewing the situation in the US: '… a customer-oriented approach involves customising and improving infrastructure through the efforts of engineers and planners working directly with users and other stakeholders. Such an approach risks conflicting with the normal lines of accountability and authority in public organisations, which place elected officials as the proper conduit for public input in policy and decisions' (p 64). He asserts that this customer-oriented approach is necessary to win back public support for any infrastructure projects.

It would seem easy enough to invent a process that includes both the elected officials and the customer-based groups from civil society and the private sector. This is happening in the United States through Transportation Management Organisations (TMO's) set up under TEA-21 for any corridor or region seeking to examine options for the future.

The best models for doing this in Australia need to be worked out. There are examples in other areas of life such as landcare groups where the people directly involved are given key roles in working out priorities. It is not hard to imagine that regional and urban transport planning bodies could be assembled from local authorities, local transport groups, private sector groups and State Government agencies and could be referred to as Regional Transport Councils, with powers to provide Regional Transport Plans.

5   THE LINKAGE OF TRANSPORT AND LAND USE SHOULD BE ENCOURAGED BY THE INVOLVEMENT OF THE PRIVATE SECTOR WHERE IT IS CLEAR THAT THEY WILL BENEFIT FROM THE INFRASTRUCTURE; A PROCESS OF USING DIFFERENTIAL RATES SHOULD BE INSTITUTED TO RECYCLE 'BETTERMENT' TO HELP PAY FOR THE INFRASTRUCTURE.

The role of the market in transport decisions has been as 'downplayed' as much as the role of civil society. There are real opportunities for solving the age-old problem of land use–transport linkages, but they invariably require close partnerships to be formed between public and private enterprise. The places where this is done most are where the Federal Government (or national government) provides no funds for transport and thus the cities and regions need to be innovative about their futures.

Everyone wants a more integrated approach to transport and land use; this is the 'smart growth' issue. The transport funding process could be structured in ways that involve developers and landowners in the funding of infrastructure as a market-oriented approach to integration. The best new urban rail projects, for example, are based on public-private partnerships that enable local goals to be met and a way of finding extra financing for the rail system based on the extra value it provides to the area (Scheurer et al, 2000). Where this process of joint development and value capture has been in place for some time, the development community settles into acceptance of it as a way of getting higher value uses out of land that it holds (eg Toronto). This is the way Copenhagen is building its rail system; now Denver has become the first US city undertaking a private-public joint rail venture. Brisbane and Sydney all have projects that are showing how this can be done in Australia. Such processes need to become commonplace.

SUMMARY TO FUNDING

The transport funding system in Australia needs to change. The five suggestions outlined are all intended to democratise the system. They are not going to lead to dramatic overnight changes but will allow Australian and New Zealand cities and regions to respond to their different economic, environmental and social needs. The change will be most noticed by those road lobby organisations and highway engineers that are used to finding guaranteed funds for their pet projects.

The system will demand much more of a consultative approach and a more rigorous assessment of all options. In summary, land transport funding is out of balance with community expectations and needs to be democratised. There is no reason why Federal land transport funding in the United States should be 20 per cent on public transport and almost zero in Australia. We suggest that Australia should quickly move towards having 20 per cent of all Federal land transport funds allocated to urban public transport in a democratised process. In view of gross deficiencies in mainline interstate track in Australia, additional Federal land transport funds should be allocated to intercity rail track upgrading.

CHANGING THE PLANNING SYSTEM IN AUSTRALIA

Throughout this book we have seen the need for a more integrated approach to transport. Transport can never be seen as an end in itself and even more, it can never be seen without assessing its implications for the broader economy, the environment, the nature of our community life, and now, global issues like oil and Greenhouse gases.

An integrated transport planning system would begin at the local level where Regional Transport Plans would be required (as suggested above) before any funding is made available. This would involve examining all the priorities and options. State planning would then need to add an integrated perspective involving a template of their goals and processes, including impact assessment (environmental and social), full cost-benefit analysis, regional preferences, and integration with land use planning goals for viable sub-centres, re-urbanisation and reduced urban sprawl. Federal planning would need to be incorporated at both the local and State levels, by ensuring guidelines are met on greenhouse gases, air quality, disabled access etc.

In order to achieve this it is not possible to have agencies like Main Roads holding independent planning powers. These must be removed and a broader strategic planning framework incorporated into State bureaucracies. An outcome-oriented approach can then be instigated and the funds found to build and facilitate the best options for achieving these. Governments can no longer be just project-oriented, based on isolated agencies vying for the best politically acceptable projects. Integrated planning is more network-oriented and less linear; it is more sustainability-oriented and less single-agency based. It cannot guarantee solutions to the problems raised in this book but it may stop them continuing to deteriorate and give us a chance to move 'on track'.

As part of the planning process, it is highly desirable that the level of debate on land transport issues in Australia be improved. This will require a quantum increase in the publication of accurate and timely transport data. The debate in Australia should include the New Zealand proposal for the commercialisation of roads to at least reveal the extent of present subsidies.

Too often the debate is dominated by myths such as 'taxes and charges levied on all motor vehicles make money for Government', 'heavy trucks pay their way', and 'rail freight is inefficient and subsidised'. Such myths are based on longstanding perceptions that are now out of date. The fact that some lobby groups choose to perpetuate them is no excuse for governments to continue to believe them. Instead, Government would better serve the interests of the nation if it would actively assist in encouraging a more informed debate. There is also a need to provide some balance between advertising for cars and other forms of transport.

An informed debate requires good, accurate and timely data that is freely available in the public domain. We have already noted the major deficiencies in transport data in Australia. Our recommendation is that Australia should now follow the lead of the United States and form a Bureau of Transportation Statistics or BTS. This Bureau was established following approval as part of the United States *Intermodal Surface Transportation Efficiency Act 1991* or ISTEA. The BTS has functions including compiling, analysing and making accessible information about the nation's transportation systems; collecting information on various aspects of transportation; and enhancing the quality and effectiveness of government statistical programs through research, the development of guidelines, and the promotion of improvements in data acquisition and use.

Ten years later, we are far from this situation in Australia and New Zealand.

Funding for the BTS was continued in the 1998 US Transportation Equity Act. It is now time to make a quantum improvement in Australia for the provision of land transport data. Specifically, this would include collection, analysis, and publication in easy to access format, of:

a) Characteristics of the road vehicle fleet in terms of safety, tonne mass, and energy efficiency. This would include: which are the safest cars on the basis of actual road use, how many of Australia's 9.6 million passenger vehicles have a mass under 0.8 tonnes, how many are between 0.8 and 1.0 tonnes, and so on, what is the expected range of annual kilometres driven for different sized passenger vehicles for each car.

b) More frequent, more accurate and more detailed Surveys of Passenger Vehicles Usage, with more use of odometer readings (total kilometres travelled) obtained by State authorities each time a vehicle is registered.

c) More accurate estimates of car occupancy rates, which apparently decreased in the 1990s.

d) The extent of long-distance car commuting in Australia.

e) Better data on urban public transport use.

f) Annual collection and publication of road freight and rail freight, tonnages and freight tasks (in tonne kilometres as well as tonnes).

g) Annual collection and publication of interstate and inter-regional freight movements.

In addition to the formation of a Bureau of Transportation Statistics in Australia, there is also a need for more research into rail and urban public transport to complement road research. In recent years, the Australian Road Research Board, which is funded by the Federal Government and State road authorities, has been recast as ARRB Transport Ltd. There is now a need for the Federal and State Governments to commission ARRB Transport Ltd to undertake research into urban public transport and rail rather than to continue focusing mainly on road research.

During the 1990s, the Federal Government has outlaid tens of millions of dollars to state road authorities to assist with forward planning for the National Highway System and other roads. This process assists in having 'plans in the drawer' for more road works. Adequate Federal funding for planning of major rail and urban public transport projects, with any necessary land acquisition, is long overdue.

In the absence of a National Land Transport Commission, there is also a need to form a National Rail Transport Commission to advance rail reform. During the 1990s, the National Road Transport Commission was paid over $10 million by the Federal Government, with matching funds from State Governments, to advance road reform for heavy truck and bus operators. It is difficult to see why there has been no comparable organisation for rail.

NEW ZEALAND

New Zealand also needs a similar democratisation of the transport funding system, an overhaul of the taxation and charging system, and a review of planning to ensure rail is more central to the future of transport planning. Transport problems also urgently need to be addressed in Auckland. New Zealand also warrants the publication of more extensive and up-to-date transport data.

Urban transport problems are severe in Auckland, whose population has grown rapidly in recent years. As we have noted in Chapters 2 and 7, Auckland has possibly the most poorly developed urban rail system of any OECD city of a million or more people. Consequently, the motorway systems that were developed in the 1970s (and then subject of envy by the NRMA whose 'Open Road' proposed them as a model for Sydney) have long since reached saturation point. The cost of providing Auckland's central area with road improvements to solve inner city traffic problems, albeit at the expense of creating traffic problems further out of the central area, could easily exceed $1 billion. The demand for more urban motorways, and government's limited finances, are good reasons for commercialising roads in New Zealand, and moving to user-pays urban road pricing. However, improved public transport in Auckland is also essential, and the New Zealand Government should accept its responsibilities in this area. We suggest that whilst bus options may have some appeal, Auckland would be better served by expansion and upgrading of its limited urban rail services.

It is of note that public transport usage in Wellington, with a more extensive urban rail system, is appreciably higher than that of Auckland. However, Wellington, like Christchurch, which no longer has an urban rail system, also suffers from excessive car use.

New Zealand's system of road user charges for all heavy vehicles has served New Zealand well throughout the 1980s and 1990s. The application of these mass-distance charges, combined with a more basic intercity road system and fewer heavier semitrailers and B-Doubles has allowed rail to more effectively compete for freight. However, at the end of the day, these charges are 'pay as you go' charges that do not require an up-front contribution to road upgrading. This factor can potentially distort modal choice, particularly where a resource such as timber is to be extracted from a region where roads are in place, but there is no existing rail line

New Zealand, like Australia, has significant deficiencies in land transport data. Both countries need better land transport data that is easily accessible to the public.

CONCLUDING REMARKS

The broad principles outlined in this chapter are not meant to be exhaustive. Undoubtedly there will be new technologies like 'intelligent transport systems' which will have a role to play in the future, but their evolution should not be used as an excuse by the Federal Government for further delays in getting 'back on track'. Thus, there is a need to introduce now, rather than in the next term of office, road vehicle use demand measures, and more even-handed investment between roads, rail track and urban public transport systems.

In 1990, the Federal Government produced a ten-point road safety program, with the eventual cooperation of the States and Territories. In return for additional Federal funding ($100 million) for 'black spot' works, the ten-point program produced good results during the 1990s. Box 8.1 is an example of a ten-point plan for the entire transport

BOX 8.1
A TEN POINT PLAN FOR AUSTRALIAN LAND TRANSPORT

1   Road safety measures such as those in the National Road Safety Strategy 2001-2010 for Australia need to be implemented, with stronger provisions to further reduce the loss of life and injury on the roads. Shifting passengers to all other non-car modes while reducing the need to travel, along with shifting freight to rail, should be seen as part of road safety.

2   Vehicle technology needs to be regulated to world best practice for new vehicles, with high standards for maintenance of the existing fleet through vehicle inspections. Standards need to include reducing transport greenhouse gas emissions by 2010 to their 1990 levels.

3   All 'road funds' should be replaced by 'transport funds' and Australia should instigate a more democratic funding-allocation process like the United States process of Regional Transport Plans, involving all local stakeholders linked to broad national goals including at least 20 per cent of Federal transport funds for non-road purposes.

4   All cities need to levy a CBD parking fee with proceeds used to improve urban public transport facilities.

5   All States need to ensure that their capital cities use congestion tolling on at least one major urban arterial road, and part of the National Highway System linking the city to an outlying urban area as part of a process of educating motorists in the real costs of transport.

6   All States, Territories and the Commonwealth need to increase the aggregate level of road cost-recovery from heavy vehicles to at least 25 per cent of road system costs, with development of the New Zealand style mass distance charges in the populous zone of Australia.

7   The problems of continuing oil vulnerability and the full costs of transport fuel use need to be explained to the Australian and New Zealand public. Fuel excise needs to be progressively increased so as to recover all external costs of road vehicle usage and to allow for a reduction of annual charges for small energy-efficient cars along with improvement of urban public transport and rail freight.

8   Agreed world best practice standards need to be set for delivery and coordination of urban public transport in major urban areas including high service delivery, the integration of land use, the development of public–private joint projects and fully integrated ticketing.

9   Federal taxation benefits need to be reduced for motor vehicle ownership and use, and improved for urban public transport use.

10 Formation of a National Bureau of Transportation Statistics needs to occur with the publication of accurate, comprehensive and up-to-date information on all modes of transport, including energy use and greenhouse gas emissions.

system that would be consistent with the broad principles listed above. We would further suggest that all Federal funding for transport be conditional on the States and Territories adopting such a plan. A similar plan could be developed for New Zealand. This would include improved road pricing, and development of an adequate urban rail system for Auckland.

As observed by the Industry Commission in its 1994 report on Urban Transport, the important steps are to actually start the reform process, and then to keep it moving. The process can be assisted by open Government inquiries such as an inquiry into road provision, funding and pricing as proposed by the Productivity Commission in 1999. However, an inquiry should not be used as an excuse by the Federal Government to further delay the allocation of adequate levels of investment in rail and public transport, and making an early start on road pricing reform.

The main need for both Australia and New Zealand is to urgently develop land transport systems with less reliance on cars and trucks. Many reasons, including the reduction of hidden road deficits, have been put forward in this book as to why such a 'culture change' is desirable. The prospect of higher world oil prices is yet another compelling reason why such a change must occur sooner rather than later.

APPENDIX A
AUSTRALIAN TRANSPORT AND ENERGY DATA

PHILIP LAIRD

Cars moving in urban areas are one of the least energy-efficient means of travel whilst road freight energy efficiency is about one third less than that of rail and sea freight.

From text

This Appendix gives a summary of energy inputs, along with passenger and freight transport outputs, in Australia to 1994–95 and is similar to information published by the Institution of Engineers, Australia (1999, Chapter 10). Most of the data given in these tables is rounded from data given by the Apelbaum Consulting Group (ACG, 1997). Other sources of transport energy data, with discussion, include the Australian Bureau of Agricultural and Resource Economics (ABARE, 1999), the Australian Bureau of Statistics (ABS, 1997), and, the Bureau of Transport Economics (BTE, 1996).

The ACG data is derived from ABARE, ABS, and BTE data along with other sources. However, the ACG data differs, in many cases, from similar data given by the BTE (1996). In addition, the ACG estimates of energy use are for primary energy, which are necessarily higher than the BTE estimates of end-use energy.

Table A.1 shows the dominance of cars and other passenger vehicles in Australia's domestic passenger task. This dominance goes back for many years before 1970. Here, one passenger kilometre occurs when one person moves one km. As shown by Table A.2, cars and other passenger vehicles really dominate urban passenger transport. This dominance increased in the 19 years to 1994–95, with their passenger km showing an average (compound) rate of increase of about 3 per cent per annum. Urban rail has shown limited overall growth, whilst buses, trams and ferries, have shown even more limited growth.

For non-urban (including intercity) transport, as shown by Table A.3, the car is again dominant. However, the real growth is shown by domestic aviation, where air passenger kms had more than tripled within the 19 years to 1995 (and had doubled in the five years to 1994–95). Non-urban bus travel, that showed a strong growth in the 1980s, has been pegged back in the 1990s. Overall, non-urban rail travel has gone backwards in Australia (except for Queensland since 1995). Note also that on some inter-capital corridors (Sydney–Melbourne but not Sydney–Canberra), air is now the dominant mode (BTE, 1998).

Table A.4 shows the growth in road vehicle kilometres, plus the use of diesel having an average growth rate of about 3.6 per cent per annum compared with petrol's average growth rate of about 1.5 per cent per annum in the 19 years to 1994–95. Table A.5 shows urban car etc kilometres doubling within the 19 years to 1995 (with an average growth rate of 3.7 per cent per annum) increasing at a faster rate than their passenger km which is mostly due to a decline in car occupancy rates. This Table also shows that most car use and vehicle use occurs in urban areas, and that road vehicles use most energy in urban areas. In fact, over half of all energy use in Australian domestic transport is accounted for by vehicle movements in urban areas. As shown by Table A.6, cars moving in urban areas are one of the least energy efficient means of travel, with air and ferries also performing poorly.

TABLE A.1
AUSTRALIAN DOMESTIC PASSENGER TASKS

Year	Cars etc	billion passenger km Buses	Trains	Planes	Sea
1970–71	108.4	6.6	12.8	5.20	0.70
1975–76	131.2	7.6	8.2	7.64	–
1984–85	171.6	13.3	8.4	10.34	0.70
1987–88	189.1	16.3	9.7	13.27	0.50
1990–91	203.4	17.0	9.3	14.50	0.50
1994–95	225.3	15.5	9.2	25.27	0.46

SOURCE BTE (1996) for 1970–71, then ACG (1997) Table 3.6, p 29, Table 3.12, p 41, Table 3.17, p 52 and Table 3.25, p 65

TABLE A.2
AUSTRALIAN URBAN PASSENGER TASKS

	billion passenger km				
Year	Cars etc	Buses	Trains	Trams etc	Ferries
1970–71	67	3.5	6.7	0.60	0.16
1975–76	87.8	4.0	5.8	0.53	–
1984–85	116.1	4.3	5.6	0.58	0.08
1987–88	134.8	4.5	6.4	0.66	0.10
1990–91	140.9	4.3	6.8	0.59	0.10
1994–95	155.9	4.4	7.3	0.59	0.12

SOURCE BTE (1996) for 1970–71, then ACG (1997) Table 3.6, p 29, Table 3.12, p 41, Table 3.11, p 39 and Table 3.25, p 65. Note that some rail journeys (eg Newcastle–Sydney) earlier classified as non-urban are now urban.
Trams includes Adelaide (0.015 bpkm in 1994–95) and the Sydney Monorail (0.012 bpkm in 1994–95). Note that the BTE series gives data that differ from Apelbaum for 1975–76 and later years in some cases, and, their estimate for trams in 1970–71 is broad.

TABLE A.3
AUSTRALIAN NON-URBAN PASSENGER TASKS

	billion passenger km				
Year	Cars etc	Buses	Trains	Planes	Sea
1970–71	41.0	3.0	6.0	5.20	0.54
1975–76	43.4	3.6	2.4	7.64	–
1984–85	55.4	9.0	2.8	10.34	0.62
1987–88	54.3	11.8	3.3	13.27	0.40
1990–91	62.5	12.7	2.5	14.50	0.40
1994–95	69.5	11.1	1.9	25.27	0.35

SOURCE BTE (1996) for 1970–71, then ACG (1997) Table 3.6, p 29, Table 3.12, p 41, Table 3.17, p 52 and Table 3.25, p 65
NOTE Planes refers to scheduled domestic flights, and excludes the unscheduled domestic flights, general aviation and commuter flights, which in 1994–95 amounted to 0.212 bpkm

TABLE A.4
ROAD TRANSPORT AND ENERGY USAGE

Year	Passenger (Veh. km. billion km)	Total (Veh. km billion km)	Fuel use by vehicles		Energy use by vehicles (PJ)
			Petrol (billion litres)	Diesel (billion litres)	
1975–76	78.5	101.5	13.0	1.5	562
1984–85	106.6	141.5	15.7	4.0	758
1987–88	118.4	155.6	16.4	4.7	820
1990–91	127.6	163.7	16.5	4.8	844
1994–95	142.9	185.2	17.4	5.7	935

SOURCE ACG (1997) Table 3.1, p 23 plus Tables 4.2, 4.3, p 106/107. Note energy used in Petajoules includes gas as well as liquid fuels. One Petajoule (PJ) is 10^{15} Joules, with ABARE conversion factors for energy for recent years including
1 litre of petrol = 34.2 MJ (unleaded) and 1 litre of diesel = 38.6 MJ

TABLE A.5
AUSTRALIAN URBAN VEHICLE USAGE

Year	Passenger (Veh. km. billion km)	Total (Veh. km billion km)	Energy used in urban areas (PJ)	% of all transport energy
1975–76	51.1	63.2	na	na
1984–85	73.5	92±	463	61
1987–88	85.8	107.5	535	65
1990–91	89.7	109.2	534	63
1994–95	102.6	126.2	611	65

SOURCE ACG (1997) Table 3.4, p 26 and Table 4.3 p 107
NOTE Energy used in Petajoules includes gas as well as liquid fuels

TABLE A.6
AUSTRALIAN DOMESTIC PASSENGER ENERGY EFFICIENCY

	passenger km per megajoule (MJ)				
Year	Cars etc	Buses	Trains	Planes	Ferries
1975–76	0.35	0.96	0.53	0.20	–
1984–85	0.36	0.90	0.65	0.25	0.11
1987–88	0.37	0.92	0.77	0.26	0.26
1990–91	0.37	0.98	0.76	0.28	0.23
1994–95	0.37	0.94	0.76	0.36	0.23

SOURCE ACG (1997) Table 4.9(b), p 116, Table 4.17, p 127, Table 4.22, p 136. Air passenger energy efficiencies are derived from Table 4.20, p 132 which gives energy efficiencies of 0.02 to 0.03 net tonne km per MJ on the additional assumption that each passenger with luggage has an average weight of 90 kg. Non-urban cars etc have a higher energy efficiency (0.43 pkm per MJ in 1994–95) than urban cars etc (0.36 pkm per MJ).
NOTE Non-urban buses have a much higher energy efficiency (1.50 pkm per MJ in 1994–95) than urban buses (0.72 pkm per MJ), but urban rail in 1994–95 had a higher energy efficiency (0.83 pkm per MJ) than urban buses. In 1990–91, 1987–88, and 1984–85, non-urban rail was more energy efficiency than urban rail. Load factors are critical for the energy efficiency of buses and trains as well as cars, planes and ferries

FREIGHT

Freight data is given in Table A.7 that shows road, rail and sea now having roughly equal shares of Australian domestic freight transport if pipelines are excluded. The largest growth has occurred with road freight. Table A.8 gives energy use in road freight.

Tables A.9 and A.10 give data on road freight by articulated trucks, rigid trucks, and light commercial vehicles (LCVs). One can query the boundaries between passenger and freight transport (eg is taking the shopping home a freight or passenger task) and the boundaries between urban and non-urban freight. However, with the data given, it is of note that the urban freight task, in tonne-kilometres has almost tripled within the19 years to 1995 (with an average growth rate of 5.6 per cent per annum). The non-urban articulated truck freight task has almost quadrupled within the 19 years to 1995 (with a high average growth rate of 7.2 per cent per annum).

As can be seen from the data given in Table A.11, average road freight energy efficiency is appreciably less than that of rail and sea freight operations. Note that, on average, articulated trucks are more energy efficient than rigid trucks and LCVs (with respective average energy efficiencies in 1994–95 of 0.83, 0.34 and 0.04 net tonne km per MJ). Like buses, non-urban truck operations are much more energy efficient than urban operations (with respective average energy efficiencies in 1994–95 of 0.50 and 0.24 net km per MJ).

TABLE A.7
AUSTRALIAN DOMESTIC FREIGHT TASKS

	billion passenger km				
Year	Road	Govt rail	Private rail	Total rail	Sea
1970–71	27.2	25.2	13.8	39.0	72.0
1975–76	36.7	30.8	26.3	57.1	110.7
1984–85	74.3	45.0	28.4	73.4	95.7
1987–88	81.2	50.1	31.0	81.1	93.6
1990–91	88.2	53.3	35.3 ·	88.6	93.7
1994–95	114.4	61.8	38.1	99.9	109.2

SOURCE BTE (1996) for 1970–71, then ACG (1997) Table 3.9, p 33, Table 3.15, p 45, and Table 3.22, p 62
NOTE Air freight tasks of about 0.1 btkm in the 1980s, rising to 0.3 btkm in 1994–95 (Table 4.21, p 134)

TABLE A.8
AUSTRALIAN ROAD FREIGHT TASKS AND ENERGY USED

	billion tonne km		Petajoules		
Year	Artic trucks	Rigid	LCVs	Total	Energy (PJ)**
1975–76	23.0	12.1	1.6	36.7	173
1984–85	52.7	18.6	3.1	74.3	260
1987–88	59.7	21.5	4.3	85.5	279
1990–91	62.9	20.5	4.8	88.2	266
1994–95	85.4*	24.2	4.8	114.4*	311

SOURCE ACG (1997) Table 3.9, p 33 and Table 4.3, p 107
NOTE *ABS estimates are about 5 btkm higher for both articulated trucks and all trucks
**'Other trucks' use 2 to 3 PJ of extra energy, but no freight tasks are noted

TABLE A.9
AUSTRALIAN URBAN ROAD FREIGHT TASKS

Year	Artic trucks	billion tonne km Rigid	LCV's	Total (% of all road freight)	Energy used (PJ)*
1970–71	3.0	5.4	0.7	9.1 (34)	na
1974–75	5.7	6.4	1.0	13.1 (37)	na
1984–85	13.4	9.9	1.8	25.1 (34)	120
1987–88	15.2	13.1	2.7	28.3 (34)	165
1990–91	14.0	12.2	2.9	29.0 (33)	127
1994–95	19.6	14.5	3.1	37.1 (32)	157

Source BTE (1996) for 1970–71, then ACG (1997) Table 3.9, p 33 and Table 4.3, p 107
Note ABS estimates are higher
*'Other trucks' use 2 to 3 PJ extra energy, but no freight tasks are noted
Note Lower implied energy efficiencies of urban freight movements
    ACG and ABS data for 1994–95 differ

TABLE A.10
ENERGY USED IN AUSTRALIAN FREIGHT TASKS

Year	Artic trucks	Petajoules Road freight	Rail freight	Sea freight	Domestic aviation (passengers and freight)
1975–76	42.1	173	20.9	39.4	48.5
1984–85	80.5	260	28.4	36.7	51.5
1987–88	86.6	279	30.0	37.0	61.2
1990–91	83.6	266	27.6	24.2	61.0
1994–95	102.8	311	27.6	26.2	83.6

Source ACG (1997) Table 3.9, p 33 and Table 4.3, p 107

TABLE A.11
AUSTRALIAN DOMESTIC FREIGHT ENERGY EFFICIENCY

Year	Road	Govt rail	Private rail	Total Rail	Sea
		net tonne km (tkm) per megajoule (MJ)			
1975–76	0.21	1.60	5.65	2.72	–
1984–85	0.29	1.83	7.06	2.57	2.61
1987–88	0.31	1.93	7.00	2.71	2.56
1990–91	0.33	2.31	7.79	3.21	3.86
1994–95	0.37	2.66	8.77	3.62	4.16

SOURCE ACG (1997) Table 4.11(b), p 118, Table 4.18, p 128, Table 4.22, p 136
 Air energy efficiency is given in Table 4.20, p 132 which notes energy efficiencies of only 0.02 to 0.03 net tkm per MJ
NOTE Remarks above re road freight. Line haul intercity road freight can now reach 1.00 or more net tkm/MJ. Line haul intercity rail freight depends on track condition and alignment. The high energy efficiency of private rail is due to the preponderance of iron ore haulage in the Pilbara using the world's most efficient trains.

APPENDIX B
AUSTRALIA'S GAUGE MUDDLE AND FUTURE PROSPECTS

PHILIP LAIRD

[Each Colony] … got the gauge it wanted, but the loss was Australia's.

Harding (1958, p 24)

Australia is notable as a country for having three different railway gauges in common use. These are standard gauge (1435 mm or 4'8.5"), a broad gauge (1600 mm or 5'3") and a narrow gauge (1067 mm or 3'6"). There are other gauges in less common use, such as that used by Queensland's sugar railways (610 mm or 2'). The story of Australia's gauge muddle could fill a book, with various accounts given by Harding (1958), Stevenson (1987) and Dunn (1989). More recent accounts are given by Fitch (1989, 1993), Kain (1995), Danvers et al (1995) and Laird (1995). What follows is a brief summary for the interested reader.

In 1848, the NSW Governor, Sir Charles Fitzroy was advised by the Secretary of State for the Colonies in London, Earl Grey, that with a view to the probability of various railway lines meeting, '… one uniform gauge should be established' and, that gauge should be the standard gauge of 4'8.5". However, an Irish railway engineer by the name of Shields persuaded the Sydney Railway Company that was formed to build a line to Parramatta, and then the NSW Legislature to seek approval for the Irish broad gauge of 5'3". This change of gauge was endorsed by the NSW Governor, Fitzroy and agreed to by Earl Grey in London in 1851 (Gunn, 1989). Subsequently, the Victorian Government settled on broad gauge, which was used for their first railway in 1854. The broad gauge was also used by South Australia for their first steam railway in 1856.

The matter could have rested there, except that the Sydney Railway Company then gained a new engineer, Wallace, who preferred standard gauge. The NSW Legislature then proposed, and a new Governor, Sir William Denison, agreed to revert to standard gauge in 1855. This was despite a request from the Secretary for State for the Colonies to reconsider the matter. Later that year, on 26 September 1855, a standard gauge railway was opened between Sydney and Parramatta. Shortly after the NSW Engineer-in-Chief for New Railways, John Whitton took up his post from England; he urged a change from standard gauge to broad gauge in 1857. At that stage, it would have only required the conversion of 37 km of track, four engines and some carriages. However, the NSW Government took a narrow view and decided against the move to a uniform broad gauge (Lee, 1988). This decision confirmed that Australia would have more than one railway gauge. John Whitton accepted the decision, and continued to build nearly 3500 km of standard gauge railways in NSW until his retirement in 1889. As well put by Harding (1958, p 24), each of New South Wales and Victoria '… got the gauge it wanted, but the loss was Australia's'.

In 1865, with the opening of a narrow gauge line from Ipswich to Grandchester in Queensland, Australia gained its third railway gauge. The narrow gauge was favoured for its lower track construction cost in hilly country. South Australia then used narrow gauge in 1870 (Port Wakefield–Hoyleton, later extended towards Broken Hill, Oodnadatta, and the Northern Territory) thus giving that State two gauges. The use of narrow gauge was followed by Western Australia in 1879 (Geraldton–Northampton). Meantime, Tasmania, whose first railway was opened in 1871 using broad gauge (Launceston–Deloraine) then settled on narrow gauge, with conversion to a uniform narrow gauge in that State effected by 1888.

It is of interest to note that New Zealand in the mid-1870s had all three gauges. New Zealand's first railway was opened in 1863 (Christchurch–Ferrymead) in broad gauge, followed by a standard gauge railway near Invercargill. However, in an ambitious public works program launched by Sir Julius Vogel in 1870, the decision to use narrow gauge for railways was settled on (Auckland 1873, Wellington 1874) and conversions of other gauges to narrow gauge were effected by 1877. This was in time for the advent of Christchurch–Dunedin services in 1878 and Dunedin–Invercargill services in 1879 on a uniform gauge. As it happened, the Provincial Governments were also abolished by the Central Government in 1876. This holds a lesson for Australia.

Other countries such as Britain, Canada and the United States that once had multiple gauges also made good progress in gauge standardisation in the later part of the 19th century. In Australia, interest in gauge standardisation, and a Federation of the Colonies, during the late 19th century was heightened on the linking of Sydney and Melbourne by rail at Albury in 1883 (with standard gauge meeting a broad gauge). This was followed by the linking of Melbourne and Adelaide in 1887 (with through broad-gauge track at Serviceton), and Sydney and Brisbane in 1888 (with standard gauge meeting a narrow gauge track at Wallangarra). In 1889, an English army officer, Major-General Edwards, in an official report on the Military Defences of Australia observed that (Barker, 1974, p 152): 'If, therefore, full benefit is to be obtained from the railways, a uniform gauge must be established, at all events on the through lines.'

Over 100 years later, this state of affairs was finally realised with the official opening on 4 June 1995 of the Adelaide–Melbourne gauge standardisation.

The Australian Constitution makes specific provision for the Commonwealth Parliament to make laws in respect to railway acquisition and construction. At the time of Federation, standard gauge was confined to New South Wales alone, but was favoured for future work. Under Section 51 (xxxiii) of the Constitution, and agreements with the South Australia and Western Australia Governments, the Commonwealth started in 1911, and completed in 1917, a standard gauge railway from Port Augusta to Kalgoorlie.

In 1921, a Royal Commission on Uniform Railway Gauge reported. Following the report, and agreements between the Commonwealth and relevant State Governments, construction of standard gauge links from Kyogle (in New South Wales) to South Brisbane were completed in 1930, and from Port Augusta to Port Pirie in 1937.

During the World War II (WWII) the many breaks of gauge — Kalgoorlie, Port Augusta, Port Pirie, Gladstone, Terowie, Wolseley, Mt. Gambier, Broken Hill, Tocumwal, Albury, Wallangarra and Clapham (south of Brisbane) — added immense difficulty to the war effort. This was not only in terms of use of additional locomotives and rolling stock, but also the extra manpower required '... upwards of 1600 service personnel at transfer points in addition to a large pool of civilians' for an annual average transfer of about 1.8 million tonnes of freight during WWII (Binns, 1956).

No gauge standardisation was undertaken during WWII. However, in March 1945, a major report 'Standardisation of Australia's Railway Gauges' was completed by Sir Harold Clapp (1875–1952 and former Commissioner for Victorian Railways from 1920 to 1939) for the Commonwealth. The three main proposals of the report were:

(i) Standardisation of gauges be effected between Fremantle–Perth and Kalgoorlie, the entire South Australian and Victorian broad gauge system, the South-East and Peterborough narrow gauge sections of the South Australian system, with acquisition and gauge conversion of the

Silverton Tramway between Cockburn and Broken Hill. Total cost: 44.318 million pounds.

(ii) A new standard gauge 'strategic and developmental railway' be provided to link Bourke, NSW to Townsville and Dajarra (near Mt. Isa) with new lines from Bourke via Barringun, Cunnamulla, Charleville, Blackall to Longreach, with gauge conversion from Longreach–Winton–Hughenden–Townsville–Dajarra and tributary lines. Total cost: 21.565 million pounds.

(iii) A new standard gauge 'strategic and developmental railway' be constructed from Dajarra to Birdum, and conversion of the narrow gauge Birdum–Darwin line to standard gauge. Total cost: 10.868 million pounds.

Sir Harold's report noted that for South Australia and Victoria '... If only the main trunk lines on which the interstate trains are operated were converted, it would virtually introduce within such States a multitude of break-of-gauge terminals resulting in confusion, disorganisation, and greatly increased operating costs'. This echoed a similar finding of the 1921 Royal Commission. The 1945 report also considered that the existing Perth–Kalgoorlie narrow gauge with its '... sharp curves and steep grades' could be abandoned in favour of a new standard gauge track with a new route and a third rail for dual gauge operation. This was finally achieved in the late 1960s. As well, the report found that '... standardisation without modernisation could not be justified' and economies from gauge standardisation would be secured '... not by maintaining a State outlook but by the railway systems being viewed as a whole from a national standpoint'.

However, parochial State viewpoints continued to prevail. South Australia was unhappy at the proposal for the new rail link to Darwin to go through Queensland (a debate that has continued into the 21st century), and, succeeded in having narrow gauge lines in the south eastern division (from Wolseley and through Mt Gambier, with branch lines) converted in the 1950s to broad gauge. This was on the understanding that eventually these lines would be converted to standard gauge. Western Australia and Queensland did not see '... any benefit to their particular States' in the proposals. Although NSW entered into agreements in 1946 to advance gauge standardisation in Victoria and South Australia, the NSW Government would not ratify the agreement. The net result, coupled with a change in Federal Government in 1949 from the Chifley to Menzies Government, was no progress on the conversion of broad to standard gauge. As a first step to providing standard gauge railway to Darwin through Alice Springs, some 348 km of standard gauge was provided between Stirling North and Marree, and opened for traffic in July 1957 (Harding, 1958).

The next major advance in gauge standardisation had to wait for a report of a Government Members Rail Standardisation Committee

(1956), chaired by Mr. W. Wentworth, with the main recommendation that: 'While there may be considerable doubts as to the justification for undertaking large-scale standardisation of Australian railways under present circumstances, there can be no reasonable doubt that the standardisation of certain main trunk lines is not only justified, but long over due.'

The Wentworth Committee, with the support of the Federal Parliamentary Labor Party (1956) strongly recommended three standard gauge projects: Wodonga to Melbourne, Broken Hill to Adelaide via Port Pirie, and Kalgoorlie to Perth and Fremantle. The Wentworth Committee (1956) noted the total cost at some 41.5 million pounds and considered that '... the saving in road construction costs would outweigh this many times, since, in default of gauge standardisation, our existing interstate highways would be pounded to pieces by heavy freight trailers which they were never designed to carry'. Following agreements between the Commonwealth, NSW and Victorian Governments work commenced on a new standard gauge track between Wodonga and Melbourne. In January 1962 the first standard gauge freight train ran between Sydney and Melbourne. Within twelve months, net freight tonnage increased by 32.5 per cent, followed by annual average increases of 8.6 per cent to 1973. Standard gauge passenger services (*Southern Aurora* and *Spirit of Progress*) commenced in April 1962.

A further major rail initiative of the Menzies Government was upgrading and gauge standardisation between Perth and Kalgoorlie. This was assisted by agreements with the WA Government and the establishment of an iron ore mine at Koolyanobbing and a steel mill at Kwinana. The new route included a dual gauge route through the Avon Valley from Midland to Northam, with high clearances and easy ruling grades of 1 in 200 to replace an older section with ruling grades of 1 in 40. This project made use of the 1940s survey initiated by Sir Harold Clapp, and the new line was commissioned in February 1966. The second major deviation was from Southern Cross to Kalgoorlie, through Koolyanobbing. The upgraded standard gauge line between Perth and Kalgoorlie was officially opened in August 1968. This work allowed Kalgoorlie–Perth freight train times to be reduced from 31 hours to 13 hours, and passenger train times from 14 to 8 hours (Bayley, 1973).

In 1963, following agreements between the Federal and SA Governments, a start was finally made on conversion of Port Pirie to Broken Hill to standard gauge. However, gauge standardisation did not extend to the branch lines from Gladstone and Peterborough. These two station yards then had the distinction of having three gauges, although Port Pirie was changed from three to just two gauges. The question of standard gauge from Adelaide access was deferred to another decade. A new standard gauge line was built between Cockburn and Broken Hill on an improved alignment, with compensation paid to the Silverton Tramway. The Indian Pacific Train commenced between Sydney and Perth in March 1970. Subsequently, the Esperance–Kalgoorlie and Leonora–Kalgoorlie lines were converted from narrow to standard gauge.

A new standard gauge line between Tarcoola and Alice Springs was started by the Whitlam Government in 1974, and completed by the Fraser Government in 1980. After numerous investigations, conversion of a broad gauge line to standard gauge from Crystal Brook near Port Pirie to Adelaide, on improved alignment, was finally effected in 1982. Freight services started in 1983, with passenger train services in 1984. This project was promoted by Australian National, who found that the benefits would exceed the costs over 25 years by a factor of 2.8, and raised loan funds for the project.

The remainder of the 1980's has to be seen as a lost decade for gauge standardisation. Although the Fraser Government in its last term of office had approved Commonwealth expenditure for providing standard gauge access to the main ports of Brisbane, Geelong and Melbourne, and the incoming Labor Party in 1983 promised '… Grants to States to continue gauge standardisation of intercapital rail links', not one kilometre of gauge standardisation took place under the Hawke Government. Moreover, work was stopped on the Alice Springs–Darwin railway, the State systems were starved of capital funds for rail, and some rail fuel excise was diverted to road works. The only rail achievement of the Hawke Government was the formation in 1991 of yet another rail system, the National Rail Corporation, to operate interstate rail freight services. As seen by Stevenson (1987, p 21), a Canadian authority, the Hawke Government '… appeared to attach a lower priority to rail transport than any other Commonwealth government since the Second World War. It was apparently much more interested in highway freight transport'.

A major advance in gauge standardisation occurred with the Keating Government's 'One Nation' rail capital works program announced in February 1992. After some delays to early 1993 in deciding that standard gauge from Adelaide to Melbourne should proceed through Geelong, and not Ballarat, work proceeded quickly and the converted standard gauge track was officially opened on 4 June 1995. The cost of associated works, to basic specifications, was about $167 million. About the same time V/Line Freight, converted some Victorian broad gauge grain lines to Portland to standard gauge at a cost of some $25 million. This cost was appreciably less than line closure and diversion of bulk freight to road at $30 million up front and $2.5 million a year. Some broad gauge grain lines in South Australia were subsequently converted to standard gauge. In 1997, freight trains using standard gauge were finally able to gain access to Brisbane's major port at Fisherman's Island — some 14 years after the outgoing Fraser Government had allocated funds for this.

One can ask why gauge standardisation has taken so long in Australia when North America, Western Europe and Britain had all but standardised their railway gauges before the end of the nineteenth century. The answer has to rest with parochial Colonial and State viewpoints coupled with a weak approach by the Federal Government to land transport. If the Australian Constitution had placed railways, like postal services and defence, as a full responsibility of the Commonwealth, then it is likely that at least the broad gauge tracks would have been converted to standard gauge in the early part of the twentieth century. However, probably due to the relative lateness of Federation in Australia (compared, for example, with Canada in 1867), the Constitution's main provisions for railways were limited and the States gained control of the railways. It then took 25 years for the first gauge conversion project (Kyogle–South Brisbane) to start, and 75 years for the acquisition of any State railways by the Commonwealth.

The Second World War gave a major incentive to the Commonwealth to progress gauge standardisation. Even so, the Chifley Government was unable to secure the necessary support of the States to implement Sir Harold Clapp's 1945 report. In place, the Menzies Government made progress with implementation of the 1956 Wentworth report with its more achievable but less ambitious scope. It is also likely that if Victoria had accepted the offer of the Whitlam Government to transfer their non-metropolitan railways to the Commonwealth in the 1970s, there would have been more and quicker conversion of broad to standard gauge.

There is still scope for gauge standardisation of the entire Victorian and South Australian broad gauge systems, or at least those that are not used for urban rail services. Until the remainder of the Victorian freight lines are converted to standard gauge, V/Line Freight will face increased operating costs as observed by the major 1921 and 1945 reports. A basic option, raised on the announcement of 22 February 1999 on the sale to private interests of V/Line Freight is providing standard gauge access to the Port of Geelong, reported (The *Age*, March 8, 1999) at a cost of $39 million with annual economic benefits of about $12 million. The cost of conversion of most of the broad gauge lines in rural Victoria was also estimated, and quoted at $180 million with annual economic benefits of up to $40 million, whilst the cost of conversion of the entire system, including metropolitan lines was estimated at $300 million (The *Age*, March 8, 1999, see also, Kain, 1995 for older estimates). As seen by the Maunsell report quoted by The *Age* (March 8, 1999), '... standardisation had the potential to improve transport efficiency for the whole of south-east Australia, integrating three states into one rail system'. Here, there is a case for some Commonwealth funding. The fact that V/Line freight was privatised in 1999 should not stop such funding. Coupled with standard gauge access to the Port of Geelong, there is a good case for standardisation of an existing broad gauge mainline, with all branches north of Benalla, between Albury to Melbourne. This would leave a broad gauge line between Melbourne and Mangalore Junction for later standardisation along with the remainder of the Victorian non-metropolitan system. Such an option would have benefits for Melbourne–Sydney/Brisbane land freight.

The question of gauge standardisation of Queensland's narrow gauge tracks is raised from time to time. However, Queensland Rail is now the strongest rail system in Australia, and has consolidated this position by the large Mainline Electrification projects of the 1980s, and the $590 million Mainline Upgrade program of the 1990s. Both projects included the construction of 160 km of high quality rail deviations to replace the sections of old track with steep grades and/or tight curvature. Accordingly, improving the rail links between Queensland and the remainder of Australia is now more important than gauge standardisation in Queensland. At present, Queensland is linked to NSW by a disused line at Wallangarra (where two gauges met — operating from 1888 to 1988), and the NSW North Coast standard gauge line from Maitland via Kyogle to Brisbane. This current rail connection is a 'long and winding track' with excessive tight radius curvature. A third possible connection is from near Boggabilla in NSW to east of Goondiwindi in Queensland, which would improve access from the Moree area to Brisbane's port. Newly developed dual gauge rolling stock could be used to advantage in such a situation.

If traffic warrants, and if a new tunnel is built under the Toowoomba Range, as currently proposed by Queensland Rail, a dual or standard gauge line could be built from east of Goondiwindi to Brisbane. Such a route, combined with minor upgrading of the existing secondary lines in NSW west of the Great Divide (from Cootamundra via Parkes, Dubbo, west of Werris Creek, Gunnedah and Moree) would have good potential to attract the bulk of Melbourne–Brisbane freight (Laird et al, 1998). This route could also have overhead clearances high enough to allow for the passage of double stacked containers. From near Goondiwindi, a standard gauge line could be later extended through an inland route towards Gladstone and its deep-water port, and possibly on to Darwin. A Queensland rail connection to Darwin has long been advocated, not only by Sir Harold Clapp, as above, but over 100 hundred years. More recent proposals include those of Endersbee (1994), and an Australian Transport and Energy Corridor (ATEC) Company that attracted the interest of the Prime Minister, Mr Howard in 1998. It is likely that an Alice

Springs–Darwin railway will be constructed, and an ATEC commissioned pre-feasibility study conducted in 2000 with the support of the Commonwealth and three State Governments showed some promise (BTE, 2000b).

It remains to be seen how long Australia will proceed into the 21st century with multiple railway gauges impeding significant freight flows. However, more important than standardising narrow gauge railways in Australia is the question of gaining a truly efficient land freight system. This will require the upgrading of mainline rail track with selected rail deviations and residual gauge standardisation of broad gauge lines.

APPENDIX C
FEDERAL FUNDING OF AUSTRALIAN LAND TRANSPORT

PHILIP LAIRD

> The Commonwealth is a big spender on roads, at the expense of
> rail and urban public transport.
>
> From text

The total Federal outlay in grants for roads and the maintenance and enhancement of roads, including the National Highway System (NHS), along with rail funding, is given in Table C.1. Table C.2 indicates that the total Federal expenditure on the NHS from 1 July 1974 to 30 June 1999 was approximately $17.9 billion in constant 1998–99 prices. This estimate exceeds that of $11 million given by HORSCTCMR (Federal Department of Finance, 1997, p21). Of the $17.9 billion, a broadly estimated $3.9 billion ($3.66 billion from Table C.2 plus say $250 million maintenance from 1980 to 1991) has been expended on the reconstruction and maintenance of the Hume Highway (Laird, 1999).

Table C.1 gives items of Commonwealth expenditure on rail for each financial year in summary form, as current, whilst expenditure in constant 1998–99 dollars is given in Table C.2. Both tables exclude outlays under structured Urban Public Transport programs administered by the Department of Transport, which are given in Table C.5, as a total of some $1.5 billion. For each financial year from July 1975 to June 1992, the largest item of expenditure on rail was for Australian National (AN) in the form of revenue supplements. Table 2 also shows a general reduction of deficits by AN over time.

The main items of Commonwealth expenditure on rail to 30 June

1999, excluding AN, are for National Rail, the 1992–95 'One Nation' rail capital works program, and loan advances that were made under the National Railway Network (Financial Assistance) Act 1978. The total of Federal allocations for rail from 1 July 1974 to 30 June 1999 in constant 1998–99 dollars was approximately $5.4 billion, of which $4.2 billion was for AN revenue supplements. This left, in broad terms, about $1.2 billion for rail capital works plus National Rail equity.

These outlays have partly been offset by Commonwealth revenue from loan repayments and interest to the Commonwealth. Details from 1 July 1974 to 30 June 1999 for AN loans and advances to the States are given in Tables C.3 and C.4 for current and constant 1998–99 prices respectively. In constant 1998–99 prices, this revenue was about $755 million, leaving a net Federal outlay of some $4.6 billion over 25 years (cf $3.86 billion in 1996–97 prices over 20 years (HORSCTCMR, 1998, p 121)); also, the net outlay by the Commonwealth on rail capital works plus National Rail equity from 1974 to 1999 is less than $1 billion in 1999 terms. Further analysis shows that the Commonwealth financially gained from the National Railway Network (Financial Assistance) Act 1978.

A further aspect of Commonwealth revenue from rail has resulted from the liability of the rail systems from August 1982 to June 2000 to pay fuel excise on diesel. Estimates of this revenue in current terms are presented in Table C.4 showing a total revenue to 30 June 1999 of nearly $2.4 billion in 1999 terms. In each of the financial years from 1985–86 to 1991–92 and 1995–96 and from 1997–98, Commonwealth revenue from government rail systems, including fuel excise, appreciably exceeded Commonwealth expenditure on rail.

The Commonwealth is a big spender on roads, at the expense of rail and urban public transport.

TABLE C.1
COMMONWEALTH GROSS EXPENDITURE ON RAIL AND
ROADS $ MILLION — CURRENT DOLLARS

Year	AN rev sup etc	AN subtotal	Other rail
1974–75	46.5	62.5	0.2
1975–76	58.5	98.4	0.0
1976–77	47.6	76.2	0.1
1977–78	63.6	93.9	0.1
1978–79	63.8	110.1	0.2
1979–80	58.1	97.9	5.5
1980–81	56.0	78.6	15.6
1981–82	70.4	79.6	25.1
1982–83	106.0	114.5	22.3
1983–84	91.3	100.6	0.4
1984–85	87.9	111.9	0.5
1985–86	72.5	99.8	0.6
1986–87	64.5	73.5	0.0
1987–88	54.9	64	0.0
1988–89	51.0	61.3	0.0
1989–90	60.3	72.9	0.3
1990–91	70.6	77.5	40.8
1991–92	59.0	82.2	49.5
1992–93	59.0	87.6	286.0
1993–94	38.2	66.9	262.0
1994–95	27.0	59.2	203.0
1995–96	74.3	85.5	38.8
1996–97	30.1	389.2	6.1
1997–98	19.9	21.8	0.0
1998–99	0.0	0.0	40.0

SOURCES For Rail; to 1985–86 Holthuyzen (1987); thereafter to 1996–97, Department of
Finance and Administration (1997) with data converted to current values, and AN total
including free and concessional fares and to exclude all loan repayments; 1997–98 Dept
of Transport Annual Report. Laird (1994) gives details of expenditure to 1992–93.
For Road; to 1990–91, Laird (1994), then to 1997–98, Minister for Transport Media
Statement TR 87/97 (21-8-96), then Budget Papers.
RAIL KEY AN Rev Sup etc, AN annual revenue supplement, etc
AN total — Australian National total expenditure including annual revenue supple-
ments, payments for free and concessional fares and freight, and capital expenditure
Other rail — Commonwealth expenditure includes *National Railway Network (Financial
Assistance) Act 1978, National* Rail Corporation, and 'One Nation' rail capital program
ROADS KEY See Table C.2

| Total rail | Roads | | All tied | Untied |
	Hume	NHS	outlays	outlays
62.7	38	109	368	
98.4	46	134	442	
76.3	58	158	434	
94	68	175	478	
110.3	64	186	508	
103.4	55	205	565	
94.2	45	253	628	
104.7	39	303	685	
136.8	63	386	851	
101	63	519	1195	
112.4	74	542	1242	
100.4	120	559	1245	
73.5	119	578	1245	
64	113	549	1245	
61.3	107	474	1217	
73.2	91	521	1335	
118.3	141	554	1561	
131.7	197	661	1253	353
373.6	229	872	1701	363
328.9	208	790	1024	508
262.2	133	819	825	687
124.3	80	834	841	729
395.3	41	728	846	758
21.8	55	702	845	761
40	68	668	838	819

TABLE C.2
COMMONWEALTH GROSS EXPENDITURE ON RAIL AND
ROADS $ MILLION — 1998–99 DOLLARS

Year	Inflation indices	AN rev sup etc	Total rail
1974–75	4.357	272	273
1975–76	3.737	368	368
1976–77	3.353	255	256
1977–78	3.095	291	291
1978–79	2.901	319	320
1979–80	2.647	259	274
1980–81	2.390	188	225
1981–82	2.148	171	225
1982–83	1.934	221	265
1983–84	1.812	182	183
1984–85	1.710	191	192
1985–86	1.597	159	160
1986–87	1.486	109	109
1987–88	1.392	89	89
1988–89	1.285	79	79
1989–90	1.207	88	88
1990–91	1.156	90	137
1991–92	1.135	93	150
1992–93	1.120	98	418
1993–94	1.109	74	365
1994–95	1.098	65	288
1995–96	1.067	91	133
1996–97	1.045	407	413
1997–98	1.030	22	22
1998–99	1.000	0	40
Total		4 184	5 365

Sources Inflation indices are based on the Gross Non-Farm product price deflators, as per Table 5.
Rail Key See Table C.1
Roads Key The Hume Highway outlay is for all construction, plus maintenance to 1980 and then from 1988, with data to 1992–93 from reply from Minister for Transport to Question on Notice No 1851 (see Hansard for 16 December 1992) except from 1981–82 to 1985–86, which is from Department of Transport Annual Reports, as is data from 1993–94 to 1997–98, with advice from this Department for 1998–99 and other data

	Roads		Tied	Untied
Hume		NHS	total	
163		473	1604	
172		501	1652	
193		530	1454	
210		541	1479	
184		539	1474	
146		542	1496	
108		605	1501	
83		650	1471	
121		747	1646	
115		940	2166	
126		927	2123	
191		893	1988	
177		859	1851	
158		765	1733	
138		609	1565	
110		629	1611	
162		641	1805	
223		751	1423	400
256		976	1904	406
231		876	1136	564
146		899	906	754
85		890	897	778
43		761	884	792
57		722	870	784
68		668	838	819
3 664		17 933	37 476	5 297

NHS — Commonwealth expenditure on National Highway System
Roads tied total — Commonwealth tied expenditure on all roads
Road untied — Commonwealth untied grants to States with a view to road expenditure

TABLE C.3

ESTIMATES OF COMMONWEALTH REVENUE FROM RAIL $MILLION
— CURRENT DOLLARS

Year	AN total	States total
1974–75	0.01	7.19
1975–76	0.04	5.25
1976–77	0.37	5.23
1977–78	0.42	5.2
1978–79	11.64	3.61
1979–80	4.44	5.16
1980–81	4.22	6.85
1981–82	4.22	7.03
1982–83	4.22	6.44
1983–84	4.89	15.46
1984–85	6.28	20.13
1985–86	28.21	19.79
1986–87	10.19	19.09
1987–88	12.77	19.06
1988–89	9.47	19
1989–90	4.49	15.85
1990–91	11.02	15.59
1991–92	50.2	14.69
1992–93	3.05	14.35
1993–94	4.94	14.04
1994–95	7.33	12.87
1995–96	1.71	12.63
1996–97	11.2	12.12
1997–98	0.00	9.4
1998–99	0.00	3.1

SOURCES The AN and States loan repayments include interest, and are from Department of
Transport Annual Reports to 1997–98, with advice from this Department for 1998–99.
See Key on Table 4 for details of loans and Laird (1994) for disaggregation to 1992–93.
Fuel estimates to 1994 derived from various sources, as per Laird (1994), then from
rail systems to 1997, then broad estimates

Total	Estimated fuel use (M.litres)	Excise rate (c/L)	Untied
7.20			
5.29			
5.60			
5.62			
15.25			
9.61			
11.07			
11.25			
10.66	600	5.2	31
20.35	614	9.0	55
26.41	600	9.5	57
48.00	590	12.3	73
29.28	589	19.7	116
31.83	602	20.5	123
28.47	553	21.8	121
20.34	536	23.5	126
26.60	492	25.2	124
64.89	455	25.9	118
17.40	460	26.2	121
18.98	491	*	137
20.20	474	*	111
14.34	468	33.7	158
23.32	480	34.6	166
9.40	470	34.7	163
3.10	470	34.7	163

Fuel excise in cents per litre is an estimate of the average rate for each financial year
*Estimates for total fuel excise are modified for the use of light fuel oil in 1993–94 and
1994–95 at a then much lower excise rate — see James (1995) and Laird (1996)

TABLE C.4
REAL COMMONWEALTH REVENUE FROM RAIL EXCLUDING FUEL
EXCISE ($MILLIONS — CONSTANT 1998–99 DOLLARS)

Year	AN total	States total	Total	Rail fuel excise	Total
1974–75	0	31	31		31
1975–76	0	20	20		20
1976–77	1	18	19		19
1977–78	1	16	17		17
1978–79	34	10	44		44
1979–80	12	14	25		25
1980–81	10	16	26		26
1981–82	9	15	24		24
1982–83	8	12	21	60	81
1983–84	9	28	37	100	137
1984–85	11	34	45	97	143
1985–86	45	32	77	116	192
1986–87	15	28	44	172	216
1987–88	18	27	44	172	216
1988–89	12	24	37	155	192
1989–90	5	19	25	152	177
1990–91	13	18	31	143	174
1991–92	57	17	74	134	207
1992–93	3	16	19	135	154
1993–94	5	16	21	152	173
1994–95	8	14	22	122	144
1995–96	2	13	15	168	184
1996–97	12	13	24	174	198
1997–98	0	10	10	168	178
1998–99	0	3	3	163	166
Total	292	462	755	2384	3139

SOURCE Table C.3 and the inflation indices in Table C.2
KEY
AN Total — Australian National loan repayments and interest for AN
States Total — loan repayments and interest from the states for gauge standardisation
    advances to NSW, Vic and WA before 1973 and for the National Railway Network
    (Financial Assistance) Act 1978 (NRN(FA)) outlays
Rail fuel excise — Commonwealth revenue from rail fuel excise
Total Rev — denotes estimates of revenue from loan repayments, interest, and Federal fuel
    excise

TABLE C.5
COMMONWEALTH EXPENDITURE ON URBAN PUBLIC TRANSPORT

($millions — current dollars)		($millions — constant 1998–99 dollars)	
Year	Total UPT	Product deflator	Index
1974–75	45.0	277	4.357	196.1
1975–76	33.9	323	3.737	126.7
1976–77	58.4	360	3.353	195.8
1977–78	51.0	390	3.095	157.8
1978–79	40.0	416	2.901	116.1
1979–80	40.0	456	2.647	105.9
1980–81	45.0	505	2.390	107.6
1981–82	0.0	562	2.148	0.0
1982–83	2.5	624	1.934	4.8
1983–84	19.9	666	1.812	36.1
1984–85	24.6	706	1.710	42.1
1985–86	31.7	756	1.597	50.6
1986–87	35.0	812	1.486	52.0
1987–88	49.2	867	1.392	68.5
1988–89	22.4	939	1.285	28.8
1989–90	0.0	1000	1.207	0.0
1990–91	42.2	1044	1.156	48.8
1991–92	86.2	1063	1.135	97.9
1992–93	93.2	1078	1.120	104.4
1993–94	0.0	1088	1.109	0.0
1994–95	0.0	1099	1.098	0.0
1995–96	0.0	1131	1.067	0.0
1996–97	0.0	1155	1.045	0.0
1997–98	0.0	1172	1.030	0.0
1998–99	0.0	1207	1.000	0.0
720.2				1539.8

SOURCE Annual Reports of the Department of Transport. Laird (1994) gives more details
NOTE These amounts exclude Commonwealth allocations under the Better Cities programs
Gross Non-Farm product price deflators are multiplied by 1000

APPENDIX D
AUSTRALIAN ROAD PRICING AND HEAVY TRUCKS

PHILIP LAIRD

'... there is ample evidence that heavy vehicles are currently not paying for the damage they impose on Australian roads'.

Bureau of Transport Economics (1984)

Considerable efforts have been made by Government in Australia over the years to estimate what road system charges can be reasonably attributed to different types of heavy trucks along with estimates of revenues from road-user charges. Early work included that of the Board of Inquiry into the Victorian Land Transport System (Bland, 1972) and the Commission of Enquiry into the NSW Road Freight Industry (McDonell, 1980, Vol. IV). During the 1980s, further work included that of the National Road Freight Industry Inquiry (1984), three reports of the Inter-State Commission (ISC, 1986,1987,1990), the Bureau of Transport Economics (BTE, 1988) and the Royal Commission into Grain Storage, Handling and Transport (1988).

With the exception of the Grain Commission, there was agreement in the above cited reports that the heavier articulated trucks hauling long distances were making less than adequate contributions to road system costs. Even using a broad definition of revenue to include sales taxes and customs duties as well as registration charges and all fuel taxes, McDonell (1980) found that '... the road freight industry is making less than equitable contributions towards road construction and related costs'.

Following a review of this and 11 other studies into various aspects of the road freight industry, the Bureau of Transport Economics

(1984) concluded that '... there is ample evidence that heavy vehicles are currently not paying for the damage they impose on Australian roads'. The National Road Freight Industry Inquiry (1984) also found hidden subsidies to articulated truck operations on arterial roads.

The ISC (1987) found that although the general taxes paid by the owners of heavy vehicles are high, road-user charges in the form of registration fees and those fuel taxes applied directly to road works are low; and, that these taxes and charges do not cover the fully distributed financial costs of road works attributable to heavy truck operations.

A Commission of Audit for the New South Wales Government (Curran, 1988) also acknowledged under recovery of road system costs. This report also noted that the transport 'playing field' is not level, and under taxation of heavy vehicles disadvantages the State Rail system.

Significant changes in road pricing for heavy trucks took place in the 1980s, following abandonment by the States of a system of road maintenance charges in 1979 after widespread truck blockades. These charges were introduced in the late 1950s (following the decision of the Privy Council in London to overturn an earlier High Court decision that had allowed the States to restrict interstate trucking) and were based on the distance travelled and assigned mass of the truck. The removal of the road maintenance charges was followed by all States except Queensland imposing a diesel fuel franchise fee, and the Federal Government increasing fuel excise taxes. In 1987, following a report by the ISC (1986), the Federal Government introduced a Federal Interstate Registration Scheme (FIRS) in 1987 that included the option of mass-distance charging.

As part of a national relaxation of mass and dimension limits, NSW and Victoria introduced a permit scheme in 1987–88 for heavy vehicles that operated above the then standard mass limits. This included an option for a six-axle articulated truck lifting its Gross Vehicle Mass (GVM) from 38 tonnes to 42.5 tonnes, with an annual NSW permit fee of $3120 in addition to a current annual registration fee of about $4000. A modification of FIRS in 1988 also allowed the option of a six-axle articulated truck lifting its GVM from 38 tonnes to 42.5 tonnes for a registration fee of $3285. This was met with truck blockades in July 1988 and an apparent undertaking by the Federal Government not to increase these fees until a full review had taken place.

The ISC (1990) recommended that the heavier long distance trucks pay a mass-distance charge along with an annual registration fee and fuel taxes, and, that a national scheme be established for the registration and charging of all vehicles operating in Australia.

THE NATIONAL ROAD TRANSPORT COMMISSION

Following an agreement made by the Commonwealth, all States and the ACT Government at the July 1991 Special Premiers Conference (SPC), a National Road Transport Commission (NRTC) was established. In June 1992, the NRTC (1992) gave its determination on heavy vehicle road-user charges. These charges were subsequently approved by a Ministerial Council with a view to implementation by July 1995. However, Western Australia did not agree on the grounds that the proposed charges were too high, and New South Wales did not agree until 1996 to implement the charges on the grounds that the proposed charges would cost that State up to $75 million a year, and, that the proposed charges for trucks were generally too low.

In essence, the heavy vehicle road-user charges determined by the NRTC (1992) included that:

a The component of diesel fuel excise regarded as a road-user charge (as opposed to a general tax) be set at 18 cents per litre.

b Annual charges for freight and passenger carrying heavy vehicles be given by a schedule with uniform rates across Australia and that the charges for each type of articulated truck (by number of axles) be the same, irrespective of GVM.

The NRTC annual charges were also designed, in aggregate for heavy vehicles over 4.5 tonnes GVM, to be 'revenue neutral' compared with current road-user charges, and to raise an aggregate amount of about $370 million throughout Australia as compared with current 1992–93 registration revenues of about $362 million (NRTC, 1992).

The NRTC faced considerable difficulties in arriving at road-user charges for Australia-wide heavy truck operations. These difficulties included:

a A long-standing variation in road-user charges across the 9 different jurisdictions (Federal, 6 States, 2 Territories) for a given type of truck at a given GVM.

b Wide ranging views on what revenues from heavy truck operators should be treated as road-user charges, and what revenues should be treated as general taxation.

c Wide ranging estimates for road system costs attributable to heavy truck operations including those noted in Chapter 4 from $4000 to $44 000 for six-axle articulated truck annual average road costs. Further to these estimates was advice to truck operators from the Federal Land Transport Minister, the Hon. Bob Brown MHR, by way of letter in September 1991, that the annual charges for the heavier articulated trucks would likely be in the $7000 to $8000 range.

d Federal involvement in road-user charging (except for the ACT) mainly restricted to the Federal Interstate Registration Scheme (FIRS).

e Abolition of the Inter-State Commission (ISC) in 1990. During its operation since 1984, the ISC had produced three definitive reports on road cost recovery from heavy trucks, and had developed considerable expertise in this area.

f Failure over the years of the Australian Transport Council (comprising Australia's many Transport Ministers) to effectively deal with issues of road cost recovery from heavy trucks.

g A very strong road transport lobby, that had made clear its preference for fuel only taxes, and its strong aversion to mass distance charges.

To allow the NRTC to work towards full road cost recovery from heavy vehicles by 1995, and to try and allow for the different annual registration charges around Australia, the NRTC was given specific options, including:

a There would be two zones—a higher charging Zone A comprising NSW, Victoria, Tasmania and the ACT and a lower charging Zone B with Queensland, SA and WA.

b There would be three levels of charge for each type of truck (the OAG concept) based on GVM; effectively for light, medium and heavy mass options. The lower limit was for trucks where no mass-distance charges would be required, and the higher limit for six-axle articulated trucks would apply for those trucks with a GVM of 42.5 tonnes.

c Road trains could be charged at lower rates, to allow full cost recovery to be phased in by the year 2000.

In setting road-user charges in 1992, the NRTC dispensed with zones, charges dependent on GVM, and a form of mass distance charges for the heavier trucks hauling large annual distances offset by lower rates for road trains operating in remote areas. The concessions granted to the road industry by the NRTC set back many of the advances made during the 1980s, and invite attention, as follows:

1 The heavy reliance on fuel use as a charging mechanism.

2 A substitution of average gross operating mass (AGM) for equivalent standard axles (ESA) for the attribution of separable pavement costs.

3 The view that demand for trucking services would not be appreciably affected by the road-user charges.

As noted in Chapter 5, the resultant NRTC charges fell far short of 'user pays'. Indeed, the former NRTC chairman confirmed ('Recession puts truck plan off road', *Sydney Morning Herald* April 13, 1992) that 'it would be "untenable" to stick to the agreement to make operators pay by 1995 for all their [road] damage'. Moreover, the NRTC (1993, page 9) openly acknowledged that there is '... under-recovery from six axle and larger articulated trucks'.

Although the NRTC annual charges generally represented an increase in annual registration fees for trucks registered in most States, they decreased charges for many trucks registered in NSW, with a marked decrease for B-Doubles registered under FIRS (from over $11 000 a year as set in 1991 by the Federal Parliament to $5500 a year (8 axle)). The NRTC charges have cost NSW over $50 million a year since their introduction in 1996.

FUEL CHARGES

The NRTC (1992), in addition to giving consideration of a Fuel-Only Charge Option (with further consideration given by NRTC, 1993), assigned as part of the diesel fuel tax (excise) as a road-user charge a value of 18 cents a litre. This was nearly 3 cents per litre above what the ISC (1990) had considered as fair.

Reservations about the use of fuel taxes as a way of charging for road use are longstanding. For example, the former Industries Assistance Commission (IAC, 1986) noted that although such taxes had an '... intuitive appeal', this approach had deficiencies and raised the need for consideration of alternative charging instruments, including congestion charges and vehicle-kilometre charges (including mass-distance charges as raised by the ISC (1990)). The IAC (1986, p115) took the view that steps should be taken to replace fuel taxes '... with other better targeted charging devices' as soon as possible.

One problem with fuel use as a road-user charge is that fuel use, in litres per 100 kilometres varies appreciably between similar trucks depending on many factors including the skill of the driver, the type of truck engine, terrain and road conditions along with the Gross Vehicle Mass (and hence the axle loads). The NRTC noted that (average) fuel use by six-axle articulated trucks varied between States from 53.8 to 58.0 litres per 100 km. A Land Freight Transport Energy Evaluation project (Laird and Adorni-Braccesi, 1993) found that the average fuel use in Australia for six-axle articulated trucks from the 1991 SMVU was 51.7 litres per 100 km, as opposed to about 55 litres per 100 km in 1988 with a wide variation of fuel use based on a respectable ABS sample size of about 2200, also, the average distance travelled by six-axle articulated trucks tended to increase the GVM. Moreover, for the heavier six-axle articulated trucks, as well as a wide variation of fuel use, there were significant numbers of heavier trucks using fuel at a low rate of 45 litres or less per 100 km travelled.

In terms of the fuel component of road-user charges set at 18 cents per litre, for a six-axle articulated truck hauling say 120 000 km per year, and using fuel at the NRTC average rate of 55.5 litres per 100 km, a charge of $11 988 would be imputed. However, there are some six-axle articulated trucks hauling 120 000 km per year using fuel at a high rate with a charge of at least $14 000 being imputed. There are even more such trucks using fuel at a low rate with a charge of at most $9720 being imputed. The difference in imputed road-user charge between these two categories of fuel use for a heavy six-axle articulated truck is then over $4000 a year.

This is one of many problems with heavy reliance on fuel taxes for road pricing. A further problem is that since the 1990s, there has been a clear increase in average gross operating mass for six-axle articulated trucks along with an increase in fuel efficiency. Whilst this is commendable for improving productivity and energy efficiency, it does have implications for economically efficient road pricing.

COST ATTRIBUTION FOR ROAD WORKS

Road wear and tear is obvious on any road that is used extensively by heavy trucks. The cost of maintaining an arterial road constructed and paved to reasonable standards depends mainly on the road pavement wear and tear that is quantified by using the concept of an Equivalent Standard Axle Loading (ESAL) where road pavement usage is related to the fourth power of the axle loading. A six-axle articulated truck with 38 tonnes Gross Vehicle Mass (GVM) has an ESAL of 3.38, and an average sized family car has an ESAL of about 0.0003 (ISC, 1986, p476). These figures give rise to an oft-quoted rule that the pavement damage done by the passage of a loaded semi-trailer is about 10 000 times the damage of an average car.

During 1987 and 1988, there was a two stage relaxation in NSW of gross vehicle mass (GVM) limits for six-axle articulated trucks from 38 tonnes to 42.5 tonnes. Whilst this increase in GVM appears slight, the number of ESALs increases sharply from 3.38 to 5.06 ESALs or by 50 per cent. This is about 15 000 times the pavement wear and tear of an average car.

A fully laden B-Double has 20 000 times or more the ESALs.

In road cost allocation, there is general agreement that costs for a particular vehicle over a given road can be determined as a function of vehicle kilometres, Passenger Car Units (1 for a car, 2 for a rigid truck, and 3 for an articulated truck etc), average gross operating mass kilometres (AGM kms) and equivalent standard axle kilometres (ESA kms).

The ISC (1990) had allocated 60 per cent of pavement construction and maintenance costs on the basis of ESA kms. The NRTC, after consideration, chose to retain ESA kms for separable pavement maintenance costs and to substitute AGM km for ESA kms for separable pavement construction costs. Changes of this nature were noted by a consultant to the NRTC in 1992 as reducing the road track cost for a six-axle articulated truck travelling 120 000 km a year by almost $5000 a year.

This major change in road cost allocation methodology by the NRTC clearly favoured the heavier long distance trucks. Excluding ESA kilometres for pavement construction costs does not take into account the additional costs incurred when either providing 'crawling lanes' for heavier trucks on multi lane highways, the cost of strengthening bridges for heavier loads, or the extra cost of providing 'rigid' pavements in highway construction.

The NRTC methodology for calculating charges for the heavier articulated trucks results in lower charges than almost all studies conducted during the 1990s, as per Table D.1.

TABLE D.1
ESTIMATES OF ROAD SYSTEM COSTS ATTRIBUTABLE TO ARTICULATED TRUCKS

Study	Year	Road system	Road system costs ($ million)	costs attributable to articulated trucks ($ million)	%
NRFII	1981–82	Arterial	1276	389	30.5
NSW	1984–85	All roads	1595	369	23.1
BTCE	1985–86	Arterial	4200	1963	46.7
ISC	1989–90	Arterial	2630	563	21.4
NRTC	Early 90s	Arterial	4515	702	16.9
Australia	1997–98	All roads	7014	1995	27.9

SOURCES National Road Freight Industry Inquiry (1984), Laird (1990), BTCE (1988), ISC (1990), NRTC (1993) and text for 1997–98

DEMAND FOR TRUCKING SERVICES

It is an old argument how demand for trucking may be influenced by road pricing. Often, it will suit a government agency such as the NRTC to conclude that demand for trucking services will not appreciably depend on road pricing for heavy trucks. This argument deserves questioning, and some counter examples include:

1   Removal of a former $2–50 per tonne surcharge for certain road haulage of grain in South Australia leading to a shift from rail to road, and hence a transfer of costs to Local Government, and then the State Government following the Commonwealth's 1989 legislation that, inter alia, deregulated grain transport. This was well documented by the Industry Commission (1991a, Vol I, p115) in their report on Rail Transport.

2 An estimate, due to Australian National (IC, 1991b, Vol II, p53), of potential transfer of road freight to rail freight of 4.2 million tonnes of net freight by 1998–99 following upgrading rail to improve rail delivery times and other standards.

3 A broad estimate from a RORVL study (NAASRA, 1985), which gave a potential transfer of 3 million tonnes a year from rail to road with use of B-Doubles with their lower unit operating costs. One example was the transfer of oil from Brisbane to Maryborough from rail to B-Doubles.

The NRTC's charter includes a provision to seek improvements in transport efficiency. Higher NRTC road-user charges for heavy vehicles were introduced on 1 July 2000. However, as a result of a fall in excise, as seen by the Bureau of Transport Economics (1999d), competitive neutrality between road and rail would become worse.

THE NEW ZEALAND SCHEME

In New Zealand, all vehicles over 3.5 tonnes Gross Combination Mass (GCM) have been required to purchase distance licenses since 1978 (Laird, 1990). The actual road-user charges depend on the axle configurations and loadings for the vehicle and any trailers. The charges now include a 12.5 per cent Goods and Services Tax (GST). To aid compliance, each vehicle paying road-user charges must be fitted with an approved distance-measuring device such as a hubodometer. Efforts to minimise the evasion of road-user charges were addressed with 1989 Transport Law Reform legislation that included particular attention to hubodometers.

During 1995–96, road-user charges for heavy vehicles raised a total of $NZ425 million out of Transit New Zealand's road revenue of $NZ888 million — that is, about 48 per cent of the main source of road funds (New Zealand Ministry of Transport, 1997, p61). This is far in excess of the NRTC level of about 17 per cent of road funds being met from heavy vehicle charges, as per Table D.1.

Whilst the New Zealand scheme is not perfect, and would be difficult to implement in the remote areas of Australia, its underlying basis as recognised by the ISC (1990), does have merit for Australia's populous zone.

ESTIMATED 1997–98 ROAD SYSTEM COST ATTRIBUTABLE TO HEAVY TRUCKS

A general description of the approach adopted by the Commission of Enquiry into the NSW Road Freight Industry (McDonell, 1980, Vol. IV, Appendix 3.1) to calculate road system costs due to heavy trucks for 1997–98 was given by the ISC (1986, p267). Using this methodology, the total NSW road system costs attributable to all trucks were later calculated as $340 million for 1978–79, $488 million for 1981–82 and $666 million for 1984–85 (Laird, 1990).

It is stressed that these figures, like the ones that follow, are approximations based on limited data. McDonell (1980, Vol. IV, p1/3) noted there are serious data deficiencies affecting the road freight industry. Some 19 years later, the Productivity Commission (1999, p8) noted that 'There is a lack of up-to-date transport data in Australia, impeding public debate and sound policy formation'.

In brief, the approach used by the NSW Commission was a pay-as-you-go one to gain an estimate of the to improve and maintain the NSW road system for various categories of vehicle. These included light rigid trucks with less than 4.1 tonnes carrying capacity, heavier rigid trucks, articulated trucks and all other vehicles. Costs were identified as separable pavement costs (trucks), separable other costs (trucks), separable costs (non trucks), and common costs. For heavy vehicles, including buses, separable pavement costs were allocated using unit costs for equivalent standard axles when a heavy truck passed over one kilometre of average Australian road that were developed by NAASRA. Other separable costs for trucks such as easier grades, overtaking lanes and stronger bridges were found by using broad estimates provided by the NSW Government; as suggested by the ISC, these other separable costs may be allocated on the basis of gross vehicle weight kilometres. After making an allocation for separable costs for the various classes of vehicles, all other costs are regarded as common costs, which are allocated on the basis of 'passenger car equivalents'.

A modified version methodology developed by McDonell is now applied for 1997–98. The seven step process we use is as follows:

1   Determine the total expenditure T for the given financial year for expenditure on all roads, and, the combined figure R for arterial road maintenance and construction costs, by all levels of government.

2   Allocate separable pavement costs P due to all heavy vehicles using ESA kms.

3   Find 'other separable costs of heavy vehicles' Q for the larger roads, stronger bridges, extra passing lanes plus easier grades to accommodate heavy vehicles. Take Q as 15 per cent of R with allocation between each class of vehicle on the basis of AGM kms.

4   Assign separable costs S of all other vehicles as 11 per cent of T.

5   Evaluate the remaining costs as common costs, $C = T - P - Q - S$.

6   Allocate these common costs to various classes of vehicles on the basis of passenger car unit equivalent kilometres using 1 for a car, 2 for rigid truck, 3 for an articulated truck, 4 for B-Doubles and smaller road trains and 5 for larger road trains (NRTC, 1998).

7   Calculate the total attributable costs to each class of truck and other vehicles.

There is nothing to say that the modified McDonell methodology is 'correct'. In the same way, no one can claim that the methodology currently used by the NRTC is correct. What can be said is that both methodologies use estimates of data, and, make some use of each of ESA kms, AGM kms and passenger car equivalent kilometres.

From the 1998 Annual Report for the NRTC an estimated $4210 million (R) was applied to construction and maintenance of arterial roads. According to the BTE (1999), Federal, State and Local Government expenditure for construction and maintenance amounted on all Australian roads in 1997–98 to $7015 million, which is the amount T.

There is a question of the unit cost for an equivalent standard axle kilometre (ESA km). On the basis that the ISC (1990, p84) used 6.104 cents per ESA km for arterial roads in 1989–90, and using NSW Roads and Traffic Authority road cost indices (1999 RTA Annual Report, p78), a unit cost of 7.45 per ESA km is used. It will be argued by some that that this cost is either too high, and, will be argued by others that this unit cost is too low.

Using these assumptions, detailed NRTC (1998) data for 1997, as summarised in Table D.2, and the methodology outlined above, it is found that attributable road system costs in 1997–98 amounted to approximately $1955 million for all articulated trucks, and $545 million for all rigid trucks including truck-trailers. Under the NRTC scheme, cost recovery was in two parts, with annual charges totalling $422 million (NRTC, 1998, p23) and a fuel charge at 18 cents per litre. Using NRTC (1998, Table B.1) estimates, the fuel charge would be $793 million. This data also shows cost recovery of about $720 million from all articulated trucks, and $495 million from rigid trucks and truck-trailers. The resulting under-recovery of road system costs is seen to be about $1235 million from all articulated trucks, and $50 million from rigid trucks and truck-trailers.

If we accept the estimate of the articulated road freight task as 99.12 billion tonne km (the ABS, 2000b estimate for 1998–99), then the average hidden subsidy for road freight moved by articulated trucks is 1.25 cents per net tonne km. For haulage on lightly constructed regional roads, the hidden subsidy is higher, with earlier estimate of the NSW Roads and Traffic Authority noted by the Industry Commission (1991a) as 3 cents per net tkm.

NSW ROAD CRASH AND ENVIRONMENTAL COSTS

The cost of a road crash fatality was noted by the BTE (2000a) in 1996 as $1.5 million, the cost of a road crash requiring hospitalisation as $325 000, and the average unit cost of other injuries as $12 000. With Roads and Traffic Authority data for 1996 for NSW road crashes involving articulated trucks indicating 56 fatalities, 208 serious injuries

and 439 other injuries, the cost of NSW road crashes involving articulated trucks in 1996 is estimated as nearly $157 million.

From ABS (2000b) estimates for the road freight task for articulated trucks operating in NSW in 1998–99 as about 32.9 billion tonne
kilometres, the average unit cost of NSW road crashes involving articulated trucks is about 0.48 cents per net tonne km. We suggest a unit
cost in Australia of 0.5 cents per net tonne km.

For allocation of environmental costs of noise and air pollution, the
Inter-State Commission (1990, p 227) suggested inclusion of an externality charge of 8.1 cents per litre for diesel (and 5.1 cents per litre for
petrol) on 1989–90 data. Indexed to 1997–98 using data from Table
C.5, this is 9.96 cents per litre for diesel. Using NRTC (1998) estimates for fuel use, this results in environmental externality costs of
$282 million for articulated trucks, and $157 million for rigid trucks
and truck-trailers. These estimates are considered as conservative.

TABLE D.2
NRTC ROAD USE AND VEHICLE DATA 1997

Vehicle class	Distance travelled (million km)	PCU-km (million PCU-km)	AGM-km (million AGM-km)	ESA-km (million ESA-km)	Number of vehicles
Motor cycles	1531	1531	0	0	288185
Passenger vehicles	125588	125588	0	0	8610095
Light commercial vehicles	31351	31351	0	0	1709198
All rigid trucks	5146	10292	7974	2485	254780
Truck trailers	328	985	11982	925	4038
Articulated trucks					
3 axles	47	141	982	124	2234
4 axles	235	705	5796	519	5794
5 axles	489	1467	14417	1048	8195
6 axles	3373	10119	118571	8353	30218
More than 6 axles	12	36	508	46	124
B-Doubles					
Less than 8 axles	46	184	1583	54	172
8 axles	372	1488	18008	730	1725
More than 8 axles	144	576	8109	412	707
Road trains					
Two trailers	452	1808	29495	1993	3295
Three trailers	351	1404	29042	1335	1827
Articulated trucks — total	5521	17928	226511	14614	54291
Bus total	369	2738	9330	573	43156
Special purpose vehicles	132	264	2992	138	8900
All vehicles	170966	191438	303060	18734	10972605

APPENDIX E
TRANSPORT AND LAND USE PLANNING INTERACTIONS: A SYSTEMS APPROACH

MARK BACHELS AND PETER NEWMAN

It is better to deal incompletely with the whole than to
deal wholly with the incomplete.

Daly, 1980, p 12

This appendix provides a detailed systems analysis of the 49-city data set and identifies some of the key feedback mechanisms affecting car dependence in our cities. These results are largely taken from Bachels, Peet and Newman (1999).

There is complexity in the interaction between individual transport decisions and transport system effects. This complexity is shown in the systems analysis and diagrams below. We make our individual transport decisions based upon a number of factors including travel time, safety, cost, and access. In turn, our transport system decisions are made based upon very similar factors, in the short-term affected directly by individual decisions, and in the long-term affected by transport improvement decisions (like building additional road capacity or improving public transport networks). Our transport systems and individual modal choice decisions are also affected by land use changes and vice versa.

49-CITY DATA SET — INDICATORS AND REGRESSION ANALYSIS

This analysis utilises a set of data collected on urban transport and land use indicators. The indicator framework was developed for the Global Cities Study (Newman and Kenworthy 1989, 1998; and Kenworthy et al, 1997). The framework focuses on land transport characteristics of urban areas, including specific indicators on transport systems and their use, land use, economic activity and transport investment, and consequent environmental effects in terms of energy consumption and estimated air emissions.

Over 40 indicators were collected for 49 metropolitan areas for cities in the USA, Australia/New Zealand, Europe, Canada and Asia for 1990. For detailed results of city data refer to Newman and Kenworthy (1998); Kenworthy, Laube et al (1999); and Bachels, Newman and Kenworthy (1999).The 49-city data set is referred to as the Global Cities Data in this research.

Systems models (described below) are developed to qualitatively capture proposed influences between transport and land use policies, and transport choices. The Global Cities Data set is used to test the correlation relationships between the variables of these proposed influences.

PROPOSED SYSTEMS MODELS — DEVELOPMENT AND TEST RESULTS

Only the summary results of this research are presented; for further detail refer to Bachels (1999). Qualitative feedback models were developed for a number of planning policy issues including urban area and population density, road building, public transport provision and use, traffic safety and slow mode use, and traffic demand management measures. Variables for each of these system models were developed from the Global Cities Data. Regression analysis was then conducted for the 'strength' of relationship between variables as a means of 'testing' the validity of proposed qualitative feedback models. The results of the tests on each proposed systems model are presented below.

For each of the systems models shown, influences were proposed between variables and each influence was assigned an equation number (eg, 1a, 1b, 2, 3, etc.). Using the indicators collected in the Global Cities Data, each of the influence variables were assigned relevant indicators. Correlation analysis was then conducted on the relationship between variables of each systems model in order to test:

- the strength of the relationship between variables (the correlation of determination (r2) value);
- the statistical validity of the relationship (P value); and
- the 'polarity' of the proposed relationship (the positive or negative influence between variables).

Note higher values of the correlation of determination (r^2) indicate a stronger relationship between variables; P values less than 0.005 were generally obtained suggesting statistically valid results.

Figures for each of the proposed systems models are presented below in an influence diagram, where influence between variables is indicated by an arrow and a sign of polarity (+ or −). Statistical correlation results from testing the relationships (r^2, P values and mathematical 'polarity') are then presented in tables for each of the proposed systems models.

'ROAD BUILDING' SYSTEMS MODEL TEST

The road building systems model is shown Figure E.1 and proposes that building more roads (and road capacity) results in increasing car use, which with current planning policies results in increasing demand for road infrastructure, and overall a positive unchecked feedback. Note that one significant policy instrument is depicted — the benefit-cost evaluation criteria which is typically used in decisions to increase road capacity.

Figure E.1 includes the relative 'weighting' of influence where a heavier line indicates a higher r^2 value — the result of the correlation analysis shown below in Table E 1 (e.g., the influence (r^2) of population density on car use (equation 1) had a reasonably high r^2 value and thus received a heavy line, whereas the relationship between urban area and car use (equation 2) showed a statistically significant but lower r^2 value and is indicated by a dotted line).

FIGURE E.1
ROAD BUILDING SYSTEMS MODEL

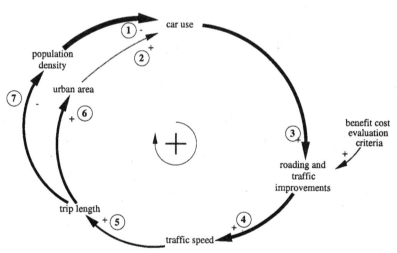

The results of correlation analysis on each influence factor of the road building systems model are shown in Table E 1. The correlation results indicate a strong mechanism for positive unchecked feedback increasing car use from independent planning policies — where increasing roading provision increases travel speed and trip length, increasing the urban area and decreasing population density which both lead to increasing car use, which again leads to a need to build more road capacity. Importantly, all of the polarity signs of influence of the systems model are supported by the mathematical functional relationships (negative/positive power functions), supporting the premise of unchecked positive system feedback of the 'road building' model.

TABLE E.I
TESTING ROAD BUILDING SYSTEMS MODEL — CORRELATION ANALYSIS RESULTS

Systems Model Equation	Correlation of determination r^2 (or % change in Y explained by change in X)	Statistical significance (P value)	Mathematical relationship
I	0.816	0.000	negative power
2	0.177	0.003	positive power
3	0.751	0.000	positive power
4	0.671	0.000	positive power
5	0.431	0.000	positive power
6	0.437	0.000	positive power
7	0.477	0.000	negative power

THE URBAN FORM (AREA AND DENSITY) SYSTEMS MODEL

The 'urban form' systems model was developed proposing a number of interactions between urban land use policies and transport choices, shown in Figure E.2.

FIGURE E.2
URBAN FORM SYSTEMS MODEL

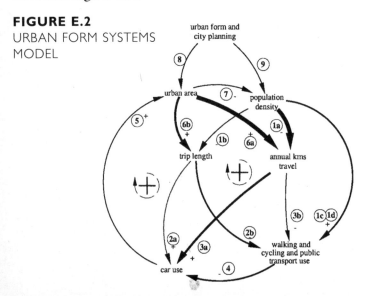

TABLE E.2

TESTING URBAN FORM SYSTEMS MODEL — CORRELATION ANALYSIS RESULTS

Systems Model Equation	Correlation of determination r^2 (or % change in Y explained by change in X)	Statistical significance (P value)	Mathematical relationship
1a	0.816	0.000	negative power
1b	0.477	0.000	negative power
1c	0.572	0.000	positive power
1c	0.548	0.000	positive power
1c	0.644	0.000	positive power
1d	0.636	0.000	positive power
2a	0.165	0.015	positive power
2b	0.277	0.001	negative power
2b	0.418	0.000	negative power
2b	0.376	0.000	negative power
3a	0.674	0.000	positive power
3b	0.551	0.000	negative power
4	0.696	0.000	negative power
5	0.221	0.003	positive power
6a	0.912	0.000	positive power
6b	0.437	0.000	positive power
7	0.226	0.001	negative power
8	policy		
9	policy		

The correlation analysis conducted to test the urban form systems model clearly indicates that increasing urban area and decreasing population density results in increasing trip length and travel per annum, decreasing use of alternative transport, and overall, positive unchecked feedback for increasing car use, with positive and potentially unintended increases in private car use (and subsequent transport energy use).

PUBLIC TRANSPORT SYSTEMS MODEL — SERVICE PROVISION AND USE

The proposed public transport systems model shown in Figure E.3 suggests that increasing service quality results in increasing use and increasing fares revenue, which when combined with funding policies, can result in increasing service provision and generally a positive feedback loop (or conversely, decreasing public transport use results in less service and in turn less use).

FIGURE E.3
PUBLIC TRANSPORT SYSTEMS MODEL

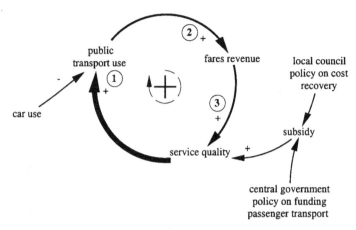

The correlation analysis for each proposed influence is shown in Table E.4. Overall, the correlation analyses confirms that increasing service delivery yields both increasing public transport use (trips per capita) and increasing fare revenue (where cost recovery was used as a proxy for fares revenue), with highly significant statistical correlations for all relationships modelled.

TABLE E.3
TESTING PUBLIC TRANSPORT SYSTEMS MODEL — CORRELATION ANALYSIS RESULTS

Systems Model Equation	Correlation of determination r^2 (or % change in Y explained by change in X)	Statistical significance (P value)	Mathematical relationship
1	0.825	0.000	positive power
2	0.450	0.000	positive power
3	0.423	0.000	positive power
4	0.635	0.000	negative power

Importantly, the results of the correlation analysis support a positive feedback mechanism for public transport, which when affected by increasing car use, quickly turns to a vicious cycle of reducing public transport use.

SLOW MODE SAFETY SYSTEMS MODEL

The 'slow mode safety' systems model shown in Figure E.4, proposes that increasing car traffic speeds and volumes deter cyclist and pedestrian activities.

The results of the correlation analysis are shown in Table E.6. The results generally confirm that positive feedback is exhibited where increasing traffic decreases safety for slower modes which decreases their use. And importantly all of the polarities of influence tested were confirmed, supporting the positive feedback suggested by the 'slow mode safety' systems model. Overall, there were some limits found in utilising the Global Cities Data set for testing the slow mode safety influence diagram. Generally, the Global Cities Data set does not capture time-sensitive indicators like traffic volume or congestion; data on cycling and walking are rather limited (only a combined indicator for the journey-to-work is available); and traffic safety data are also somewhat limited (where traffic fatality data are for the total transport not a specific mode).

TABLE E.4
TESTING SAFETY SYSTEMS MODEL — CORRELATION ANALYSIS RESULTS

Systems Model Equation	Correlation of determination r^2 (or % change in Y explained by change in X)	Statistical significance (P value)	Mathematical relationship
1	0.244	0.001	positive power
2	0.532	0.000	negative power
3	0.674	0.000	positive power
4	0.146	0.016	negative power
5	0.146	0.016	negative power
6	0.244	0.001	positive power
7	0.532	0.000	negative power
8	policy		
9	policy		
10	policy		
11	policy		
12	0.586	0.000	positive power
13	0.158	0.018	positive power
14	0.158	0.018	positive power
15	0.334	0.000	negative power
16	0.334	0.000	negative power

TRAFFIC DEMAND MANAGEMENT–BALANCING FEEDBACK

The introduction of traffic demand management (TDM) measures as possible 'balancing' or negative feedback policies are the final systems model tested using the Global Cities Data set.

Using the Global Cities Data a number of traffic demand management approaches are tested including. The traffic demand management measures which could not be tested using the Global Cities Data set include such measures as traffic calming, induced traffic in roading project evaluations, integrated land use and transport planning , improved accessibility, and pricing other externalities like air emissions, etc.

- Priority for public transport using a ratio between public transport and private transport speeds;

- Pricing externalities using the variable (or marginal) cost of car use;

- Parking controls using the variable for the central business district (CBD) parking provisions ('1000 CBD Worker per parking space').

FIGURE E.4
SLOW MODE SAFETY SYSTEMS MODEL

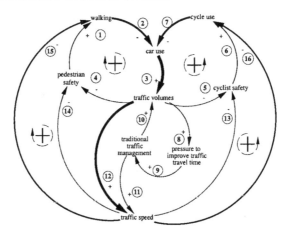

FIGURE E.5
TRAFFIC DEMAND MANAGEMENT SYSTEMS MODEL

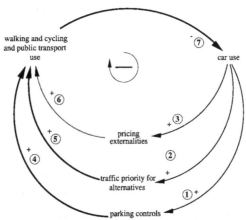

The results of the correlation tests of the systems model are shown in Table E.5. The correlation analysis results of the Global Cites Data set confirm that the traffic demand management policies tested could be used as 'balancing' or negative feedback for increasing car use.

TABLE E.5
TESTING TRAFFIC DEMAND MANAGEMENT SYSTEMS MODEL — CORRELATION ANALYSIS RESULTS

Systems Model Equation	Correlation of determination r^2 (or % change in Y explained by change in X)	Statistical significance (P value)	Mathematical relationship
1	policy		
2	policy		
3	policy		
4	0.480	0.000	positive power
5	0.639	0.000	positive power
6	0.184	0.006	positive power
7	0.696	0.000	negative power

COMPLEXITY OF INTERACTIONS — CONNECTING SYSTEMS MODELS

Although not explored in detail in this appendix, linking the various systems models reveals the complexity of the interactions affecting transport choices, as well as transport and land use interactions. Figure E.6 shows the links between various transport planning policies explored which affect transport choices, and Figure E.7 shows some of the interactions between land use and transport planning. Although not pursued in detail here, the complexity of these interactions suggests that quantitative systems modelling could reveal more about the planning policy interactions affecting urban transport choices.

FIGURE E.6
INTERACTING TRANSPORT PLANNING

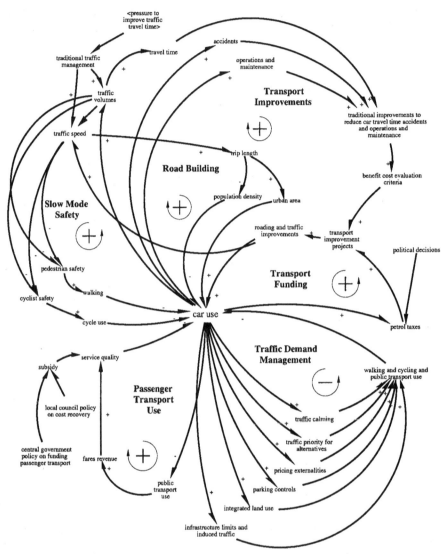

CONCLUSIONS OF SYSTEM MODEL TESTS

As the results of correlation analysis across data for 49 cities between dependent and independent variables indicate, there are significant positive feedback mechanisms occurring between independent planning policies and transport choices — all of which may lead to unintended increasing car use. In all cases the correlation relationships supported the contention of 'polarity' between factors developed in the proposed systems models. Also importantly most of the correlation of determination results were highly statistically significant (generally with a P value less than 0.005), suggesting that the relationships were statistically accurate.

In some models the positive influence between variables appeared to be very strong (with correlation of determination results showing r^2 above 0.8), in others there were moderately strong relationships (r^2 about 0.5) and others with a weaker but still statistically significant correlation (r^2 of 0.2). Overall the correlation results supported the predicted influence polarities in the proposed systems models. To determine more accurate respective strengths of each influence and quantitative modelling of effect would require multivariate regression analysis and further research (including improving some of the identified 'gaps' in the data).

FIGURE E.7
COMPLEXITY OF LAND USE AND TRANSPORT PLANNING INTERACTIONS

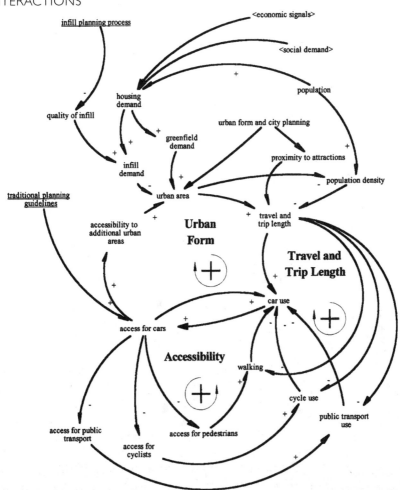

REFERENCES

Allen Consulting Group (1993) *Land Transport Infrastructure, Maximising the Contribution to Economic Growth*, Australian Automobile Association, Canberra

Apelbaum Consulting Group Pty Ltd (1997) *The Australian Transport Task: Primary Energy Consumed and Greenhouse Gas Emissions*, DPIE, Canberra

Australian Academy of Technological Sciences and Engineering (1997) *Urban Air Pollution in Australia*, Melbourne

Australian Bureau of Statistics, Canberra (1997) *Australian Transport and the Environment* Cat. No 4605.0

— (2000a) *Survey of Motor Vehicle Usage for 1998*

— (2000b) *Survey of Motor Vehicle Usage for 1999*

Australian Greenhouse Office (AGO 2000) *National Greenhouse Gas Inventory*, Canberra

Australian Rail Track Corporation (2000) *Annual Report* 1999–2000

Australian Road Research Board (1991) *Improving Truck Safety in Australia*, Melbourne

Australian Transport Advisory Council (1979) *Transport and Energy Overview*, Canberra

Australian Transport Council (1995) *National Competition Policy in the Australian Transport Sector*

— (2000) *The National Road Safety Strategy* 2001–2010

Austroads (1997) *Australia at the Crossroads; Summary Report*, Sydney

Bachels M (1996) Developing positive feedback for sustainable transport: learning from car-dependence *Sustainable Energy Forum Conference*, March, Tauranga, New Zealand, (contact author)

— (1998) Opportunities and threats for sustainable urban transport: Getting the right balance, *Urban Transport Forum*, March 2–3, 1998, Wellington (contact author)

— (1999) *Development of Sustainable Urban Transport Energy Policy — Transport and Land Use Planning Implications*, unpublished PhD Thesis, University of Canterbury, Christchurch

Bachels M, Newman P and Kenworthy J (1999) *Indicators of urban transport efficiency in New Zealand's main cities*, a study prepared for a number of New Zealand government bodies and published by the Institute for Science and Technology Policy, Murdoch University (contact ISTP at Murdoch University)

Bachels M, Peet J and Newman P (1999) Using a systems approach to unravel feedback mechanisms affecting urban transport choices, *Systems Modelling Conference: Systems Thinking for the Next Millennium*, July 20–23, Wellington, New Zealand

Barker TJ (1974) *The Way It Was*, NSW Government Printer, Sydney

Bernick M and Cervero R (1997) *Transit Villages in the 21st Century*, McGraw-Hill, USA

Bossel H (1994) *Modelling and Simulation*, AK Peters Ltd, USA

Bayley WA (1973) *Standard Gauge Railway Across Australia*, Austrail Publications, Bulli, NSW

Binns, Brigadier LG (1956) Appendix 1, *Government Members Rail Standardisation Committee Report*

Bland, Sir H (1972) *Report of the Board of Inquiry into the Victorian Land Transport System*

Brindle, RE (1994) Lies, damned lies and 'automobile dependence' — some hyperbolic reflections, *Proceedings of the 1994 Australasian Transport Research Forum*, Melbourne, pp 27–42

Brindle R, Houghton N and Sheridan G (1999), *Transport-generated Air Pollution and its Health Impacts*, ARRB Transport Research

Brotchie J et al (1999) *Cities in Competition*, Longman Cheshire, Melbourne

Bureau of Industry Economics (1995) *International Performance Indicators — Rail Freight 1995*, AGPS, Canberra

Bureau of Transport (and Communications) Economics (1984) *Overview of the Australian Road Freight Industry*, AGPS, Canberra

— (1988) *Review of Road Cost Recovery*

— (1995a) *Greenhouse Gas Emissions in Australian Transport in 1900 and 2000*

— (1995b) *Information Sheets 4, 5, 7 and 8*

— (1996) *Transport and Greenhouse: Costs and Options for Reducing Emissions*

— (1999a) *Public Road — Related Expenditure and Revenue in Australia*

— (1999b) *Urban Transport — Looking Ahead*

— (1999c) *Trends in Trucks and Traffic*

— (1999d) *Competitive Neutrality Between Road and Rail*

— (2000a) *Road Crash Costs in Australia*

— (2000b) *Brisbane–Melbourne Rail Link: Economic Analysis*, Working Paper 45

Cairns S, Hass-Klau C and Goodwin P (1998) *Traffic Impact of Highway Capacity Reductions: Assessment of the Evidence*, Landor Publishing, London

Calthorpe P (1993) *The Next American Metropolis: Ecology and Urban Form*, Princeton Architectural Press, Princeton, New Jersey

Camph DH (1999) *Transportation, the ISTEA, and American Cities*, Surface Transportation Policy Project, Washington DC

Castells M (1989) *The Informational City: Information Technology, Economic Restructuring and the Urban Regional Process*, Blackwell, Oxford

— (1996) *The Rise of the Network Society*, Blackwell Publishers, Cambridge and Oxford

Castells M and Hall P (1994) *Technopoles of the World*, Routledge, London

Claap, Sir H (1945) *Standardisation of Australia's Railway Gauges*, Commonwealth of Australia Parliamentary Papers — General and Finance, Session 1945–46, p 1309

Commeignes H (1991) *Road Traffic Congestion: An Issue for the 90's*, prepared for the NSW Roads and Traffic Authority

Commonwealth Bureau of Roads (1975) *Hume Highway Corridor Study* (Goulburn to Albury–Wodonga), first report

Curran C et al (1988) *Review of the NSW State Taxation*, NSW Government Printer

Daly H (1980) *Economics, Ecology, Ethics: Toward a Steady-state Economy*, WH Freeman, San Francisco

Danvers M, Jay C and Affleck F (1995) *Across One Nation*, National Rail Corporation

Diesendorf M, Hutabarat R and Banfield K (1999) Sydney's passenger transport: Accounting for different modes, *Papers of the Australasian Transport Research Forum*, Perth, 23: 269–86

Duany A, and Plater-Zyberk E (1991) *Towns and Town-making Principles*, Rizzoli, New York

Ellis B (1998) *Abolish the Consumer*, Penguin

Endersbee L (1994) *The Asian Express, a Proposed Fast Freight Service to Asia*, Australian Academy of Technological Sciences and Engineering

Engwicht D (1993) *Towards an Ecocity: Calming the Traffic*, Envirobook, Sydney

— (1999) *Street Reclaiming: Creating Livable and Vibrant Communities*, New Society Press, Vancouver

Federal Department of Finance (1997) *Submission to the House of Representatives Standing Committee on Communications, Transport*, and *Microeconomic Reform Inquiry into Federal Road Funding*, Canberra

Federal Parliamentary Labor Party (1956) *Report on Rail Standardisation*, Commonwealth of Australia, Parliamentary Papers — General Session 1956–57, p 1103

Finemore R (1992) As quoted in the proceedings of the Annual Conference of the Chartered Institute of Transport in Australia

Fitch RJ (1989) *Making Tracks*, Kangaroo Press, Kenthurst

— (1993) *Railroading at its Wildest*, Kangaroo Press, Kenthurst

Fleay BJ (1995) *The Decline of the Age of Oil*, Pluto Press, Sydney

Franz JD (1989) *Views of Bay Area Residents on Traffic and Growth Issues*, Metropolitan Transit Commission, San Francisco, July

Freeman C (ed.) (1996) *The Longwave in the World Economy*, International Library of Critical Writings in Economics, Elgar, Aldershot

Freeman C and Soete L (1997) *The Economics of Industrial Innovation*, Pinter, London, 3rd edition

Freeman C and Perez C (1988) Structural crises of adjustment, business cycles and investment behaviour. In G Dosi, D Freeman, R Nelson, G Silverburg and L Soete (eds) *Technical Change and Economics Theory*, Pinter, London

Ffrost G (1997) *They Came like Waves*, Kangaroo Press, Sydney

Frost L (1991) *The New Urban Frontier: Urbanisation and City Building in Australasia and the American West*, UNSW Press, Sydney

Gifford JL (1999) Increasing the social acceptability of urban transport projects, *Transportation Quarterly* 53(4): 49–66

Government Members Rail Standardisation Committee (1956) Report, Commonwealth of Australia, Parliamentary Papers — General Session 1956–57, p 1129

Gunn J (1989) *Along Parallel Lines*, Melbourne University Press, Melbourne

Hall P (1997) Reflections past and future in planning cities, *Australian Planner* 34(2), 83–9

Hamer M (1987) *Wheels Within Wheels: A Study of the Road Lobby*, Routledge and Kegan Paul, London

Harding E (1958) *Uniform Railway Gauge*, Lothian Publishing, Melbourne

Healthy Cities Illawarra (with Environment Protection Authority) (1993) *Traffic Noise Study*

Hensher D (2000) November edition of *The Drawing Board*, Institute of Transport Studies, University of Sydney

Hillman M (1996) Curbing car use: The dangers of exaggerating the future role of public transport, *Traffic Engineering + Control*, January

Hilmer, FG, Rayner M and Taperell G (1993) *National Competition Policy — Report by the Independent Committee of Inquiry*, Canberra

House of Representatives Standing Committee on Communications, Transport and

Arts (formerly Microeconomic Reform) AAA *see* Australian Automobile Association
— (1997) *Planning not Patching*
— (1998) *Tracking Australia*
— (2000) *Beyond the Midnight Oil*
House of Representatives Standing Committee on Road Safety (1977) *Heavy Vehicle Safety Report*
Holhuyzen F (1987) The finances and performances of Australia's rail systems, *Proceedings of the 12th Australian Transport Research Forum*, Brisbane, 1: 17–42
Hoyle J (2000) Rail — slowly sinking from public view, *Railway Digest*, 38(May issue): 26–9
Industries Assistance Commission (1986) *Certain Petroleum Products — Taxation Measures*, Report No 397
Industry Commission (1991a) *Rail Transport, Final Report*
— (1991b) *Costs and Benefits of Reducing Greenhouse Gas Emissions*, Final Report
— (1992) *1991–92 Annual Report*
— (1994) *Urban Transport*, Final Report
Institution of Engineers, Australia (1999) *Sustainable Transport — Responding to the Challenges*
Inter-State Commission (1986) *Cost recovery arrangements for Interstate Land Transport*
— (1987) *Federal Registration Charges for Interstate Vehicles*
— (1989) *Waterfront Investigations, Special Study, 'Rail access to Ports'*
— (1990) *Road Use Charges and Vehicle Registration: A National Scheme*
Jacobs J (1984) *Cities and the Wealth of Nations*, Penguin, Harmondsworth
James D (1995) *Revenue Before Rhetoric: A Critique of Fuel Taxation in Australia, Current Issues Brief*, Parliamentary Research Service (PRS), Commonwealth Department of the Parliamentary Library, Canberra
Johnston, WB (ed.) (1965) *Traffic in a New Zealand City*, Christchurch Regional Planning Authority, p 23
Kain J (1995) *A Spirit of Progress? Assessing Australian Rail Transport Policy*, Research Paper No 31, Commonwealth Department of the Parliamentary Library, Canberra
Katz P (1994) *The New Urbanism: Toward an Architecture of Community*, McGraw-Hill, New York
Kenworthy J (1995) Automobile dependence in Bangkok: An international comparison with implications for planning policies, *World Transport Policy and Practice* 1(3): 31–41
Kenworthy J and Laube F (1999) *The Significance of Rail in Building Competitive and Effective Urban Public Transport Systems: An International Perspective*, Global Mass Transit, 69–74, November
Kenworthy J and Newman, PWG (1993) *Automobile Dependence: The Irresistible Force?*, ISTP, Murdoch University, Perth
Kenworthy JR, Laube FB, Newman PWG, Barter PA, Raad T, Poboon C and Guia B (1999) *An International Sourcebook of Automobile Dependence in Cities 1960–1999*, University Press of Colorado, Boulder
Kirby D (1981) Report of the Commission of Inquiry into the Kyeemagh–Chullora Road, NSW Government Printer, Sydney
Klaassen LH, Bourdrez JA and Volmuller J (1981) *Transport and Re-urbanisation*, Gower, England
Laird, PG (1986) A tale of two ports, *Current Affairs Bulletin*, August, pp 24–31
— (1990) Road cost recovery in Australia and New Zealand, *Transport Reviews* 10: 215–27
— (1994) *Rail and Urban Public Transport: Commonwealth Funding and Policy Issues. Upgrading Options*, Background Paper, Parliamentary Research Service, Canberra

— (1995) Sir Harold Clapp's 1945 report — fifty years on, *Australian Rail Historical Society Bulletin* 46: 363–82

— (1996) *Intercity Land Freight Transport in Eastern Australia*, Working Paper, Centre for Resource and Environmental Studies, Australian National University

— (1998) Rail freight efficiency and competitiveness in Australia, *Transport Reviews* 18(3) 241–56

— (1999) Interstate rail and road investment and access pricing, *Papers of the Australasian Transport Research Forum*, Perth, 23: 27–42

— (2001) Rail freight competition and efficiency gains in Australia, papers, Canadian Transport Research Forum, Vancouver, 36: 512–29

Laird PG and Adorni-Braccesi G (1993) *Land Freight Transport Energy Evaluation*, Energy Research and Development Corporation, Canberra

Laird PG, Michell M and Adorni-Braccesi GA (1998) Melbourne–Brisbane rail upgrading options — Inland or Coastal, *Australasian Transport Research Forum*, Sydney, 22: 243–58

Lee R (1988) *The Greatest Public Work*, Hale and Iremonger, Sydney

Linstone HA, and Mistroff J (1994) *The Challenge of the 21st Century: Managing Technology and Ourselves in a Shrinking World*, State University of New York, New York

Lonie WM (1980) Victorian Transport Study, Report on Interstate Rail Services

Lowe I et al (1998) *State of the Environment (SOE) Australia 1996 Report*

McDonell G (1980) *Report of the Commission of Enquiry into the New South Wales Road Freight Industry*, Volume IV, Government Printer, Sydney

McKenzie JJ and Walsh MP (1990) *Driving Forces: Motor Vehicle Trends and their Implications for Global Warming, Energy Strategies and Transportation Planning*, World Resources Institute, Washington DC

Maddison D, Pearce D, Johansson O, Calthrop E, Litman T and Verhoef E (1996) *The True Costs of Road Transport*, Earthscan, London

Manins P (1997) Transport: The future is clearer, Paper presented at Outlook '97, Canberra

May AD and Gardener KE (1990) Transport policy for London in 2001: the case for an integrated approach. *Transportation* 16: 257–77

Mees P (2000) *A Very Public Solution: Transport in the Dispersed City*, Melbourne University Press, Melbourne

Mercer Management Consulting (1996) *Infrastructure, Access and Railway Restructuring*, Prepared for Queensland Railways

Metcalfe S (1990) Evolution and economic change. In A Silburton (ed.) *Technology and Economic Progress*, Macmillan, London

Moudon A, Hess P, Snyder M and Stanilov K (1997) *Effects of Site Design on Pedestrian Travel in Mixed-Use, Medium Density Environments*, Prepared for Washington State Transportation Commission, May. Research Report T9903, Task 65

Naisbett J (1994) *Global Paradox: The Bigger the World Economy, the More Powerful its Smaller Players*, Allen & Unwin, Sydney

National Association of Australian State Road Authorities (1985) *Review of Road Vehicle Limits*, Sydney

National Strategy for Ecologically Sustainable Development (1992) Transport, AGPS, Canberra

National Road Freight Industy Inquiry (1984) *Report*, AGPS, Canberra

National Road Transport Commission (1992) *Heavy Vehicle Charges: Determination*

— (1993) *Investigation of Fuel Only Charges for Heavy Vehicles*

— (1998) *Updating Heavy Vehicle Charges*, Draft policy paper

National Transport Planning Taskforce (1994) *Building for the Job*, Main report

— (1995) Commissioned Work, *BTCE Report* Vol 1, AGPS, Canberra

Newcastle and Hunter Business Chamber (1998) *Draft Hunter Region Transport*

Infrastructure Strategy

Newman, PWG (1996) Transport. In UNCHS, *An Urbanising World: Global Report on Human Settlements*, UNCHS, Habitat and UNEP, Nairobi

Newman P and Kenworthy J (1988) The transport energy trade off: Fuel-efficient traffic versus fuel-efficient cities, *Transportation Research* 22A(3): 163–74

— (1989) *Cities and Automobile Dependence*, Gower Technical, Aldershot

— (1999a) 'Relative Speed' Not 'Time Savings': A New Indicator for Sustainable Transport, *Papers of the Australian Transport Research Forum*, Perth, 23: 427–42

— (1999b) *Sustainability and Cities: Overcoming Automobile Dependence*, Island Press, Washington DC

Newman PWG, Kenworthy JR and Laube F (1999) The global city and sustainability: Perspectives from Australian cities and a survey of 37 global cities. In *East–West Perspectives on 21st century Urban Development: Sustainable Eastern and Western cities in the new millennium*, Brotchie, J, Newton, P, Hall J , and Dickey, J, Ashgate, Aldershot.

Newman PWG et al (1996) Human settlements. In *Australian State of the Environment Report*, Department of Environment, Sport and Territories, AGPS, Canberra

Newman PWG et al (1997) *Car-free Copenhagen: Perspectives and ideas for reducing car-dependence in Copenhagen*, Royal Danish Academy of Fine Arts, Copenhagen

New South Wales State Coroner (1990) *Report on the adjourned hearing into the inquest ... as the result of a collision between a semi-trailer and a motor coach at Cowper, near Grafton, on 20th October, 1989*

New Zealand House of Representatives Transport Committee (1996) *Report on the inquiry into truck crashes*

New Zealand Ministry of Transport (1994) *Land Transport Strategies and Network Funding*

— (1995) *National Roading Account, Roading as an Economic Good*

— (1996) *Land Transport Pricing Study, Environmental Externalities*

— (1997) *Land Transport Pricing Study, Options for the Future*

New Zealand Prime Minister (1997) *Road Reform: The Way Forward*

Noland RB (2001) Have highway 'improvements' improved traffic safety?, Seminar presentation, White House Conference Centre, 4 January — see also 2000 Transportation Research Forum papers

NRMA (1975) *Hume Highway NRMA Highway Survey No. 14*

— (1991) *Country or Coast, A Motorist's Comparison of the Pacific and New England Highways*

— (1994) *Newell Highway NRMA Highway Survey No. 49*

— (1999) *Central Coast Commuters: Their Home, Work and Journey*

NSW Coal Development Strategies Industry Task Force (1990) Report issued by NSW Department of State Development, p 59

OECD/IEA (1997) *Transport, Energy and Climate Change. Energy and Environment*, Policy Analysis Series, OECD, Paris, France

OECD/EMT (1996) *Urban Travel and Sustainable Development*, OECD, Paris

Ogden K (1992) *Urban Goods Movement*, Ashgate, London

Productivity Commission (1996) *Stocktake of Progress in Microeconomic Reform*

— (1999) *Final Report on Progress in Rail Reform*

Putnam R (1993) *Making Democracy Work: Civic Tradition in Modern Italy*, Princeton University Press, Princeton, New Jersey

Rail Projects Taskforce (1999) *Revitalising Rail: The Private Sector Solution*, Department of Transport and Regional Services, Canberra

Rainbow R and Tan H (1993) *Meeting the Demand for Mobility*. Selected Papers, Shell International, London

Royal Commission into Grain Storage, Handling and Transport (1988) *Report*, Vol 1, AGPS, Canberra

SACTRA (1994) *Trunk Roads and the Generation of Traffic*, report by The Standing Advisory Committee on Trunk Road Assessment, Department of Transport, London, HMSO, December

Scheurer J, Newman PWG, Kenworthy JR and Gallagher T (2000) *Can Rail Pay? Light Rail and Urban Redevelopment with Value Capture Funding and Joint Development Mechanisms*, ISTP, Murdoch University, Perth

Searles B (1986) Overseas investigation: Road safety countermeasures, *Proceedings of 13th ARRB Conference*, ARRB, Melbourne, p 162

Selman P (1996) *Local Sustainability: Managing and Planning Ecologically Sound Places*, Paul Chapman Publishing, London

Senate Environment, Communications, Information Technology and the Arts Reference Committee (2000) *The Heat is On: Australia's Greenhouse Future*

Senate Select Committee on National Competition Policy (2000) *Riding the Winds of Change*

Serageldin I and Barrett R (1993) *Environmentally Sustainable Urban Transport: Defining a Global Policy*, World Bank, Washington DC

Simpson R and London J (1995) *An Economic Evaluation of the Health Impacts, of Air Pollution in the BCC Area*, Report to the Brisbane City Council

STAYSAFE NSW Parliamentary Committee on Road Safety (1982) *Alcohol, Drugs, and Road Safety*

— (1989) *Alert Drivers, and Safe Speeds for Heavy Vehicles*

Stells M and Hall P (1994) *Technopoles of the World*, Routledge, London

Stevenson R (1987) *Rail Transport and Australian Federalism*, Australian National University, Canberra

Surface Transportation Policy Project (1998) *An Analysis of The Relationship Between Highway Expansion and Congestion in Metropolitan Areas: Lessons From the 15 Year Texas Transportation Institute Study*, Washington DC

Troy PN (1996) *The Perils of Urban Consolidation*, The Federation Press, Sydney

United Kingdom Department of the Environment and Department of Transport (1994) *Planning Policy Guidance: Transport* (PPG 13), HMSO, London

United Kingdom Deputy Prime Minister (1998) *A New Deal for Transport: Better for Everyone*, Government White Paper on the future of transport

United Nations (1996) *An Urbanizing World: Global Report on Human Settlements*, United Nations Centre for Human Settlements, Oxford University Press

Vanselow RG (1989) Productivity improvements in heavy haul railway operations — The Hamersley experience, *Proceedings, Fourth International Heavy Haul Railway Conference*, Brisbane

Victoria, State Transport Authority (1986) Fuel conservation guides for Train Controllers and Locomotive Drivers

WA Department of Transport (2000) *Survey of Transport Funding Priorities*, Report By Marketforce, Western Australian Department Of Transport, Perth

Waslin N and Widdup JDA (1988) The Australian National Highway, *Proceedings of the Institution of Civil Engineers* 84: 217–34

Webber M (1963) Order in diversity: Community without propinquity. In L Wingo (ed.) *Cities and Space: The Future Use of Urban Land*, Johns Hopkins University Press, Baltimore

— (1964) The urban place and the non-place urban realm. In *Explorations in Urban Structures*, University of Pennsylvania Press, Philadelphia

— (1968) The post city age, *Daedulus* 97(4): 1093–99

Whitlam G (1997) *Abiding Interests*, University of Queensland Press, Brisbane

Whitelegg J (1993) *Transport for a Sustainable Future — The Case for Europe*, Belhaven Press, London

Willoughby K (1994) The 'local milieu' of knowledge-based industries. In J Brotchie, P Newton, P Hall, E Blakeley and M Battie (eds) *Cities in Competition*, Longman Cheshire, Melbourne

Winger AR (1997) Finally: A withering a ways of cities? *Futures* 29(3): 251–56

Wingo L (ed.) *Cities and Space: The Future Use of Urban Land*, John Hopkins University Press, Baltimore

World Bank (1996) *Sustainable Transport: Priorities for Policy Reform: Development in Practice*, The World Bank, Washington DC

Yonge J (1985) *New Zealand Railway and Tramway Atlas*, Quail Map Co, Exeter

Zeibots M (1994) *The Economic Role of Cities*, Honours Thesis, Institute of Science Technology Policy, Murdoch University, Perth, p 48

INDEX